KAPLAN
ADVANTAGE™

KAPLAN
ADVANTAGE™

ACADEMIC SKILLS

This publication is designed to provide accurate and authoritative information in regard to the subject matter. The publisher is not providing legal, accounting, or other professional advice or services. If any such advice or other expert assistance is required, contact an appropriate professional.

Permissions

Cover photos reproduced by permission from Dave & Les Jacobs, Fuse, Klaus Tiedge, Jetta Productions/Dana Neely, moodboard, ERproductions Ltd, Hill Street Studios, PhotoAlto/Frederic Cirou, Kate Kunz/Corbis.

Microsoft, Windows, Office, Word, Excel, PowerPoint, Windows Media Player, Windows Fax and Picture Viewer, Outlook, and Internet Explorer are either registered trademarks or trademarks of Microsoft Corporation in the United States and/or other countries.

Apple, Mac, Safari, and iChat are registered trademarks of Apple Inc.

Dell and the DELL logo are trademarks of Dell Computer Corporation.

Hewlett-Packard is a registered trademark of Hewlett-Packard Company.

IBM is a registered trademark of International Business Machines Corporation.

Screenshots from the following pages were used with permission from Microsoft: 47, 48, 52, 54, 57, 59, 60.

Google and Google Books are either registered trademarks or trademarks of Google, Inc. in the United States and/or other countries.

Some illustrations in this book have been acquired from Web sites and are used for demonstration and educational purposes only. Online availability of the text and images does not imply that they may be reused without the permission of the copyright holder.

Printed in the United States of America

10 9 8 7 6 5 4

ISBN-13: 978-1-60978-637-3

Contents

UNIT 1 Welcome to Academic Skills. 2

UNIT 2 Human Behavior 14

UNIT 3 Understanding Communication 28

UNIT 4 Computer Applications and the Internet 42

UNIT 5 English Fundamentals: Language Arts 64

UNIT 6 English Fundamentals: Writing Process 86

UNIT 7 Internet Applications 104

UNIT 8 Applying Communication Techniques in the Workplace. 120

UNIT 9 Math Fundamentals 1 138

UNIT 10 Math Fundamentals 2 172

Glossary. 209
Index 215

Introduction

Congratulations! By committing to developing your skills, you have made an important investment in yourself. Entering a higher education program requires many sacrifices, and we recognize your courage in taking this step. We admire your willingness to do what it takes to reach your goals.

If you have been working for many years, it may have been some time since you were in school; even if it hasn't been that long, you may have some anxiety about taking on a higher education workload. Many students are concerned when they enter a higher education program—they may feel nervous about working on computers, or about reading, or writing, or math. This book is designed to revive and strengthen your foundations—to review the **Academic Skills** that you need in order to succeed in your academic program. Part of the Kaplan Advantage™ is making sure that you have the skills you need now, in the first two terms of your program, so you can apply them throughout your studies and approach your program with confidence.

It's okay if it's hard

You may be worried that you will struggle in a specific area. Many students have had a bad educational experience in the past and are therefore concerned about a certain subject, such as writing or math. Others have simply been out of school for a long time and need a little time to get back into the rhythm of assignments and quizzes. If you need a little extra time to get up to speed, that's what this book is for—to cover the key academic skills, so you have the tools you need.

It's also okay if it's easy. You may be a very confident student—computer savvy, comfortable with reading and writing, and not afraid of math. If that's the case, you may feel very comfortable as we review the critical academic skills. That's great! Take this opportunity to develop your communication skills by providing support to any classmates who may be having a tougher time adjusting. You can also develop your teamwork skills, which are critical to success in every work environment.

Why are we doing this again? Most students would prefer to take only core courses that align with their intended career. Hands-on activities and labs are some of the most exciting parts of an academic program. However, skills in computers, communications, and calculations are critical foundational capabilities that are necessary for success in every career. If you want to have an advantage over your peers in the job market, these skills are the difference makers. Ignore them at your peril. If every job candidate has the core skills, then the employer will choose the individual who is the best communicator. Now is the time to solidify your academic skills.

Keep professionalism in mind. You have learned about the Four Pillars of Professionalism, or the EDGE: Empowered, Dependable, Goal-Oriented, and Engaged. You will be studying these concepts in depth during your Professionalism modules, but we will also remind you of them in this book. Look for the "Practice Now" features, which will give you ideas for how to improve your professionalism skills while you work on your career skills.

We are here to help

Keep this book as you work through your program. Each unit covers an important academic skill that can be useful to you throughout your journey to success.

1. Welcome to Academic Skills

In this unit, you will work through a brief overview of the skills covered in the course. You will learn about the types of skills and discuss critical issues, such as academic honesty, that will be important throughout your program.

2. Human Behavior

You may not be a psychologist, but you can still learn from the study of human behavior. Employees who understand the dynamics of personality are more likely to make good choices in communication and be effective in teams. In this unit, we identify the forces that affect personality and examine how those forces influence career choices.

3. Understanding Communication

You know what you intend to communicate when you speak, but do others understand what you mean? This unit examines not only what you say intentionally, but also the many things that you communicate unintentionally by your facial expressions, the things you do, and the things you do not say.

4. Computer Applications and the Internet

Today, there are very few jobs that do not involve a computer. In most organizations, you will need to be able to use a Web browser with confidence, manipulate common software products, and use digital tools to complete tasks. In this unit, we will go into computer tools in depth, practicing the most highly valued skills.

5. English Fundamentals: Language Arts

Employers make assumptions about candidates based on their ability to communicate in English. If your writing has poor grammar, misspellings, or style errors, it could cost you your job. In this unit, we will cover the most important rules and help you improve your language arts skills.

6. English Fundamentals: Writing Process

In school, you will need to be able to write clearly and effectively in order to meet your goals. In this unit, we will discuss how effective writers consider their audience, plan their writing, and draft successfully.

7. Internet Applications

Having already practiced browser skills, in this unit, you will practice more complex Internet applications. Most importantly, you will practice Web surfing, research, and using the online library to find credible sources. We will discuss the criteria that make one source more reliable and convincing than another.

8. Applying Communication Techniques in the Workplace

This unit applies the communication concepts from units 2, 3, 5, and 6, pulling them all together into some concrete skills that you can use to improve your success on teams and in other workplace situations. You will learn how to meet customer needs, deal with conflicts, and approach diversity.

9. Math Fundamentals 1

Math is the foundation of critical problem solving in many careers. It is important in pharmaceutical equivalencies, in medical dosage calculations, in crime scene measurements, and in construction conversions. In this unit, we will look at applications of basic math operations, measurements, and metric conversions.

10. Math Fundamentals 2

In this unit, we will connect math to problem-solving situations. We cover the most commonly applied aspects, including decimals, ratios, and proportions. You will practice these skills in your digital sessions to build facility. When performing calculations becomes second nature, you can focus on the larger question.

Take advantage of this time

The competencies learned in *Academic Skills* are applicable across all jobs and careers. Take advantage of the time in this course to build these skills to the highest level possible. If your skills are rough, build up to confidence. If you are already confident, become an expert. If you feel expert, tutor your classmates. Work until you have reached your highest capacity, because you will need these skills. The Kaplan Advantage focuses on skills that you really need—throughout your career and your life. If you sharpen them now, you will do better in your program, and you will be more prepared for your new career.

Acknowledgments

hank you to the following editors for their contributions.

Kaplan Higher Education Corporation
Chicago, Illinois

Karen Baldeschwieler, MBA, PhD
VP, Academic Programs

Aimee Brown
VP, Marketing

Kari Costello
Executive Director, Career Services

Sarah Croft
Manager, Research and Curriculum Design

Jon Eads, PhD
Executive Director, Research and
Curriculum Design

Chakana Fowler
Director, Curriculum Operations

Yvonne Gasik
VP, Product Development

Murray Matens Kimball
Instructional Designer

Maegan K. Murphy
Executive Director, Student Experience

UNIT
1

Welcome to
Academic Skills

Identifying the goals of this course

Describing key academic skills

Applying academic skills to your educational program and your career

Y ou've probably met students who make school look easy. They always turn in their assignments on time, say just the right thing in class, make instructors nod and smile, and receive high scores on every test. What's their secret? Most people think that being an excellent student is a matter of natural ability—either you're born "school smart" or you're not. However, research shows that academic superstars rely not only on talent, but also on a set of skills that anyone can develop with practice and hard work. This unit is an introduction to the skills you'll be developing throughout this course in order to succeed in your academic program. There's no secret; all you need are a few tools and you'll be well on your way toward academic success.

From Potential to Actual: Academic Skills

This course is about converting your potential—what is *possible* for you—into a series of actual, measurable successes. Along your educational path, these successes will take many forms: an A on an assignment, a well-received oral presentation, or a difficult mathematical problem solved. Academic skills are the keys to unlocking your potential. Think of them in terms of a mathematical statement:

$$\text{potential} + \text{skill} = \text{actual achievement}$$

Course Goals

With the above equation in mind, let's review the goals of this course. By the time you complete this course, you should be able to do the following:

- Identify skills that help you succeed at school.
- Apply those skills to your academic program, your career, and your life.
- Perform basic mathematical operations.
- Write effectively in academic and professional environments.
- Demonstrate strong computer and online research skills.

What Are Academic Skills?

If you want to be good at something, you can use talents, skills, or—ideally—both. A **skill** is an ability that you learn, develop, and master through practice and effort. We typically use the word **talent** to describe a natural ability—you're born with it, though you may choose not to use it. The advantage of skills is that you can use them to supplement your talents, or even to overcome a lack of talent in a certain area. Thus, you may never be a *talented* mathematician, but you most certainly can become *skilled* at mathematics.

An **academic skill,** therefore, is a learned ability that helps people succeed in school. Here are just a few reasons why academic skills are important:

They translate directly into academic achievement. Superior writing skills translate into good grades on tests and writing assignments. Computer skills lead to success at digital classroom and research tasks. Communication skills impress your instructors during classroom discussions and group activities. The list goes on.

They increase your confidence. It's human nature: When you're good at something, doing it makes you feel able and confident. When you face an academic task, such as a quiz, you can say to yourself, "I've *got* this. I have the skills to do it, and I've used them before."

They build on each other. Academic skills work together. When you spend time mastering one skill, you'll find that your abilities in other areas grow. For example, honing your critical thinking skills will make you a more skilled reader because you will ask more questions and make deeper connections as you read.

They are transferable. Academic skills will easily—and often automatically—enhance your performance on the job and in your personal life. You'll find yourself solving work problems more creatively, making life decisions more intelligently, and forming more satisfying relationships.

This unit is not meant to teach you every critical academic skill. During this course, you will learn about several skills in greater detail. Also keep in mind that being able to identify academic skills is just the first step. It's up to you to develop and master them, and that takes practice and effort. This course will help. Consider the rest of this book a how-to manual for honing the skills introduced in this unit.

Types of Academic Skills

Some academic skills apply to every educational task, while others are more specialized. Below are several types of skills, along with examples of how to apply them to your schooling.

Thinking skills. Education is about learning, and learning is about exercising your brain. The following thinking skills will aid you as you approach a wide variety of academic tasks:

Thinking critically. When you think critically, you look at an idea or issue from many different perspectives and question its truth and validity. You withhold immediate judgment, avoid making assumptions, and try to view it without bias—a preference or inclination that prevents impartial judgment. Critical thinking is useful whenever you're reading or processing new information. As you ask critical questions, your understanding deepens. This skill also applies to performing research and evaluating the reliability of online sources.

Problem solving. Problem-solving skills include identifying the problem, choosing the right problem-solving tools, inventing creative solutions, and implementing one or more solutions. You might apply these skills when an instructor presents you with a moral or professional dilemma.

Decision making. To make a good decision, you must weigh all options, articulate advantages and disadvantages, make a final choice, and then follow through with your decision confidently and effectively. This applies to educational tasks such as picking a topic for a presentation or choosing which course(s) to take.

Classifying. To **classify** means to sort—to divide objects or information into groups. In an

academic environment, you use classification skills to sort your course materials, to organize information for a research paper, or to line up the elements of a mathematical problem.

Communication skills. Good communication skills are essential for developing strong relationships, showing and earning respect, and interacting with people in any setting. You'll find the following especially helpful:

Presentation skills. At school you'll need to make oral presentations, which require skills like these: speaking slowly and clearly, choosing appropriate words, making eye contact, using appropriate hand gestures, displaying confident body language, and using visual aids effectively.

Listening skills. In the classroom, active listening is just as important as effective speaking. Listening skills include showing receptivity through eye contact and other nonverbal clues, keeping your mind focused and engaged, and determining what information is most important. For instance, if you listen for details about assignments, definitions of key terms, and any information likely to end up on a test, you will be more likely to get higher grades on test day.

Leadership skills. Think about the good leaders you know. Their skills probably include motivating others, communicating well, planning, teamwork, and decision making (notice the crossover with thinking skills!). When you apply leadership skills to group activities and class discussions, you'll receive positive feedback from instructors and classmates—and you'll be recognized as a team player.

Conflict-resolution skills. Some examples of conflict-resolution skills are keeping an open mind, seeking compromise through negotiation, controlling your emotions, and respecting differences in opinions. While in school, you'll receive feedback on your work almost constantly, and you might not always agree with it. You will avoid unnecessary conflict if you learn not to take criticism personally.

Navigating diversity. To succeed in any group, you'll need to communicate effectively with people from a variety of backgrounds. A related skill is avoiding stereotypes based on gender, nationality, and other categories. Apply this to your education by showing interest in classmates and instructors who are different from you.

You'll learn more about communication skills throughout Units 3 and 8.

Practice
Critical Thinking

Scenario: Edgar, Will, and Lia are working on a group presentation. Edgar is a talented artist and has his own computer, so Will and Lia have asked him to make all the visual aids and to do all the typing for the report. Edgar is comfortable in this role, but he doesn't want to end up doing more than half of the work for the project. He thinks Will and Lia are taking advantage of him.

Questions: Is there a clear "right" and "wrong" in this situation? How would you help Edgar, Will, and Lia resolve their team conflict? What types of communication skills would help them?

Research skills. Whenever you seek information that doesn't come from your own prior knowledge and experience, you are doing research. You will probably be required to conduct research for at least one assignment in every higher education course you take. We'll cover several important research skills in Unit 7. For now, here is a basic introduction:

Finding sources. Once you have established your research question—for example, "What are the main diseases requiring respiratory care?"—you'll need to find sources that answer the question.

Evaluating sources. Let's say you've found six sources that answer your research question, but the information in those sources conflicts, and you don't know which information is correct. Evaluation skills will help you judge the reliability of your sources.

Taking notes. Once you've identified reliable sources, it's time to record information. Note-taking skills, such as classifying information (another crossover with thinking skills!) and using abbreviations, will help you record what you've learned from your research.

Citing sources. Because a research project involves using other people's ideas, you must

cite, or give credit to, your sources. Giving credit where it's due is one of the fundamental principles of higher education.

Language arts skills. It's a basic fact: To do well in school, you must develop your ability to speak and write according to the rules of the English language. Whether you're expressing an opinion in class or writing an email message to an instructor, it is critical to use words, phrases, and sentences appropriately and correctly. In many cases, your use of language helps form the first impression you make.

In Unit 5, you'll hone your skills in the following areas of language arts:

- Grammar: parts of speech (such as nouns and verbs) and their uses
- Spelling: learning the rules and knowing the exceptions
- Punctuation: correct use of marks such as periods, commas, and parentheses
- Capitalization: when to use uppercase letters versus lowercase letters
- Word analysis: determining word meanings by breaking them down into parts

Applying Academic Skills to Your Academic Program—and Beyond

Every time you begin a task for school, take the opportunity to practice one or more of your academic skills. The task could be a

---

Building **Background:** Avoiding Plagiarism

When you commit plagiarism, you fail to cite outside sources when you use them in your own work. Plagiarism is a form of academic dishonesty; it means you have used someone else's information, ideas, or words without crediting that person. The consequences of this offense can range from a zero on the assignment to expulsion from school. If a graduate student or professor is caught plagiarizing, he or she may be expelled from the community of scholars. To avoid plagiarism, always give credit to your sources through proper citation.

reading assignment, a set of math problems, a group activity, a class discussion, a research paper, a test or quiz, a video, or selecting a new course. Ideally, you'll be able to practice multiple skills as you set out to accomplish your task. For example, imagine you've been assigned a group presentation as the final project for a course. A complex project like this will require you to utilize skills from every category we've discussed so far. Continued practice will propel you along the path to your educational goal.

Academic skills are also applicable to your chosen career. Job success requires problem solving, excellent communication, the ability to find and organize information (research), and skilled use of language. For example, in the medical field, your daily tasks may include resolving a scheduling conflict, discussing an insurance issue with a patient, researching side effects of a medication, and writing a letter to a medical supply vendor.

TrueStory

"I had to do a research project for my course on managed health care. I had never done serious online research before, so I met with a librarian at my school's media center. He sat down with me for three hours and showed me how to find sources that I never knew existed. Now I get mostly A's on research-based assignments. My friends even ask me to help them find the best deal when they want to buy something online. The world of information is really powerful."

Your Electronic Assistant: Computer Skills

Computer use has entered every aspect of schooling, and it's here to stay. Today people can complete an entire higher education program online, without ever meeting their instructor or another student in person. For this course, a significant part of your coursework consists of online digital sessions. If you learn to make the most out of your computer, you'll be able to turn it into your own electronic assistant. In Units 4 and 7, we'll address computer and Internet skills in greater detail. Below are a few of the topics we'll cover.

Identifying Computer Components

In order to make a computer work for you, you need to know its main parts and their functions—and if you're preparing for an information technology (IT) career, you need to know much more than that. What is a hard drive, anyway? What's the difference between storage memory and RAM? How do you connect your computer to a projector in order to make a PowerPoint presentation? Since you'll be using computers at school, you will probably have to troubleshoot computer problems at some point, too. Knowing a computer's main components and how they function will aid you throughout your academic and professional careers.

Basic User Skills

Once you've turned a computer on, you need to know how to interact with it and tell it what to do. This involves skills such as the following:

- Using keyboard commands
- Using a mouse or trackpad
- Creating and saving files
- Creating and organizing folders
- Opening, closing, and toggling between windows
- Opening and closing programs
- Navigating menu bars
- Inserting and removing DVDs and CDs
- Attaching external equipment such as cameras, phones, and printers

Practice Now: Goal-Oriented

Students who are goal-oriented take initiative by going above and beyond what is asked of them. When using a new computer program, take some extra start-up time to familiarize yourself with the program's features so that you can learn how to fully utilize its capabilities. You may learn some special shortcuts or commands that will save you time when entering data or help you create an interesting graphic for a presentation. Getting to know a program's specialized functions will help you use your time efficiently and create a comprehensive finished product.

Using Programs

Last but not least, you'll need to develop skills associated with using programs, also called applications. Programs used for educational purposes include word processors, such as Microsoft Word®; Internet browsers, such as Mozilla Firefox® and Internet Explorer®; presentation programs, such as Microsoft PowerPoint®; and video viewing programs, such as Windows Media Player®. Each application is its own miniature system, with unique menus, functions, and features.

Cool and Calculated: Math Skills

Math students are constantly asking their instructors, "When am I going to use this in the real world?" If you consider school and work parts of the real world, then here's the answer: all the time. Whatever field you're entering, whether it's medicine, IT, or electricity, you will thank yourself every day for the time you spent mastering mathematics skills. People often refer to math skills as "hard" skills because they are concrete. You either possess

them or you don't; there is simply no faking this sort of knowledge—especially on the job.

Operations

Operations are the classic mathematical calculations: addition, subtraction, multiplication, and division. Performing operations accurately and quickly is an invaluable skill. Here are some examples of how to apply them to your education and career:

- Financing your educational program (calculating student loan amounts, calculating interest rates)
- Calculating your grade point average
- Figuring out required numbers of credits
- Paying, recording, calculating, and reconciling bills (This applies to billing work in any industry, as well as your personal finances.)

Systems of Measure

This set of skills involves identifying, using, and converting units of measure involving distance, area, volume, weight, and so on. In an academic setting, you might use measurement skills to create visual aids for a presentation or to figure out how much time it will take you to write a five-page paper. Any scientific job setting, such as pharmacy sciences, requires extreme precision and the ability to use measurement tools. HVAC and electrical technicians must expertly calculate and evaluate measurements such as square footage, current, resistance, and volume in order to properly install equipment.

Solving Mathematical Problems

Using mathematics to solve problems is a highly transferable skill. You use math to solve school-related problems such as managing and prioritizing your time, setting budgets for books and other materials, and even figuring out transportation issues (taking into account factors such as mileage, gas prices, and cost of public transportation). At work, you may tackle mathematical problems related to billing and reimbursement, readings on advanced technical equipment, or computer networking.

By the Letter: Writing Skills

Writing is a challenging task, but again, you can break it down into manageable tasks once you've mastered the right skills. And master them you must, because much of your success in higher education will depend on your ability to communicate effectively in writing. Important academic writing skills include the following:

- Generating ideas
- Organizing and connecting ideas and information
- Following instructions for writing assignments
- Choosing effective and appropriate words and sentence patterns
- Following the steps of the writing process (planning, drafting, revising, editing)
- Catering to your audience

So you see, there really are no secrets to academic success. The tools for your academic success are within reach, and you can make them yours. This course is your opportunity to become that awesome student—on top of your game, at the top of the class, and looking as if you've had the edge all along. Remember to take it one skill at a time, and success can be yours.

Unit Summary

- Educational achievement isn't just about talent; it requires skills that anyone can develop.
- A skill is an ability that you learn and eventually master through hard work and practice.
- Areas of academic skills include thinking, communication, research, language arts, computers, math, and writing.
- Academic skills can help you succeed not only in school, but also in your career and personal life.

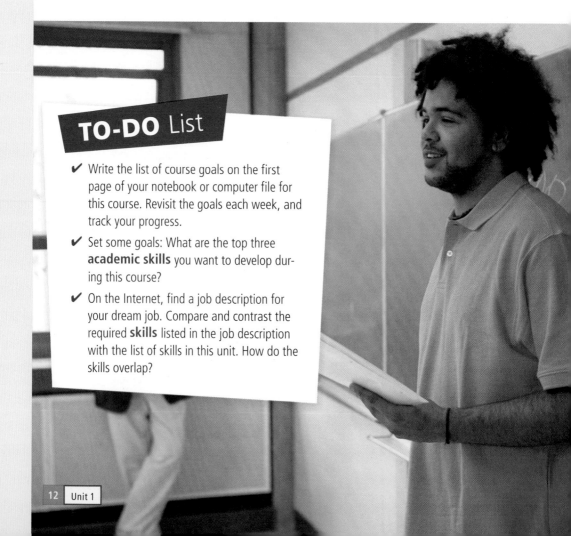

TO-DO List

✔ Write the list of course goals on the first page of your notebook or computer file for this course. Revisit the goals each week, and track your progress.

✔ Set some goals: What are the top three **academic skills** you want to develop during this course?

✔ On the Internet, find a job description for your dream job. Compare and contrast the required **skills** listed in the job description with the list of skills in this unit. How do the skills overlap?

Important Terms

How well do you know these terms? Look them up in the glossary if you need help remembering them.

skill   **academic skill**

talent   **classify**

Online Resources

Academic Tips
www.academictips.org/acad/

Computer Skills
www.ctdlc.org/remediation/indexComputer.html

Guide to Grammar and Writing
grammar.ccc.commnet.edu/grammar/

Communication Skills
www.mindtools.com/page8.html

Math Practice
www.math.com/students/practice.html

Exercises

1. In a notebook, respond to the following question: When you decided to return to school, what skills did you hope to gain or develop?

2. Do a personal skills inventory. For each skill introduced in this unit, give yourself a score from 1 (not skilled) to 5 (highly skilled). Be honest with yourself. Share this information with instructors, fellow students, or media center professionals. Ask them about ways to draw on your existing skills as you practice new ones.

3. For each skill covered in this unit, think of at least one additional way to apply that skill to your educational program.

4. Visit the Online Resources, and compare the information you find there with the content of this unit. What new academic skills did you learn about? How will you apply them in school?

UNIT 2

Human Behavior

Defining the term *personality*

Identifying several elements of personality

Describing how personality and behavior affect your career choices and
professional performance

Identifying forces that shape personality

Defining the term *behavior*

Explaining how personality and behavior are related

C lose your eyes and picture two people you consider to be effective
leaders. What are their dominant qualities? How do they act? What
makes them good leaders? How do their leadership styles differ?

Just as no two people are exactly alike, leaders can vary widely in their
personalities. Some, like Martin Luther King, Jr., are assertive and charismatic;
others, like Mohandas Gandhi of India, are quiet yet persuasive; and others,
like Golda Meir of Israel, are direct and sensible. These three world leaders
also differed in their behavior, their approaches to solving problems, and their
decision-making strategies. Yet each was an effective and powerful leader
who brought about profound changes. In this unit, we will explore the concepts
of personality and behavior. In particular, we will discuss how personality
affects people's career choices and professional style.

Your Personality at Work

Defining and understanding personality is one of the main missions of **psychologists**—scientists who study the human mind and behavior. Over the years, psychologists have proposed several different theories and models of personality and behavior. At the same time, people who study organizations have tried to figure out how to harness the power of personality to build winning teams of employees. In this section we will simplify the wealth of information about personality and focus on its relevance in a professional setting.

Personality Defined

Personality is a set of emotional and behavioral **traits,** or characteristics, that distinguish you from others. Basically, your personality is what makes you *you.* It includes your values, thoughts, preferences, opinions, desires, beliefs, attitudes, and actions.

Think about how you have used the word *personality* or heard it used. It might sound something like this:

- "She's got a great personality." (I really enjoy her; she has positive characteristics.)
- "I never knew he had such personality." (He's a real character, perhaps a bit quirky.)
- "I've always had an outgoing personality." (I tend to be social and friendly.)

Take a look at the partial list of personality traits in Figure 2.1. Which words describe you? If you're like most people, many of these traits have applied to you at some point in your life. At any given moment, the characteristic you display may depend on the day, your mood, your age, and your surroundings. But personality is based on dominant patterns or tendencies— the ones that show up with surprising regularity. You might display several traits within a lifetime or even within a day, but which ones

Personality Traits	
kind	wasteful
honest	mature
determined	selfish
jealous	sympathetic
rude	self-disciplined
respectful	distant
responsible	independent
cold	eager
curious	funny
open-minded	arrogant
humble	relaxed
picky	anxious
bossy	affectionate
loyal	sensitive
forgiving	creative
driven	moody
decisive	talkative
cooperative	disorganized
joyful	patient
shy	brave
outgoing	stable
organized	adaptable
rebellious	persuasive
trusting	polite

Figure 2.1 Personality traits

define you most? Which traits are central to your identity? When you interact with people, solve problems, or face stressful situations, which characteristics guide you most strongly?

These questions can be difficult to answer. Human beings are complex creatures with traits that sometimes conflict. For example, you might be shy and reserved in a private setting but dramatic and charismatic when performing on stage or leading a group. What does this mean about your personality? You're only one person, but you have many different facets. No one is easily defined.

Here is another question to ponder: Is your personality the same today as it was when you were 16 or when you were a baby? Some psychologists believe that an individual's personality is set in stone, but recent research suggests that it can—and does—change.[1] As with many questions of human nature, the truth may lie somewhere in the middle: Some aspects of personality change, while others do not.

Personality and Your Career

According to experts who study **organizational behavior**—the way individuals and groups act in organizations such as businesses and schools—personality influences the jobs people choose, the way they approach and complete work-related tasks, and the roles they play on a team. For instance, certain personality traits probably attracted you to your chosen career. If you're helpful and compassionate, you may have gravitated toward jobs in health care or customer service. Practical people who like to work with their hands tend to thrive in hands-on careers like electrical work or appliance installation and repair. Self-disciplined individuals with a strong commitment to fairness and social service may find criminal justice careers appealing. Simply put, you are more likely to stick with—and succeed in—a job that meshes well with your personality.

As part of the job application process, or once you have started a new job, you may be asked to complete a **personality test.** This is a survey or questionnaire intended to identify your dominant traits and behavior patterns. You, your supervisor, and your co-workers may use the results of a personality test in the following ways:

- Assess job candidates during the interviewing process.
- Make hiring decisions.
- Predict how you will behave on the job.
- Maximize your job performance (and thus help your company achieve its goals).
- Help co-workers and supervisors understand your style of communicating, learning, interacting with customers, problem solving, decision making, and functioning on a team.
- Match you with co-workers who will complement or benefit from your professional style.
- Help you develop and grow as an employee.

In most cases, the results of a personality test assign you a specific **personality type**—one of several predetermined categories used to group people with common traits. Have you ever heard anyone talk about type A and type B personalities? These predominant categories are often used to describe people or to explain their behavior: They are goal-oriented and practical (type A) or easy-going and emotional (type B). Do these categories sound like stereotypes? They certainly can be—but it depends on how you use them.

[1] Dwek, C.S. (2007). *MindSet* (New York: Ballantine Books), 4.

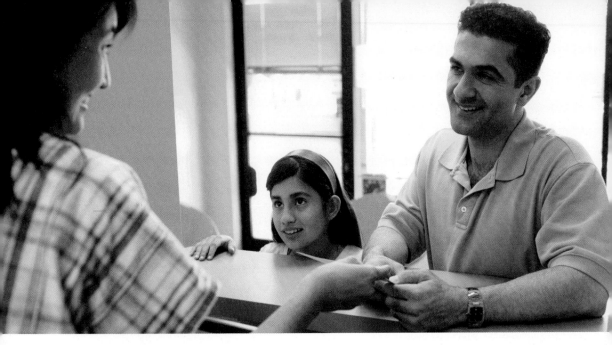

If an employer (or potential employer) asks you to take a personality test, don't get worried or stressed. This isn't a traditional test like the ones you take in school. There are no grades, and there are no right or wrong answers. Be as honest as possible, and think of the test as a way to get to know yourself better. Personality tests are just tools. They do not define who you are, and they do not place limits on your potential. You might find it difficult or even uncomfortable to answer the questions on a personality test because they might ask you to commit to an extreme—for example, "Are you trusting or suspicious?" Base your answer on traits or behaviors that apply to you *more* reliably.

Shaping Me, Myself, and I: Influences on Personality

What shapes your personality? How did you become who you are? What determines who you will become in the future? In this section, we will explore four categories of influences: biological, environmental, cultural, and social. Keep in mind that psychologists continue to debate this topic. As you read about each influence, ask yourself, "Does this affect my personality?" Your opinion counts here.

Nature: Biological Influences

Anyone who spends a lot of time with infants will tell you that every person is born with a unique personality. Have you ever noticed that some babies are "easy"—good-natured, smiley, and unlikely to cry—while others are fussy and "difficult"? We begin showing certain traits immediately following birth, and we have little or no control over them. Even as we grow up and start defining ourselves more actively, part of our personality is a simple matter of biology, or nature.

Genetics, temperament, and the Big Five. We inherit some of our personality traits from our parents and our species. Genetics and instinct combine to create our **temperament,** or inborn personality, which comes across as an overall mood or attitude. Your temperament guides your emotional reaction to various situations, and it is unlikely to change.

Evidence suggests that temperament consists of a few basic personality dimensions that are determined before birth. Psychologists refer to them as the Big Five:[2]

1. **Openness.** Are you open to many types of experiences, or do you have a limited comfort zone? Do you have wide-ranging interests or just two or three main passions? How intuitive, curious, imaginative, and intelligent are you?

2. **Conscientiousness.** Are you well organized or all over the place? Do you tend to finish tasks, or do you leave them undone? Do you plan things thoroughly with attention to details and goals, or do you leave life events to chance or to someone else's leadership?

3. **Extraversion.** Are you sociable, or do you prefer being alone? Do you get your energy from within yourself or from interaction with others? Do you express your emotions or hold them in? Are you forceful and assertive, or do you have trouble insisting that you get what you want?

4. **Agreeableness.** Would people describe you as warm and affectionate or distant and reserved? Do you find it easy to sympathize with and care for others, or do other people's complaints and problems turn you off? Are you agreeable or disagreeable?

5. **Emotional stability.** Do you tend to be anxious, worried, irritable, and tense? Or are you generally calm, stable, and even-tempered? Are you prone to depression, or are you happy most of the time?

Gender. Gender appears to have some effect on the development of personality. What remains up in the air is whether or not male and female personalities are somehow genetically different. Are men and women just as likely to possess certain characteristics, displaying certain tendencies only because of social and cultural expectations? Or are gender personality differences based, at least in part, on biology? Psychologists and biologists still aren't sure.

Health and physical appearance. Although you have direct control over some aspects of your health and the way you look, other aspects are matters of biology. These factors affect how you experience the world, how you view yourself, and how others view you, and there is little doubt that they influence the development of your personality.

---

[2] Nettle, D. (2009). *Personality: What Makes You the Way You Are* (New York: Oxford University Press), 29–30.

Health issues. Some people are born with health limitations such as a genetic disease or disorder. Others sail through life with few health problems or physical abnormalities. The presence or absence of physical limitations, whether mild or severe, contributes to the way you feel, act, and present yourself.

Body type. Are you tall or short, large-boned or petite, flexible or stiff? Different body types may bring out different personality traits, partly because of the way others view you and partly because of how your physicality affects your experiences in the world.

Skin color and race. Your skin color and race do not determine who you are, but they might influence your personality. This factor comes into play more strongly in diverse societies, in which people of many races live together and perceive each other as different. It is less of a factor in places where everyone has the same racial characteristics.

ON THE JOB

The Myers-Briggs Type Indicator

The Myers-Briggs Type Indicator (MBTI) is one of the world's best-known personality tests. A mother-daughter team developed the test in the 1940s and perfected it over the next 20 years. Each year, an estimated 2 million people take the MBTI in the United States.[3] Although the MBTI is based on several personality dimensions, it is probably best known for popularizing the opposing personality types of extrovert (abbreviated as E) and introvert (I).

Thousands of organizations around the world give the MBTI to their employees, students, or members. On the job, you can use your MBTI type to understand your co-workers, to approach problems and decisions, to manage stress, and more. Like any personality test, however, it has limitations. Always beware of stereotyping yourself or others.

Birth order. There are many psychological theories about how (and whether) birth order impacts personality. Your status as an only child, firstborn, middle child, or youngest sibling may bring out traits such as rebelliousness, reliability, responsibility, perfectionism, intuitiveness, sociability, or helplessness.[4]

Stage in life. It may not surprise you that another central goal of psychology is to determine how personality changes as people mature, become more independent, and progress through life stages, such as puberty and parenthood. Psychologist Erik Erikson identified certain traits, patterns, and central concerns that he associated with different life stages:

- Infancy: developing trust, meeting basic needs
- Childhood: mastering skills, conquering shame, satisfying curiosity, acting imaginatively, differentiating ourselves from others
- Adolescence (roughly ages 13 to 18): defining identity, establishing beliefs, determining social roles
- Adulthood: exploring intimacy, finding love, finding meaningful work, establishing stability
- Old age: searching for purpose and contribution, appreciating wisdom

[3] Griffin, R.W. and Moorhead, G. (2009). *Organizational Behavior: Managing People and Organizations* (Mason, OH: South-Western College Pub.), 64.

[4] Neal, R. "Personality Traits Linked to Birth Order." *CBS News*, June 11, 2002. http://www.cbsnews.com/stories/2002/06/10/earlyshow/living/parenting/main511694.shtml

You can also consult your own experiences and memories to guess how human personalities tend to develop over time. What parts of your personality did you express most when you were a child? What were you like when you were 15? How are your beliefs, opinions, motivations, and qualities different today?

Nurture: Environmental and Cultural Influences

So far, we've discussed personality influences that are more internal, or *you*-focused. We've answered the question, "What is it about *me* that shapes my personality?" Now we'll shift gears to discuss external factors, or influences that come from the outside. We'll turn to the question, "What is it about my surroundings that shapes my personality?"

Your environment and culture—elements collectively referred to as nurture—have a major impact on who you are and who you become. How much they directly affect your dominant personality traits is debatable. Review these factors to see for yourself:

Geography. Believe it or not, your geographic location might influence your personality—or at least help determine which parts of it you express. Do you live on or near a body of water? Is your region mountainous, hilly, or flat? Do you live in a part of the world where natural disasters such as tornados or floods happen regularly? Is the air around you polluted or clean?

Climate and weather. Most people agree that climate and weather influence our day-to-day moods, but some research suggests they can also affect or enhance certain personality traits. For instance, some people experience cycles of depression and happiness based on seasonal changes such as length of daylight and fluctuation of temperature.[5]

Laws and government. Some people live in nations with strict laws governing personal and social behavior, while other governments emphasize individual freedoms. Your geographical location *within* your state or country also comes into play: Do you live near a regional or national border and thus come into contact with people who live under different laws and leaders?

Morals and religion. It would be difficult to argue that moral and spiritual beliefs do *not* influence your personality. There is a two-way relationship here: Your personality helps guide your sense of right and wrong, while your surroundings and cultural traditions affect your morals and beliefs.

Schooling. Starting the day you enter school, you receive strong messages about values, priorities, and success. Educational practices vary from culture to culture and affect individuals differently. For example, does your educational system prioritize memorization of facts or critical thinking? Is individual achievement valued over group work?

Experiences. The events and places you witness or participate in are also potential influences on your personality development. Have you traveled abroad? Have you lived through a war or other history-making event? Some people report how a single moment marked a new

[5] Partonen, T. and Pandi-Perumal, S.R. (2009). *Seasonal Affective Disorder: Practice and Research* (New York: Oxford University Press).

stage in their personal development; it made the difference between who they were beforehand and who they became afterward.

Social Influences

Strictly speaking, people are part of your environment. Social surroundings have such a profound influence on personality that they deserve their own category. To some extent, your per-

sonality becomes aligned with what other people expect from you and believe about you.

Who defines *you*—you or the people who interact with you? Are you your own person, or are you a reflection of what you see in other people's eyes? The answer is that all of these possibilities are true. This explains the difference between your self-perception and others' perceptions of you. The feedback we receive from others shapes and reinforces our personalities. In fact, the concept of personality would be meaningless if we all lived solitary lives. Our personality is a product of our social interactions.

Your family is an enormous influence on the person you become. Your parents or other caregivers, your siblings, and your extended family members set the tone for how you are expected to interact with others. They are the first people to observe your personality, and your self-perception is partly based on their stories about your childhood. Whether your caregivers are strict or easygoing, involved or distant, their

TrueStory

"When I was 13, I moved from the East Coast to the West Coast. Lots of people would hate to move at that age, but it was freeing for me. In my hometown everyone had me pegged as acting a certain way or being a certain person. When I moved, nobody had those kinds of expectations. I started expressing parts of my personality that I didn't even know were inside me. None of my new teachers knew my older brothers and assumed I was a troublemaker too. I became a lot more outgoing."

child-rearing style makes a lifelong imprint on you. You might find yourself trying to be like certain family members, or you may do just the opposite—rebel against them.

As you grow up, your friends, teachers, coaches, spiritual and political leaders, and acquaintances all leave their marks on your personality. When you think about your values, major life decisions, priorities, career goals, and political views, you can probably point out people who helped shape each one. Even the media plays an important role. What we watch on television, read in newspapers or magazines, or hear on the radio affects us in both direct and subtle ways.

Acting It Out: Personality and Behavior

Does your personality shape your behavior, or does your behavior determine your personality? Are your personality and behavior linked at all? These questions have stumped philosophers and psychologists for centuries. Even today, you'll get different answers from different sources. In this section, we will take a closer look at behavior and how it relates to personality. Then we will discuss how patterns of human behavior play out in the workplace.

What Is Behavior?

Behavior is how we act and react in response to our environment. If personality is a set of observable traits, behavior is one of the main ways you announce your personality to the world. It could be said that your behavior is a window into your personality. Since others cannot see into your brain, they must rely on your actions and words to figure out who you are. For example, if you frown and look downward every time you enter a meeting, your co-workers will probably conclude that you are antisocial, introverted, or grumpy.

Have you ever made a New Year's resolution that you didn't keep? More than likely, you found it difficult to adjust your usual behavior. Like personality traits, behaviors happen in patterns. It is said that history repeats itself; so do our behaviors. If you pay close attention, you'll observe distinct patterns occurring in your close relationships, at the workplace, in your financial dealings, in your schooling, and in many other areas of your life.

This is where the agreement ends and the debate begins. Psychologists can generally agree on the definition of behavior, but they differ widely in their views on two topics: (1) how behavior relates to personality, and (2) how much control people have over their own behavior. Let's approach these topics one at a time.

How Are Personality and Behavior Related?

Here are two theories about how personality and behavior interact. The first comes from the work of Austrian psychologist Sigmund Freud (1856–1939); the second comes from the field of behaviorism.

Behavior is dependent on personality. According to Freud, one of the fathers of modern psychology, our behavior is determined by the three aspects of personality—the id, the ego, and the superego. It helps to think of these elements in terms of the controls of a car.

If your personality were an automobile, the **id** would be the gas pedal, telling you to go. Your id consists of basic, instinctual urges aimed at survival and pleasure: protection, hunger, sex, and warmth. It demands instant gratification and ignores anything but animal desires. If you were stranded on an island with no supplies, your id would drive you to find sources of food and water at all costs. Even though the id is based on instincts that all humans share, people act on and prioritize their urges in different ways. Hunger may be a particularly strong desire for one person, while another individual may be driven more by a need for protection.

The **ego** is the clutch, helping you change gears depending on the driving conditions and the situation. Your ego tells you to proceed with *caution*. Aware of the realities of your environment, your ego tells your id to cool off by activating your conscience. How does this translate into behavior? Let's return to the island you're stranded on. You find a lone palm tree with eight coconuts on it. Your id presses the gas pedal and says, "Eat them all!" Your ego reasons that this tree might be your only food source for days or even weeks. It presses the clutch and shifts you to a lower gear. In the end, you eat one coconut and decide to eat one more per day.

Finally, the **superego** is your brake pedal, telling you to *stop*. It demands that you modify your behavior to fit moral principles or to please others, and it controls your sense of guilt. Another nickname for the superego is "the police," because it controls your sense of right and wrong. Imagine that you're stranded on an

Building **Background**

Coping strategies are behavior patterns that people develop—often without being aware of it—in order to protect themselves from anxiety or pain. Many people think that all coping strategies are bad habits, but human beings need them in order to survive. You may not have complete control over your behavior, but with some help, you can identify destructive coping strategies and learn to face stressful situations more productively instead. See the chart below for examples of coping strategies.

Coping Strategies

Less Healthy Coping Strategies	More Healthy Coping Strategies
withdrawal: hiding from anxiety	reducing your commitments (saying no)
denial: refusing to admit you are anxious	anticipating anxiety and planning ahead
aggression: taking out your anxiety on others	channeling anxiety into a productive activity, such as volunteer work or art
addiction: trying to escape anxiety through drugs, alcohol, smoking, overeating, starving yourself, etc.	spending quality "you" time—exercising, meditating, writing in a journal
regression: acting like a child in the face of anxiety	asking for help

Behavior Patterns at Work

Negative or Destructive Patterns	Positive Patterns
shifting your responsibilities onto others	taking responsibility for your work
stereotyping your co-workers and treating them accordingly	learning and nurturing other employees' strengths
playing favorites or forming alliances	maintaining balanced relationships with all co-workers
hiding your faults and mistakes	communicating delays or other problems honestly and directly
complaining about what you don't get	asking for what you want

island, but you're with two children this time. You come across the lone palm tree, but there is only one coconut on it. Your id screams, "Eat the whole thing!" Your ego points out, "It might be to your advantage to keep everyone alive; you can cooperate." Your superego says, "No way are you going to take food from a child. That's plain wrong." In the end, you give half to one child and half to the other.

Behavior happens with no regard to personality. Behavioral psychologists, such as Ivan Pavlov, John B. Watson, and B. F. Skinner, proposed that our actions have nothing to do with our personality traits or our state of mind. Human behavior happens automatically, in the same way for all animals:

1. Something happens or changes in your environment.

2. You respond. (This is the behavior.)

3. Your behavior has a positive consequence (a reward) or a negative consequence (a punishment).

4. You learn to repeat behaviors that are rewarded and to stop behaviors that are punished.

Here is a very simple example to illustrate this process:

1. A pot of boiling water starts to fall off the stove.

2. You reach out to grab it.

3. You get a second-degree burn on your hand.

4. In the future, you avoid reaching out to catch a hot object.

If this theory is true, behavior may influence your personality—observations about your behavior will still lead to conclusions about your defining characteristics—but not the other way around.

Who's right? In short, neither theory. So far, no scientist has come up with a model that fully explains the relationship between personality and behavior. The trophy is up for grabs. What do you think?

Behavior Patterns on the Job

Just as your personality traits affect your attitudes toward work and performance in the workplace, behavior patterns are part of the impression you make as a job candidate or employee. Review the chart above of positive and negative professional behavior patterns. When you are at work, try to minimize actions from the left-hand column and maximize actions from the right-hand column.

After reading this unit, you might find your mind filled with more questions than answers. Welcome to the study of human behavior!

Unit Summary

- Personality is a set of observable traits that makes an individual unique.
- Research suggests that your personality can change over time.
- Both personality and behavior affect your career choices and your professional style.
- Personality tests can be useful tools in the workplace, but they do not fully assess who you are or how you act.
- Your personality is shaped by biological, environmental, and social forces.
- Behavior is how you act and react in response to your environment.

TO-DO List

- ✔ Determine which aspects of your **personality** led you to your current career goals.
- ✔ Research free online **personality tests.**
- ✔ Talk to family members about which personality **traits** might have been passed down through multiple generations.
- ✔ Identify some of your values, and describe how they shape your personality and **behavior.**
- ✔ Make a list of five actions you took yesterday, and try to figure out why you behaved the way you did. In each case, were you simply reacting to your environment, or did you intentionally decide to take that action? How did your actions reflect your personality, if at all?

Important Terms

How well do you know these terms? Look them up in the glossary if you need help remembering them.

psychologists	personality test	coping strategies
personality	personality type	id
traits	temperament	ego
organizational behavior	behavior	superego

Online Resources

The Myers and Briggs Foundation
www.myersbriggs.org

Stress Management
www.helpguide.org/mental/stress_management_relief_coping.htm

National Institute of Child Health and Human Development
www.nichd.nih.gov/

Common Careers for Personality Types
www.personalitypage.com/careers.html

Great Ideas in Personality
www.personalityresearch.org/

The Five-Factor Model of Personality in the Workplace
www.personalityresearch.org/papers/neubert.html

Exercises

1. Review the list of personality traits on page 16. Choose the five traits that you feel are most central to your personality. Then show the list to two people who know you well. Which five traits did these people choose for you? Are they different? If so, why?

2. Find one or two online personality tests and complete them. Based on the results, think of at least five ways you can draw on your personality to perform well in your future career.

3. In a notebook, write a few paragraphs about the person who has shaped your personality the most. Why do you think this person was (or is) so influential? How do you think you would be different today if you had never met this person?

4. Use the four-step behavior process on page 25 to come up with three more examples of how you might learn to behave in a certain way in response to your environment.

KEYS TO
success

Distinguishing between communication and expression

Recognizing that we communicate with and without words

Learning to listen actively

Using good communication skills in the workplace

how would your life be different if you couldn't communicate? Think of all the ways you communicated today. How did you let someone know what you were thinking or feeling? Did you use words? Did you smile? Did you frown? Maybe you asked questions when you didn't understand something clearly. Maybe you drew a picture to describe something. When you communicate, you let others know what you are thinking or how you are feeling. But communication is not just about expressing yourself. It's also about listening and about really hearing what the other person says.

Communicating—or not communicating—can make a huge difference everywhere in our lives, including the workplace. This unit will help you become more aware of the different ways in which we communicate.

Communication Versus Expression

Communication requires a connection between an individual who is sending a message and an individual who is receiving that message. If the message is not received in the way that the sender was hoping it would be received, then effective communication did not occur. Communication requires engagement between two people.

Expression

When you express yourself, you might say, write, or even paint or dance about what you are thinking or feeling. You might talk or sing where no one will hear you—say, in the shower—or write in a journal that no one else will read. In fact, when you express yourself, you do it for yourself and not others. The term *self-expression* says it all. Expression comes from the self, for the self.

When you express yourself, you do it because it helps you feel better or it helps you sort out your thoughts. For example, if you let out a yell because your car has a flat tire, the yell doesn't fix your tire, but for an instant it makes you feel better. Doing a victory dance when your team scores a touchdown won't help them score another one, but it expresses your happiness. No one may ever see the journal you keep, but the thoughts you express help you sort out your feelings at the end of every day. When you express yourself, you are not especially concerned about whether someone else correctly interprets your message—or is even listening at all.

Communication

Communication may begin with an expression of ideas or feelings, but it includes sending that information to another person. If you do not express yourself clearly, in a way that your listener can understand, you are not communicating. When you communicate, you are not talking or writing just for yourself. Instead, you are tailoring your message to a certain audience.

As you communicate, you use **feedback,** the verbal or nonverbal response to a communication, from your audience to adjust your message because you care whether your audience understands what you are saying. Thus, the audience communicates with you, as well. For example, if the other person communicates by leaning toward you, you know that he or she is excited by or interested in what you are saying. If you post on Facebook and your wall fills up with questions, you should consider the wording of your posting. What caused all of the questions? Did you include too many details or not enough? The questions you receive give you feedback so you can adapt your message to your audience—and make a clearer posting next time!

Being able to identify and use feedback, even when it's not spoken, will strengthen your ability to communicate at home, at work, and at every place in between. In this unit, we will provide some tips that will help.

Communicating With and Without Words

Your friend asks whether you are ready to go to lunch. You might reply by saying yes, or you might just smile and nod your head. We communicate in more ways than with just our words.

Verbal Communication

Verbal communication means using words to speak or write, but in this unit we'll focus on speaking. Did you know that *how* you speak can be as important as the words you say? The same words, spoken in different ways, can have different meanings.

For example, your instructor might ask, "Are you finished yet?" to find out about the completion of a project. You say yes or no. However, what if your instructor asks, *"Aren't you finished yet?"* emphasizing *Aren't* and *yet?* Now your instructor sounds impatient. You worry that it is taking you too long to complete the project. You might get nervous and feel insecure. The simple addition of one word completely changes the tone of the message.

Consider these elements when you speak:

Word Choice. The words you use tell people how professional you are. If your supervisor asks you to do something, reply, "Okay," or "No problem" instead of "You got it, babe." Even if you get along well with your supervisor, it's better to use words that show respect. Avoid using slang expressions at work or school.

Also, remember that the point of communication is understanding. If a co-worker is having problems with a computer program, try to explain the problem and give the solution in terms that he or she will understand. Sometimes, using too many technical terms leads to confusion instead of clarity. The goal is not to impress the person with your knowledge. It is to help your co-worker understand how to use the computer. Watch how your co-worker behaves in response to your instructions and then adjust your communication until he or she understands.

When posting comments on a discussion board, remember who your audience is. Stay on topic and choose words that communicate your thoughts clearly. If you agree with someone else's comments, you might want to post, "Yes, I agree," instead of, "Ain't it the truth!"

Practice
Critical Thinking

Think about how you communicate verbally. Do people often ask you to repeat yourself? Might you be speaking too softly or not clearly enough? Has someone recently asked you to speak more slowly? Do you often end up protesting, "That's not what I meant!"? Think about your word choices, along with the tone and pitch of your voice and the other aspects of your verbal communication. What are your strengths? What might you need to watch more carefully?

Now think about how you communicate nonverbally. Do you always face a speaker and show your interest by making eye contact? Do your facial expressions match what you say? Do you use gestures meaningfully? Do your clothes and appearance look professional? Remember that we are always communicating, whether we intend to or not.

Tone. The tone of your voice indicates whether a sentence is a statement or a question. Tone also indicates whether you feel confident or uncertain about your message. For example, consider the difference between saying, "You can't find the file?" if a colleague asks for your help, instead of, "Can't you find the file?" The first response sounds helpful; the second sounds irritated or annoyed by the request.

Tone can definitely send a message. You might say "Really?" to show that you are impressed and amazed by what you just heard. However, spoken in a different tone, "Really?" can indicate that you aren't fooled by whatever the other person just said.

Pitch. The pitch—highness or lowness—of your voice is determined by the thickness and length of the vocal cords in your throat. However, when you are excited or angry, your pitch tends to rise from its usual level. A higher pitch can communicate your true feelings, even if you are trying not to share them. "WHAT did you say?" is an example of a higher pitch. You can hear the emotional reaction. "What did you say?" is an example of a lower pitch. Even though the words are the same, you can tell that the speakers have very different emotions.

Rate. The more excited or nervous you are, the faster you tend to talk. You got an "A" on your test and are so excited to tell your friend that your words come gushing out of you. Take your time. Slow down. Remember to breathe. And remember that your goal is to share information. Being aware of how your feelings affect your speaking rate helps you communicate more effectively.

Building **Background**

The word "clarity" can refer to the way words are pronounced or to the ideas expressed by those words. Clarity of speech and clarity of ideas are both essential to good communication.

If you remember the two ways that clarity—or the lack of it—can affect the message, you'll communicate more clearly.

Stress or Inflection. Stress or inflection refers to the word or words emphasized in a sentence. The words you choose to stress can communicate many different meanings. Here are some examples:

- ***You*** *are doing a good job.* The speaker really wants you to know you're special.
- *You **are** doing a good job.* Stressing **are** is reassuring. There's no doubt you're succeeding.
- *You are doing a **good job.*** By emphasizing **good job,** the speaker emphasizes the strength of your performance.

Before you say something important, try stressing different words to see how the meaning changes. What do you notice?

"Words mean more than what is set down on paper. It takes the human voice to infuse them with shades of deeper meaning."
—Maya Angelou, American poet

Clarity. Saying words clearly shows confidence. It also indicates that you are considerate of your listeners. You want to make it easy for them to understand you. Mumbling, on the other hand, makes speech difficult to understand. It also shows a lack of awareness or concern about listeners. In addition, listeners often assume that a mumbling speaker lacks knowledge, confidence, or both.

Volume. It's appropriate to speak in a normal volume both at work or in school. A loud voice can startle your listeners, or hurt their ears. Yet a soft voice makes the speaker seem young and unsure. Be sure to use a volume that is appropriate for the situation. Jesse, for example, works at a construction site. In order to be heard, he needs to raise his voice above the sounds of the equipment, so sometimes he yells. Abby, on the other hand, works in a medical office, where patient information is very sensitive. Abby has a very loud voice. To make sure that Abby doesn't reveal a patient's private information, she needs to speak at a lower volume.

So, remember to be aware of not just what you say, but how you say it. Keep your volume and pitch at their usual levels. To help hide any nervousness, don't let the tone of your voice turn sentences into questions. It's always a good idea to speak slowly. Choose your words carefully, matching your vocabulary to your audience. Say words clearly so listeners can easily understand them, and remember that the

words you choose to stress can greatly affect your message.

Nonverbal Communication

The words you say are only part of how you communicate. The way you say those words carries its own message. In addition, you communicate nonverbally. **Nonverbal communication** simply means communicating without words. For example, you communicate by the way you stand and sit, whether you intend to send a message or not. In fact, it's impossible to stop communicating as long as another person can see or hear you. Everything about your appearance and your actions communicates something to the people around you. Sometimes your appearance or actions can communicate more than your words!

Differences in Feedback. Think about the different ways you communicated today. You probably spoke face-to-face with many people. Maybe you spoke on the phone, too. Did you post a message on a discussion board? Now think about how the person you were communicating with responded. Beyond their words,

how did you know what they were thinking or feeling? Was your friend silent on the phone when you asked her a question? Did her silence mean she was thinking of the answer? Or did it mean that your question made her nervous, and she didn't really want to answer it? When you gave your presentation in class and the instructor smiled at you, you probably assumed you did well. Nonverbal feedback lets you know whether you are communicating and how your message is being received.

When you are communicating face-to-face, your message includes not only the words you say and how you say them, but many nonverbal cues. The next section explores how you can become aware of those cues and make them work for you.

Body Language. The way you sit and stand offers a message. Leaning toward the speaker shows you are engaged and interested in the speaker and the topic. Think of how you feel when someone leans closer to hear what you have to say. On the other hand, slouching could say that you are bored or uninterested, and fidgeting implies nervousness.

Eye Contact. Eye contact means different things in different cultures. In the United States, making eye contact shows honesty and interest. Failure to make eye contact during a conversation can show nervousness, boredom, or even arrogance—as if the person speaking is not worth listening to. Making eye contact during a conversation lets the other person know that you're paying attention. When you are engaging in a conversation with someone, look at the person before you begin. When the person looks back, it is a signal that you have his or her attention and may begin. During the conversation it is natural to look away from the other person—constant eye contact can make a person uncomfortable—but glance back periodically to reestablish the connection. Looking into the listener's eyes offers the speaker feedback about how the message is being received. If you see confusion, anger, or boredom, you can adjust how you are communicating your message accordingly.

Facial Expressions. Whether it's a smile, a frown, pursed lips, or a roll of the eyes, facial expressions speak volumes about a speaker or a listener. No matter what a person says, however, the look on his or her face offers a louder message. A supervisor might say, "I really like your idea," and her face lights up as she says it. Being aware of someone's facial expressions gives you more feedback about his or her reaction.

Gestures. Gestures can help clarify a message, distract from it, or show nervousness or uncertainty. For example, someone who waves his arms around while sharing an idea may look excited—or unprofessional. Make sure your gestures are appropriate to the situation.

Clothing, Accessories, and Appearance. The way you look may communicate many messages, depending on your audience. Some businesses have dress codes or guidelines, and some jobs involve uniforms, because the

Practice Now: Empowered

How can you convince potential employers that you are empowered? Eye contact is a very powerful tool. Practice now by being aware of your use of eye contact. When you check out at the grocery store, look the clerk in the eye and smile—see whether you can get the clerk to smile back. Try it anywhere—at the gym, at work, at school. See whether you can communicate with your body language that you are positive and confident. You'll know it's working when the other person looks you in the eye, smiles, and strikes up a conversation.

employer wants employees to send a certain message about the company. Clothing, jewelry, shoes, and accessories that distract other employees or customers can be interpreted as attention-seeking or overly sexual. Uniforms solve this problem. Conservative people may interpret tattoos on a person's face, neck, or hands as a sign of aggression. For this reason, employers often require employees to conceal tattoos.

Personal Space. Standing too close to others can make them uncomfortable. Invading someone's personal space can be interpreted as aggressive or intimidating, like an attack. How close is too close? Even people within the same culture don't agree on the amount of personal space that is appropriate. If someone backs up, you're too close for that person's comfort. Don't step closer.

Recognizing Nonverbal Communication Cues

So, if someone rarely makes eye contact, is she untrustworthy? Maybe, but probably not. She might just feel uncomfortable or unsure about what is expected of her. She might come from a culture where looking down is a sign of respect and making eye contact is rude. It is important to practice the other side of communication, too—"listening" to the other person's message, even when it isn't spoken.

Identifying Possible Meanings to Some Nonverbal Cues. If someone sits with his arms crossed over his chest, is he angry? Maybe, but he might just be cold. If your suggestion is met with silence, does your supervisor hate it? Maybe, but she also might be thinking about ways to use your idea.

It is easy to misinterpret the intention of someone else's nonverbal cues. This is especially true when you are interacting with people from other cultures or even from other regions of the United States. If you're not sure how to interpret a nonverbal cue, you might ask a reflective question, such as "What do you think?"

TrueStory

"I had just started a new job, and there was a guy at work who always looked away from me when I walked by. I thought he hated me. I worried about it for weeks. Then, one day, we were in a meeting together, and I figured out that he was like that with everybody—he just couldn't look people in the eye because he was really shy. We later became good friends. What you see on the outside isn't always the whole story."

Matching Nonverbal Communication to the Intended Message. If you want others to interpret your nonverbal cues correctly, you will need to be a careful observer. Pay attention to your body language, the amount of eye contact you use, and your facial expressions. Make sure your nonverbal cues match the message you intend to share. And make sure your gestures, clothing, and other cues show that you are professional.

Practice Now: Empowered

The physical presentation that works in your community or with your friends may not be acceptable at your school or work. If you wear too much jewelry, you may be seen as dangerous or too showy. If you wear the wrong clothes, you may be perceived as sloppy or unprofessional. How can you figure out the right messages to send to your audience? Practice being empowered now by becoming an observer. Study the successful people around you—the people you admire. How do they dress? What accessories do they wear? Watching others can teach you how to communicate effectively.

What Is Active Listening?

You know what it means to listen. But **active listening** means that you are really paying attention to the speaker and are working to understand what he or she is communicating.

Listening Shows Respect

A supervisor is telling her staff about a change in the way assignments are made. Maria and Mike are clearly listening, but Carla hasn't looked up once. In fact, she seems to be texting someone! "Carla," the supervisor says, "may I have your attention?"

"I'm listening," Carla insists. "I can do two things at once. No problem."

Carla is likely to miss important information about this new procedure—and may compromise her job performance. Listening is not only a way to gather information but also a sign of respect. Good listening skills can encourage a speaker to tell you more, so you get the information you need to perform well on the job. Active listening can lead you to ask questions when you don't understand the speaker's meaning or intention. If you're not actively listening, you won't know what you don't understand. Poor listening shows a lack of interest and a lack of respect for the speaker.

Keys to Good Listening

In the scenario above, the supervisor knows that Maria and Mike are paying attention because good listening is obvious. You, too, can tell when someone is—or is not—listening to you. Good listeners show they are paying attention in these ways:

- They make eye contact and focus on the speaker without looking around the room, shuffling through papers, or checking an electronic device, including a cell phone or computer screen.

- They lean forward to hear better and avoid distractions.
- They interact with the speaker in ways that show they agree or understand.
- They ask for more information to clarify the message. For example: "When should we send that form?"
- They restate what they think they heard to confirm the message. For example: "So, we need to complete this new form every time we make a run?"
- They listen for emotions and feelings to show understanding. For example: "The last-minute change in that order must have been frustrating."

Listening Affects the Speaker, Too

Why else is good listening important? Think of how you feel when someone really listens to you. When you feel heard, you know that your ideas are valued, which encourages you to share more of your thoughts and to value others' ideas. In this way, good listening improves teamwork. Active listening can strengthen relationships and reduce conflicts. It also helps avoid miscommunications that can lead to mistakes and delays. On the other hand, poor listening, along with thoughtless responses, can strain or even destroy a relationship.

TrueStory

"I had a boss whose idea of how to run a business meeting was to go around the team and ask everyone what he or she thought we should do. Then, no matter what the team had said, our boss would tell us what we were going to do. Sometimes, we had all agreed on a solution, and then she would tell us that we were going to go with her (different) solution. Why did she even ask us if she had already made up her mind? I didn't work there for long. I found a job where the managers listened to the staff."

Communicating Effectively in the Workplace

Communicating is more than talking, and listening is more than hearing. Both take skill and practice. No matter what field you're in, communicating and listening effectively are essential.

Speak Carefully, but Speak Up

Whether it's fair or not, people judge your competence and professionalism by how well you communicate—with and without words. You need strong communication skills to build relationships with customers, clients, patients, supervisors, co-workers, team members, and others. Here are some examples:

- A patient care assistant who makes eye contact and speaks calmly, controlling pitch, rate, and volume, can help an anxious patient relax. If the assistant uses active listening while taking a medical history, a patient will be more likely to describe symptoms that may greatly affect the medical care he or she needs.
- An electrician who slowly and clearly answers an elderly customer's repeated questions is increasing his job security, as that customer is likely to call his company

again. She'll also tell her friends about this friendly, helpful technician.

- A billing clerk who tells an angry customer, "I can understand why this would upset you," is helping to defuse his anger. Showing that she understands his frustration helps him calm down. Then he will be more likely to accept her solution to the problem.

You Are Always Communicating

The key to effective communication is to be aware of your audience(s) at all times. You talk about different things with different people. You also use different words and different body language. The topics and tones that are appropriate with friends may not be acceptable in the workplace. Here are some tips for communicating in a wide variety of environments safely and professionally:

- Use standard English and grammar. You do not need to sound like a grammar teacher; just avoid swear words and slang.
- Be respectful. Using offensive names for women (or men) or for racial or religious groups can get employees fired in many workplaces and can ruin potential friends and opportunities. Telling jokes about certain groups is just another way of offending people and showing disrespect. Whenever you talk, imagine that the whole office or department is listening. Today, most cell phones can record both audio and video, so whatever you say or do could end up on YouTube. Make sure you'd be comfortable with your behavior if everyone could see it.
- Be polite. *Please, thank you,* and *you're welcome* will never be inappropriate, anywhere. These words show respect anvd consideration. Being polite helps build and strengthen relationships, no matter who or where you are.

- Talk about appropriate topics. Let's say you and other patients are sitting in a medical waiting room. Everyone can overhear the receptionists talk about the doctors, other staff, and an office party they're planning. The receptionists might even be venting their frustration about patients who don't show up for appointments. The people waiting feel uncomfortable or annoyed at this unprofessional sharing of information. If several mention it to the doctors, the receptionists may face reprimands—or even lose their jobs.

Remember, it's a wired world. You may have audiences you don't even know exist. So, communicate as if EVERYONE can hear you.

ON THE JOB

Keisha noticed how it took days to gather the required signatures on request forms before they ended up in her supervisor's inbox. She had a better idea, so she gathered her courage and approached her supervisor's desk.

"Umm… Mr. Lewis, I think…. I mean maybe…. You know those request forms?" Keisha mumbled as she stared at her shoes.

Mr. Lewis glanced up from the spreadsheet he was studying. "What about them?"

"Well, it takes a long time… I mean, I think I have an idea." By now, Keisha was practically whispering.

Mr. Lewis had already turned back to his spreadsheet. "Keisha, I'm really busy. Can we talk about this another time?"

Because Keisha mumbled and whispered, her ideas were not heard. Also, Mr. Lewis did a poor job of listening, preventing him from benefiting from the ideas. Now Keisha is discouraged, Mr. Lewis is annoyed, and the process is still inefficient.

Unit Summary

- Expression is the sharing of ideas and thoughts, perhaps just with yourself. Communication requires sending information to and receiving information from another person.

- We communicate with and without words, so we need to be aware of the messages we send, whether or not we intend to send them.

- To listen actively, use words and nonverbal cues to show your interest and to encourage the speaker to say more.

- Communicating appropriately in the workplace can help make you a trusted, respected, effective employee.

TO-DO List

✔ Keep track of the nonverbal cues that you observe during one day. Complete a chart like this:

Nonverbal cue	Possible meaning or meanings	Any verbal message	How well do the verbal and nonverbal messages match?

✔ After you complete the chart above, choose a nonverbal cue that you now know you misinterpreted. Explain why that happened and describe the correct interpretation of this nonverbal cue.

✔ Listen for another example of how someone's tone of voice, pitch, rate of speaking, word stress, or volume contradicted the words he or she said. For example, someone might say, "Lester, I'd like to hear your suggestion" in a way that implies that Lester probably isn't going to offer a usable idea. Describe the situation.

✔ Listen actively to at least one person today, in the workplace, at school, or at home. Record how listening actively differed from your usual listening. Also describe how the speaker reacted to your **active listening.**

Important Terms

How well do you know these terms? Look them up in the glossary if you need help remembering them.

Feedback

Verbal communication

Nonverbal communication

Active listening

Exercises

1. You work in a dental office. After patients have had a complicated procedure, the dentist has you give them a written set of instructions to follow at home. Are these instructions an example of expression or communication? Explain your answer. How can the dentist use these instructions to show respect for the patient?

2. Why is it important to pay attention to the nonverbal cues when you are communicating?

3. You don't have any experience with a software program you've been asked to install. You call Jeff, an installer who works in another office, and ask whether he could walk you through it. Jeff hesitates a moment, and you hear him sigh. Then he says, "Well… I guess so…. What system are you using?" What verbal message does Jeff offer? What is his nonverbal message? What are the nonverbal cues? How could you use active listening as you respond?

4. How is communicating with customers, clients, or patients different from communicating with co-workers?

success

Identifying and using basic computer parts

Opening and using a web browser

Using computers and the Internet to accomplish tasks and goals

Creating, naming, saving, and organizing files and folders

Using Microsoft Office® programs for academic and professional tasks

a t hectic times in your life, have you ever wished you had a personal assistant? Like a celebrity movie star, you could have someone do your shopping, manage your finances, get you coffee in the morning, and give you pep talks when you're in a bad mood. Or have you ever wished you had a clone? You could sit back and put your feet up while your carbon copy did all your work.

Most of us aren't movie stars, but we can still have the closest thing to a personal assistant: a computer. The whole point behind the personal computer is to make your life easier—to have another "brain" around. You can put it to work for you in your everyday life, at work, and at school. And you don't even have to pay it a salary.

Meet the Personal Computer

Your new assistant—the personal computer—can do a lot of things automatically, but it doesn't run completely on its own. This is where computer skills come in handy. This unit is a brief, practical guide to using a computer and its programs. We will walk through each task step by step and provide additional tips to keep you going.

Here are a few items to keep in mind along the way:

- This unit is an introduction. For additional help, consult your librarian or learning resource center director, your instructor, the distance education administrator at your campus, or another advanced computer user. The Internet is also an excellent resource for tips and training.
- The abbreviation *PC* stands for *personal computer*. However, it is also a general term for a computer that runs on Windows®—basically, any machine that isn't made by Apple®. For the purposes of this unit, the term *PC* refers to a non-Mac® computer such as a Dell®, IBM®, or Hewlett-Packard®.
- Every skill covered in this unit applies to Macs as well as PCs. The steps, menus, and commands may be slightly different. In some cases we have supplied Mac-specific instructions.

Basic Personal Computer Tasks

Figure 4.1 shows just a few examples of tasks you can complete on a computer. We won't cover every task in this unit, but here is a preview of what your "personal assistant" can offer.

Building **Background**

Computers haven't always been used in these ways. For example, some of the earliest computers—such as the Colossus, the Lorenz cipher machines, and the Enigma machine—were used to create or crack codes during World War II.

Functions of a Computer

At Home	At School	At Work
• Make calculations	• Do research	• Manage customer or patient information
• Write to-do lists	• Write papers	
• Download, store, and organize photograph and music collections	• Sign up for meetings	• Create invoices, payments, and receipts
	• Check grades	• Buy supplies
• Watch online videos, movies, or TV shows	• Email with instructors, classmates, and school administrators	• Schedule shipments
• Shop online		• Create budgets
• Create a budget	• Design presentations	• Write memos and reports
• Manage a calendar	• Learn software	• Design newsletters and pamphlets
• Email, chat, or video chat with friends and family members	• Complete coursework	• Email co-workers and clients

Figure 4.1

(1) **Monitor** (3) **System Unit** (5) **Speaker** (7) **Keyboard**

(2) **Modem** (4) **Mouse** (6) **Printer**

The Main Gear: Hardware

Computers have a lot of parts, but getting to know them is usually worth the time it takes. **Hardware** consists of the physical parts of your computer. In the diagram shown here, you'll see the main hardware components of a laptop and a desktop computer.

Components you don't control. These parts do a computer's work behind the scenes. You don't have to worry about controlling them. They are like the organs in your body and run on their own.

- **Processor.** This is a computer's "brain." It does most of the calculating and manipulating of data. When you execute a command, the processor carries it out. The processor is also called the central processing unit, or CPU.
- **Hard drive.** A computer's main storage device, the hard drive contains files, programs, and other data. When you save a file or install a program, it usually ends up on the hard drive.

- **RAM (random access memory).** There are two types of memory: storage memory (what the hard drive is for) and RAM. A computer uses RAM to keep programs running smoothly.
- **Monitor.** This part is the screen that displays text and graphics. Aside from making sure its power is on, you don't control it directly.

How do you get all this going? You have to start—or boot—your computer. Here's how:

1. Press the main power button on the system unit, which looks something like this: ⏻. You might also need to press the power button on your monitor.

2. You may be prompted to type a username and password. If you are not familiar with this step, you may need to follow your computer's "Get Started" instructions or, if you are borrowing a computer, consult with the owner of the computer.

3. You'll see the desktop, with a background picture and icons. Now you're ready to use your computer.

Components you control. You use these hardware parts to tell the computer what to do.

- **Keyboard.** This is the component you use to type letters, numbers, symbols, and commands. To use it, simply press down on a key and let go immediately. If you want to type several versions of the same key (for example, 15 *y*'s in a row), press the key and hold it until you're done.

- **Mouse or trackpad.** For desktop computers, you use a mouse—a handheld device plugged into the keyboard. For a laptop, you use a trackpad—a flat panel built into the keyboard. The chart below tells you how to use a mouse or trackpad. (**Note:** In this unit, when we direct you to *click* on something, we are referring to the left button of the mouse or trackpad.)

Mouse and Trackpad Commands

Command	How to Do It With a Mouse	How to Do It With a Trackpad
Move the pointer ( ) or cursor (I) around on the screen.	Move the entire mouse over a flat surface such as a desk.	Touch the trackpad with one finger, and move your finger around on the panel (maintaining contact).
Select an icon or other object.	1. Move the pointer to the object. 2. Click the left button once and release it immediately.	1. Move the pointer to the object. 2. Click the left button once and release it immediately.
Open a folder or program; highlight one word.	1. Move the pointer to the object or word. 2. Click the left button twice quickly.	1. Move the pointer to the object or word. 2. Click the left button twice quickly.
Click and drag: move an object around on the desktop.	1. Move the pointer to the object. 2. Click the left button and hold it down. 3. Move the mouse to drag the object where you want it. 4. Release the button.	1. Move the pointer to the object. 2. Click the left button and hold it down. 3. Move your finger on the trackpad to drag the object where you want it. 4. Release the button.
Scroll (go up and down within a window).	Move the round dial up and down (some mouses do not have this feature).	Press up and down on the middle button OR place two fingers on the trackpad and move both fingers up and down (some trackpads do not have this feature).
Highlight multiple words.	1. Move the pointer to the beginning of the first word. 2. Click and hold the left button. 3. Move the mouse to the end of the last word (you will see the text highlight as you go). 4. Release the button.	1. Move the pointer to the beginning of the first word. 2. Click and hold the left button. 3. Move your finger on the trackpad until you get to the last word (you will see the text highlight as you go). 4. Release the button.
Right-click: bring up a list of commands that apply to a specific object.	1. Move the pointer to the object. 2. Click the right button once and release it immediately.	1. Move the pointer to the object. 2. Click the right button once and release it immediately.

- **Optical drive.** This slot or sliding tray holds CDs and DVDs that you use on your computer. To operate a slot-loading mechanism, insert the disk into the slot. For a tray-loading mechanism, press the button next to the tray, place the disk on the tray, and press the same button to close it.

- **Input ports.** These are miniature outlets. You use them to plug in peripherals, or external devices that cooperate with your computer. Peripherals include printers, scanners, MP3 players, cameras, and portable drives. You can use portable drives to back up the contents of your hard drive or to send data from one computer to another.

On the Screen: The Desktop

The desktop is the background on your computer screen. It is always there, whether you are using programs or not. For our purposes, the most important elements on a desktop are icons, the start button, and windows.

An **icon** is a small picture or symbol that represents an object—such as a program, a folder, or a file—on a computer screen. You can customize a desktop to show more or fewer icons, in the same way you can customize a physical desk to be more or less cluttered.

The start button is at the lower left corner of the desktop. You can use it to access nearly everything on your computer. When you click on the start button, you will see a menu like the one at the bottom left.

By clicking on items in the start menu, you can open programs and folders, search for items on the computer, and turn off or restart the computer.

Every time you open a program or a folder, a window will appear. Your desktop can have 1, 3, or even 20 windows open at the same time. The three buttons at the top right-hand corner of each window help keep you organized.

- Click on the right-hand button, or X, to close a window.
- Click on the middle button to do one of two things: expand the window so it fits the entire screen, or reduce the window so it takes up only part of the screen.
- Click on the left-hand button to minimize the window. It will disappear and turn into a tab along the bottom of your screen. This allows you to see your desktop. To bring the window back up, click on the tab.

On Task: Software

Your hardware is up and running, and you know your way around a desktop. Now it's time to use some **software.** This is the term for programs—also called **applications**—that are used on a computer. Software is what you use to complete tasks. Here are some common types of programs:

- Office and school programs: word processors, presentation programs, spreadsheet programs, database programs (you'll learn a lot more about these later)
- Media programs: music and movie playback (Windows Media Player®), image viewing (Windows® Picture and Fax Viewer)
- Email programs (Microsoft Outlook®, Apple Mail®)
- Instant messaging programs (Windows® Live Messenger, Google Chat®) and video chat programs (Skype®)
- Accessory programs (Calculator, Notepad)
- PDF-viewing programs (Adobe® Reader, Adobe® Acrobat Pro, Preview)

Window size buttons

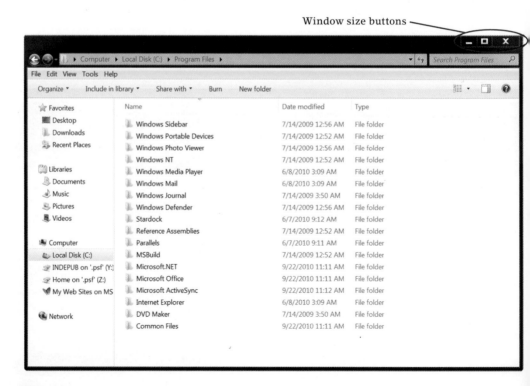

To get around most programs, you will use a combination of menus and buttons. For instance, if you open Windows Media Player®, you will click the <u>Play</u>, <u>Pause</u>, <u>Back</u>, or <u>Next</u> buttons while listening to songs or watching videos. If you're using Apple Mail, you might go to the menu at the top of the screen, click on <u>File</u>, and select <u>New Message</u> from the new menu that drops down.

Internet Basics

The **Internet** is a worldwide network of computers. Its overall purposes are to connect computers and their users and to share information widely and instantaneously. More specifically, people use the Internet for communication, research, education, personal organization, job-related tasks, gaming, entertainment, and social networking.

To access the Internet, follow these steps:

1. Make sure the computer you are using is connected to the Internet. (Internet connections can be complicated, so if you do not know whether your computer is connected, consult your computer manual or the Help Desk for your campus.)

2. From your desktop or the start menu, click on a web browser such as Internet Explorer®, Firefox®, or Safari®. A window will pop up.

3. Click on the address bar. Delete any text that's currently in it.

4. Type a **URL,** or web address into the address bar. If you want to search for a certain type of website, type the URL of a search engine such as www.google.com.

5. Press the ENTER key.

6. The website you have entered will appear in the window.

An especially helpful Internet skill is making a list of **bookmarks** (also called favorites), which are websites you save so you can return to them quickly later on. Follow these steps to bookmark a site:

1. In the top menu, click on <u>Favorites</u> or <u>Bookmarks</u>.

2. Click <u>Add to Favorites</u> or <u>Bookmark This Page</u>.

3. Whenever you want to return to a bookmarked website, click on <u>Favorites</u> and you'll see the site at the bottom. Click on it, and the browser will take you there.

By now you've already been using the Internet to "attend" your digital sessions for CS102. This is an example of using a website in an integrated, effective way. When you visit the course website to complete a session, the components of the digital session work together. From a single website, you can access the unit to-do list, get your reading assignment, watch a video, participate in an online discussion, use flash cards, play educational games, participate in activities, and retrieve and submit assignments. If you haven't done so already, bookmark Kaplan Quad on the browser you use most.

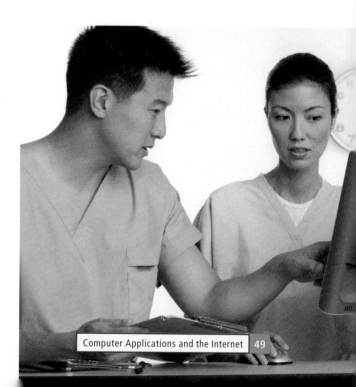

Files and Folders: Your Electronic Filing Cabinet

A physical filing cabinet is typically a large, heavy piece of furniture. Inside these cabinets are hanging folders; inside the hanging folders are manila folders; and inside the manila folders are paper documents. This system may be a bit cumbersome, but it has passed the test of time. A computer can be used as a lighter, smaller filing system. As computer files become more secure and as it becomes easier to scan and store physical documents, more and more industries are moving away from physical filing cabinets in favor of paperless systems.

Files

A **file** is a set of data that is stored on a computer. It could be something you have created, such as a word processing document, a slide presentation, or a photograph. Or it could be something you have bought or downloaded, such as an application, a song, or a movie. Depending on the program, files have specialized names. For example, a file created with Microsoft Word® is often called a document. A PowerPoint® file is a presentation or a slide show. An Excel® file is referred to as a spreadsheet or a workbook.

How do you create a file? It's one of the easiest tasks you can do on a computer.

1. Open a program, such as Microsoft Word or PowerPoint.

2. Usually a new, blank file will open automatically. If you want to create a new one, press and hold the CONTROL key and then press the N key. For Mac, hold the command ⌘ key and then press the N key. Alternatively, go to the top menu and click New. A new file window will pop up.

Once you have created a file—even before you start working on it—you should save it. Saving your work immediately and often should become as automatic to you as breathing. The following instructions for saving a file apply to most computer programs:

1. There are three main ways to command your computer to save a file. Method one is to press and hold the CTRL key (command ⌘ for a Mac) and then press S. Method two is to use the mouse or trackpad to click a button with a disk icon on it. This is often found at the upper left corner of the window. Method three is to click on File in the top menu of your screen and then click Save.

2. A window will pop up. You use this window to name your file and to determine the location where your file will be saved.

3. Along the left side of the window, click the location where you want to save the file. The two most common locations are Desktop and My Documents. Within My Documents, double click on the folders you see until you get the folder where you want to store the file. To create a new folder, click on the Create New Folder button (the icon with a folder and a starburst).

4. Now it's time to give your file a name. Type a brief name (no more than two or three short words or abbreviations) next to File name:.

5. Click the Save button.

6. As you continue working, save your work every few minutes. You will not have to name the file or select the location again; all you have to do is press or click Save.

There may be times when you want to save a file with a different name or in a different location. For example, let's say you use Microsoft Excel to create a weekly timesheet at work. You don't want to type a whole new workbook for each new timesheet; instead, you want to make small changes to the previous week's version and save it as a new file. Follow these steps:

1. Open the file that you want to save in a new way.

2. In the top menu, find Save As . . . and click on it.

3. Follow the general file-saving instructions above to choose a location and to rename the file.

4. Click the Save button. Now you have two files: the original and the newly saved one.

Folders

A **folder** is a named electronic location where you store files. It serves the same purpose as a physical hanging folder or manila folder: to organize and classify information. Imagine what your house or office would look like if you put every important document or piece of mail—that is, every file—in one big heap. If you wanted to find a specific piece of paper, it could take you hours or even days.

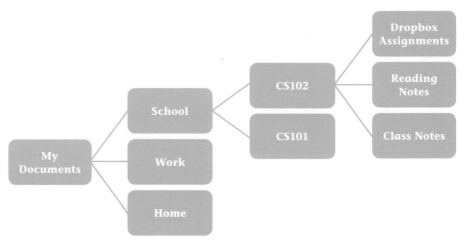

Figure 4.2

The same is true for your computer. Over time, you may create hundreds or even thousands of files of many types and functions. If you don't organize them into folders, you are defeating one of the main purposes of a computer: to simplify your life. Windows computers come with three main folders already created: My Documents, My Pictures, and My Music. It's up to you to create subfolders within these main folders.

Before you start creating folders, think about the best way to organize your electronic life. Get out a piece of paper and draw a diagram such as shown in Figure 4.2.

This computer user decided to divide all of his files into three folders: school, work, and home. Within the School folder, he created a subfolder for each course he is taking: CS102 and CS101. Then, within his CS102 subfolder, he created additional folders for dropbox assignments, notes on readings, and notes he takes in class.

Follow these steps to create new document folders (the same process applies to music and picture folders):

1. On your desktop or in the start menu, click on My Documents. A window will pop up.

2. Click on Make a new folder. A new folder icon will pop up in the middle of the window. It will contain highlighted text that says New Folder.

3. Type a name for your new folder.

4. Press ENTER.

5. To open your new folder (for example, if you want to create subfolders inside it), double-click on the icon.

6. To move back one level to the previous folder, click the Back button.

Back button

7. To delete a folder, click on the icon of the folder you want to delete. Then click Delete this folder at left.

The more time you take to create and organize folders, the easier it will be to find a file quickly. You won't have to scroll down an endless list or stare at hundreds of file icons on your desktop.

Programs With Power: Microsoft Office

Microsoft Office is a group, or suite, of computer programs used for an enormous variety of office-related tasks at home, at school, and at work. As of 2010, about 500 million customers were using Microsoft Office worldwide,[1] and the suite held more than 94 percent of the office software market share.[2] In this section, we will explain how to use three Microsoft Office applications: Word, PowerPoint, and Excel. In essence, all three programs are about manipulating words and numbers.

Common Microsoft Office Features

We'll begin by explaining features that can be used in all three programs—Word, PowerPoint, and Excel. First, look at the diagram of the main screen of Word. Then read the explanations.

- Click on the **Office Button** to create a New file, to Open an existing file, to Save a file, to Print a file, or to Send a file to someone.
- The **Quick Access Toolbar** consists of a few icons that always show on your screen. You can customize them, but the default icons are the Save, Undo, and Redo commands.
- Underneath the Quick Access Toolbar you will find several **tabs** (Home, Insert, and so on). Each tab has its own **ribbon,** or set of buttons. You can see each tab's ribbon by clicking on the tab. Together, the tabs and ribbons are your command center for any Office program.
- The **help button** is your way to say "SOS!" If you need help or advice about any feature of an Office program, click on this button. Type in your topic (for example, "print multiple copies"), and press ENTER. Scroll through the options and click on the most promising link.

[1] Mick, Jason. "Office 2010 to Launch Today, Microsoft Owns 94 Percent of the Market." May 12, 2010. *DailyTech*. http://www.dailytech.com/Office+2010+to+Launch+Today+Microsoft+Owns+94+Percent+of+the+Market/article18360.htm

[2] Fildes, Jonathan. "Microsoft Office 2010 takes aim at Google Docs." May 12, 2010. *BBC News*. http://www.bbc.co.uk/news/10107799

The following common features aren't all labeled on the diagram, but you can find them on the <u>Home</u> tab of all three programs:

- **Fonts and type size.** In any Office program, you can change the **font** (type style) and its size, measured in points. The default text size in Word and Excel is 12 point; the default sizes in PowerPoint are much higher because people need to read text from far away.
- **Copying, cutting, and pasting text or images.** One of the major advantages of using a computer is that you can quickly move words and images around. If you want to cut or copy text, use the mouse or trackpad to select the text; then click the <u>Cut</u> or <u>Copy</u> button in the ribbon. Place the cursor in the location where you want to paste the text, and click the <u>Paste</u> button. You can use the same process for an image. You can even cut text from one program (for example, Excel) and paste it into another.
- **Formatting text.** With the formatting buttons (or key commands—see below), you can make text plain, **boldface,** *italic,* <u>underline</u>, ~~strikethrough~~, or SMALL CAPS.
- **Format Painter.** This button is a huge time saver. Let's say you want to apply the formatting of one word—including its font, size, and formatting—to the rest of the text on your page. Select the word, click the <u>Format Painter</u> button, and then highlight the text that you want to apply the formatting to. Presto: all the formatting details are applied.
- **Text alignment.** Do you want your text to appear in the center of the space it's in, or do you want it hugging the left or right side (or both sides)? Use the text alignment buttons.
- **Undoing and redoing actions.** This is one of the lifesaving features of Office programs. Imagine that you've just spent an hour typing one paragraph, but then you make a mistake and delete the entire thing. Is it gone forever? No! Just click the <u>Undo</u> button in the Quick Access Toolbar, and the computer undoes your previous action. The paragraph will

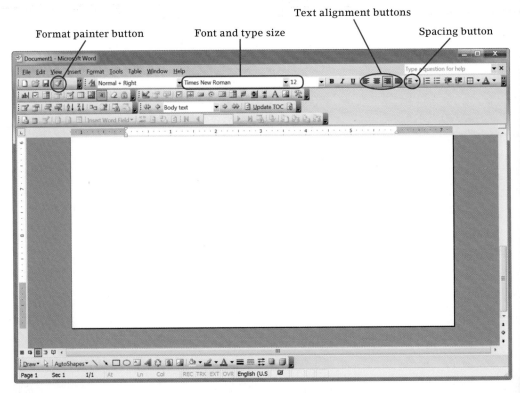

Format painter button   Font and type size   Text alignment buttons   Spacing button

reappear. If you decide that you want to redo the previous action, use the Redo feature, also in the Quick Access Toolbar.

Finally, there are several keyboard shortcuts common to all Office programs. They take the place of ribbon buttons so that you don't have to reach for your mouse or trackpad to move around and click. Whether you use the buttons or the key commands is simply a matter of preference. For the shortcuts below, press and hold the first key, press the second key, and then release both keys.

Microsoft Word Basics

If you haven't used Word yet, now is the time to get familiar with it. You can use Word to create polished, professional-looking documents—reports, essays, research papers, memos, class notes, meeting minutes, cover letters, resumes, envelopes, address labels, and more.

A new Word document looks like a blank piece of paper, just waiting to be filled with ideas and information. Here is how to create one:

1. Open the Word application. A new document should pop up automatically. If Word is already open, do one of two things: press Ctrl + N OR click on Office Button ➔ New ➔ Blank Document.

2. Your new, blank document will appear.

Now comes the creative part: writing and shaping your document. Type away! To start a new line, press ENTER. To indent at the beginning of a paragraph, press TAB. But Word allows you to do much more than type plain text. Every new version of Word gives you more options for creating, polishing, reviewing, and sharing documents. Once you've got your text written, have fun with the program. Play around with the buttons. Remember, you can always undo a change you don't like.

Common Keyboard Shortcuts

Command	Windows Shortcut	Mac Shortcut
Create a new file.	Ctrl + N	⌘ + N
Save a file.	Ctrl + S	⌘ + S
Undo your previous action.	Ctrl + Z	⌘ + Z
Redo your previous action.	Ctrl + Y	⌘ + Y
Copy selected text or object.	Ctrl + C	⌘ + C
Cut selected text or object.	Ctrl + X	⌘ + X
Paste selected text or object.	Ctrl + V	⌘ + V
Make text **bold.**	Ctrl + B	⌘ + B
Make text *italic*.	Ctrl + I	⌘ + I
Underline text.	Ctrl + U	⌘ + U
Close a window or file.	Alt + F4	⌘ + W

Here are some of the most commonly used Word features, tab by tab:

- **Home tab.** This is where you find all the formatting and text tools discussed in **Common Microsoft Office Features** above. Another important feature in this tab is the spacing button. This allows you to make lines of text more or less tightly packed together (single spacing = 1.0; double spacing = 2.0). It's good to know about this feature in case your instructor asks for papers to be double-spaced.
- **Insert tab.** Use the buttons on this tab to insert a page break (when you want to end the page and start a new one), a table, a picture, a piece of clip art, a header or footer (faded text at the top or bottom of the page), page numbers, or other symbols.
- **Page Layout tab.** Click this tab if you want to change the margins on a page, change the orientation of the page (horizontal or vertical), or put text into two or more columns.

- **References tab.** Here you can insert citations such as footnotes, endnotes, captions, and a bibliography.
- **Mailings tab.** Use the buttons on this ribbon to create mailings that will go to a number of people.
- **Review tab.** This set of features is becoming increasingly popular. With document reviewing functions you can make visible changes to a document (Track Changes) and make comments to yourself or to other viewers (New Comment). These are fantastic editing and cooperative writing tools. You can also run a spelling and grammar check and consult a thesaurus.
- **View tab.** You can use these buttons to change the way your document appears on the screen. For example, if you show the ruler, you will see the measurements of each page in inches.

Here are a few more tips for getting the most out of Word:

- Save your work often! Pressing a quick key command (Ctrl + S) will save you the inconvenience of having to re-create your work if there is a power failure or program crash.
- Don't get too crazy with fonts, especially if you're going to email your document to others or use a different computer to print your work. Other computers might not have your chosen font. Stick to common fonts such as Times New Roman, Helvetica, and Arial.
- Get to know the common keyboard shortcuts. They will save you a lot of time.
- Don't insert too many pictures and graphics in a Word document, and be wary of using images from the Internet. They slow you down and cause Word to crash more often than usual.
- Don't use too many fonts in the same document. It is distracting to your reader.

Microsoft PowerPoint Basics

PowerPoint is used to create professional multimedia presentations for any setting. While a Word document consists of pages, a PowerPoint presentation consists of slides, or individual units with a small amount of bulleted (•) text mixed with graphics. You might use this program to make a presentation for a course at school, a training session at work, or a club or team you have joined.

During a presentation, the speaker projects the PowerPoint slides onto a large screen and moves from one slide to the next. The slides do not contain the entire presentation; rather, they contain key points and graphics that serve as visual aids for the audience. PowerPoint slides are meant to *enhance* and *supplement* your presentation, not to *be* the entire presentation.

Here is what the main screen of PowerPoint looks like:

To get started in PowerPoint, create a new slide:

1. Open the PowerPoint® application. A new slide should pop up automatically. If the program was already open, do one of two things: press Ctrl + N OR click on Home tab → New Slide.

2. Click on the slide design you want. The new slide will appear.

If you make a slide you especially like, here's how to duplicate it:

1. In the Slides tab along the left side of the window, click on the slide you want to duplicate.

2. Click on Home tab → New Slide.

3. Click on Duplicate Selected Slides.

4. Your duplicate slide will appear below the original slide you selected.

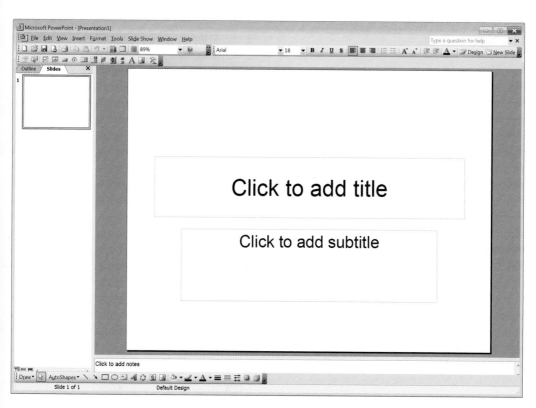

Now it's time to fill in and format your slides. To add text, follow the directions on the slide templates—click inside each rectangular area and type your text. Then use the tabs and ribbon buttons to make your slides look slick and professional:

- **Home tab.** The buttons here are approximately the same as the ones in Word®. You can format text, change alignment, and insert basic shapes.
- **Insert tab.** Use these buttons to insert tables, pictures, clip art, shapes, charts, hyperlinks (links to websites), and other items.
- **Design tab.** Here you can change the slide orientation (horizontal or vertical) or apply a colorful theme to the slide. Play around with different themes; they add visual interest.
- **Animations tab.** In this ribbon you can apply animated (moving) transitions between slides.
- **Slide Show tab.** Go here to set up a timed presentation of the slides you have created.
- **Review tab.** In this tab, you can make comments on a slide or run a spell check on your text.

- **View tab.** With these buttons you change the way your slides appear on the screen. For example, you might want to see small versions of all your slides side by side instead of just one slide.

Here are some helpful PowerPoint tips:

- Your text should consist of key words and phrases, not full sentences. Capitalize the first letter of each bullet point.
- Don't crowd your slide. Keep text on each slide to a minimum. Aim for six words or fewer and six bullet points or fewer. The whole point of bulleted lists is to provide a highly condensed version of your presentation.
- Use photos and illustrations that are related to your presentation. Don't use random graphics just because you think they're cute or pretty.
- Make sure your text is large enough to be read from the back of the room you are presenting in.

- Avoid using many different fonts, more than two or three colors on one page, or colors that are overly bright.
- Avoid overusing boldface or italic text.
- If you'll be using an unfamiliar computer (especially if you're switching from a PC to a Mac or vice versa), preview your presentation on that computer first to make sure it looks correct.
- If you're sending your presentation to other people, use common fonts (Times New Roman, Helvetica, or Arial), and use caution when inserting sound or video clips.

Microsoft Excel Basics

Excel is used to create lists, charts, and groups of data that often involve complex calculations and graphics. For instance, many individuals and companies create budget sheets in Excel. As in any table, an Excel workbook is organized into cells—small, rectangular blocks—that make up columns (vertical stacks) and rows (horizontal lines). A blank workbook looks like a simple grid.

Here is what the main screen of Excel looks like:

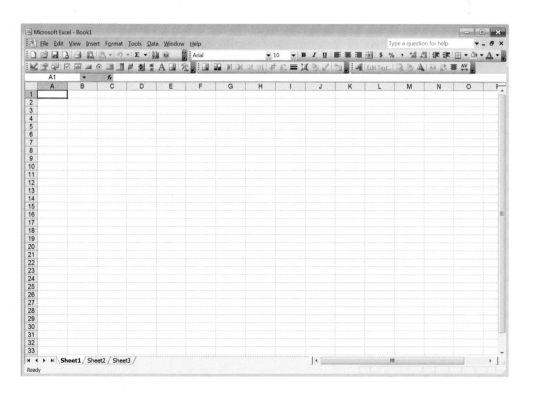

To begin, create a new workbook:

1. Open the Excel application. A new workbook should pop up automatically. If the program is already open, do one of two things: press Ctrl + N OR click on Office Button ➔ New ➔ Blank Workbook.

2. Your new, blank workbook will appear.

Now you can populate the cells. Type titles for your columns and rows, enter data in the form of words or numbers, and apply formulas and calculations if necessary. Getting the most out of Excel requires a moderate amount of training. For now, here are the tab-by-tab highlights of Excel's functions:

- **Home tab.** This tab is very similar to the Home tabs of Word and PowerPoint. You can format text, align text, merge cells (join them together), insert and delete cells, insert and delete rows, insert and delete columns, and create borders so that chart-type lines appear.
- **Insert tab.** Here you can insert preformatted tables, pictures, clip art, shapes, charts, hyperlinks, and other objects.
- **Page Layout tab.** Click on this tab if you want to change margins or page orientation (horizontal or vertical).
- **Formulas tab.** You use these buttons to apply automatic calculations within or between cells, rows, or columns. For example, if you want to divide the numbers in one column by the numbers in the column to the right, you go to this tab.
- **Data tab.** These features allow you to insert data from another source, such as a database or the web, into the cells of your workbook. A popular button in this tab is Sort, which you can use to alphabetize a list.

- **Review tab.** Go here to make comments on your workbook or to run a spell check of the text in all cells.
- **View tab.** With these buttons, you can change the way your workbook appears on the screen. For example, you might want to see where the page breaks would fall if you printed your workbook. You can also zoom in or out on your workbook (see it bigger or smaller).

Here are a few tips for using Excel:

- Make column and row titles boldface and/ or larger than surrounding text. This is an aid to the eye as readers look at your workbook.
- To move from cell to cell, you don't have to use the mouse or trackpad. Use the up, down, left, and right arrow keys instead.
- Changing text color or highlighting cells can help differentiate rows and columns.
- Don't put too much text in a cell. Excel is meant for small chunks of information. If you find yourself typing one or more paragraphs, it might be better to use Word for your task.

Job Search **Tip**

When you are searching for a job, you might apply to hundreds of different companies. Use Excel to create a spreadsheet to keep all your job lead information together and organized. Your chart might look like this:

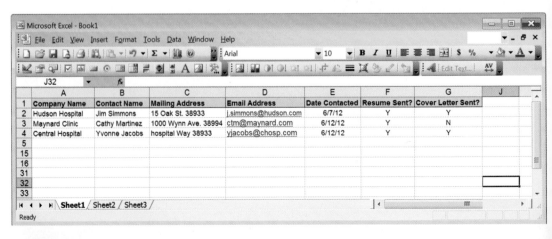

Unit Summary

- Personal computers can help you efficiently complete a wide variety of tasks at home, at school, and at work.

- Computer components can be divided into hardware (physical parts) and software (programs).

- The two main tools that you use to command a computer are the keyboard and the mouse or trackpad.

- The desktop, or your screen's background, contains various icons and a start button.

- Files and folders help keep the information on a computer organized. They work much like a physical filing cabinet.

- Microsoft Word is used to create documents such as research papers, letters, and memos.

- Microsoft PowerPoint is used to create slide presentations.

- Microsoft Excel is used to create budgets, lists, and complex charts.

TO-DO List

✔ Familiarize yourself with the **hardware** and **software** components of the computer you use most.

✔ Practice your **mouse** and **trackpad** skills on real computers by reviewing the chart on page 45.

✔ Use the instructions on page 52 to create three **folders** and at least two subfolders.

✔ Open all three Microsoft Office programs, click on each tab, and review the buttons on each ribbon.

✔ Research online tutoring websites with training videos on the Microsoft Office suite.

Important Terms

How well do you know these terms? Look them up in the glossary if you need help remembering them.

hardware	icon
RAM (random access memory)	Internet
keyboard	folder
optical drive	hard drive
portable drives	monitor
applications	trackpad
URL (uniform resource locator)	peripherals
file	software
processor	field
mouse	bookmarks
input ports	font

Online Resources

Tech Tips for the Basic Computer User
pogue.blogs.nytimes.com/2008/10/02/tech-tips-for-the-basic-computer-user/

Solutions in Office
office.microsoft.com/en-us/help/CH010168729.aspx

Learn to Use Internet Explorer
www.newbie.org/internet_explorer/

How to Create Folders
www.cybertechhelp.com/tutorial/article/how-to-create-folders

Office Tips and Tricks for Administrative Professionals
www.microsoft.com/events/series/administrativetipsandtricks.aspx

Exercises

1. Use the instructions on page 49 to bookmark three websites.

2. Create a diagram of folders to use for your personal computer files. Use the diagram on page 52 as a model.

3. In Microsoft Word, create and save a to-do list for tasks you need to complete tomorrow.

4. In Microsoft PowerPoint, create and save a three-slide presentation on the topic of your choice.

5. In Microsoft Excel, create and save a chart with the following columns: **My Personal Goals, My Career Goals,** and **My Educational Goals.**

English Fundamentals: Language Arts

Identify the nouns pictured in this street scene. Think of a sentence for each noun.

KEYS TO
success

Defining basic terms of English language study, such as *grammar, parts of speech*, and *mechanics*

Identifying and using the eight main parts of speech

Identifying and correcting common errors in grammar, spelling, punctuation, and capitalization

Proofreading your own writing thoroughly and effectively

Using knowledge of prefixes and suffixes to determine the meanings of words

What wood you think if you pickd up this textboock and their wur speling and gramar erorrs in evry paragraf? How about if u started 2 read a txtbk filled w/abbreviations & symbols like the 1s in a txt msg?

If your instructor handed you a textbook and every paragraph looked like the one above, you would have every right to be disappointed and even angry. That's because incorrect grammar and informal English have no place in a textbook. You're investing a lot of time and money in your schooling, and you expect your instructors and course materials to meet the highest possible standards of communication. Your education and career depend on it.

Don't be surprised, then, when instructors—and employers—expect you to know and apply the rules of English grammar. Abbreviations, slang words, and sentences with only lowercase letters are acceptable in some situations. In the workplace and in the classroom, however, formal language skills are key to your success. When you apply for a job, for example, your use of proper formal English can make the difference between getting hired and being next in line.

Even if you decide to break the rules sometimes, you need to know what they are in the first place. This unit will get you up to speed on the basics so that your use of language opens doors rather than closing them.

Building Blocks: The Parts of Speech

You've heard about nouns, verbs, and adjectives before. In this section, we'll identify the parts of speech. You'll learn about different types of words and how they are used. Then you will be able to understand how to use words to create meaning.

True Story

"I'm in charge of Human Resources, and I read about 50 resumes every day. I have zero patience for grammatical mistakes. People will not succeed at this hospital if they don't have the skills to communicate appropriately and correctly. If a resume has even one glaring typo or mistake, I throw it directly into the recycling bin."

Grammar and the Great Eight

Grammar is the study of words and how they function. Therefore, a grammatical error is a mistake in the way you use a word or group of words. Central to any study of English grammar is learning the eight main **parts of speech,** or categories of words and their functions. In everyday speech and writing, we use parts of speech as building blocks to create meaning. Here are the great eight parts of speech:

1. nouns   **5.** adverbs

2. pronouns   **6.** prepositions

3. adjectives   **7.** conjunctions

4. verbs   **8.** interjections

The parts of speech work together. We combine words into sentences to create meaning. One confusing point is that a particular word can act as one part of speech in one sentence and a different part of speech in another sentence. For instance, the word **show** can be a noun, as in "The show is about to begin." It can also be a verb, as in "Show me the way to go home." To determine a word's part of speech, you must determine how and where it is used in the sentence.

What follows is a brief introduction to the eight parts of speech and their roles in the English language. Once you have mastered them, you will be able to make more deliberate choices in the way you communicate.

Words of Being: Nouns, Articles, and Pronouns

A **noun** names a person, place, or thing. Think of nouns as words of **being**—words that name what exists. Most nouns name things or people that you can directly touch, see, hear, or experience in the world around you. Here are some examples:

Nouns

Person	Place	Thing
man	park	desk
woman	city	windshield
athlete	Asia	flag
student	kitchen	spoon
employee	library	book

Here are two of the main ways to classify nouns:

1. **Singular or plural.** A singular noun names only one person, place, or thing (tree, dress); a plural noun names two or more (trees, dresses). Most plural nouns end in -s or -es; one exception is **foot → feet**.

2. **Common or proper.** Common nouns refer to **general** people, places, and things (scientist, galaxy, high school). Proper nouns refer to **specific** people, places, and things (George Washington Carver, the Milky Way, Middletown High School).

We often use nouns with partner words called **articles.** Articles are special types of adjectives that indicate whether we're referring to a noun generally or specifically. There are three articles in the English language: *a*, *an*, and *the*.

Incorrect: Please give me wrench.
Correct: Please give me <u>a</u> wrench.
(general—any wrench)
Correct: Please give me <u>the</u> wrench.
(specific—that one wrench right there)

A **pronoun** is a word that takes the place of one or more nouns. Like nouns, pronouns can be singular or plural. People often use pronouns as shortcuts in everyday speech. The following chart shows the main types of pronouns and examples of how they can be used to simplify or shorten what we say.

Pronouns

Type of Pronoun	Examples	Use as a Shortcut (If Applicable)
refers to specific people or things	**Singular:** I, me, you, she, her, he, him, it **Plural:** we, us, you, they, them	**Long version:** I took Kara, Glenda, and Jimmy with me. **Shortcut:** I took <u>them</u> with me.
indicates ownership	**Singular:** my, mine, your, yours, her, hers, his, its **Plural:** our, ours, your, yours, their, theirs	**Long version:** The computer belongs to me. **Shortcut:** The computer is <u>mine</u>. OR That's <u>my</u> computer.
shows that the person or thing performing an action also receives the action	**Singular:** myself, yourself, himself, herself, itself **Plural:** ourselves, yourselves, themselves	**Long version:** He was the one who made the cookies that he brought to the party. **Shortcut:** He brought cookies that he had made <u>himself.</u>
identifies or points to specific nouns	this, that, these, those	**Long version:** Submit your drop box assignment on the website that I have projected on the screen right here. **Shortcut:** Submit your drop box assignment on <u>this</u> website.
refers to people or things in a general, nonspecific way	all, another, any, anybody, anyone, anything, both, each, either, everybody, everyone, everything, few, many, neither, none, nobody, no one, nothing, one, several, some, somebody, someone, something	**Long version:** Katie, Gerard, Andrew, Marta, and the other students have to make a presentation. **Shortcut:** <u>Everyone</u> has to make a presentation.
introduces questions	who, whom, whose, which, what	**Long version:** Do you want to buy the black metal stapler or the red plastic stapler? **Shortcut:** <u>Which</u> stapler do you want to buy?
introduces an explanatory part of a sentence	who, whom, whose, which, that	**Example sentence:** Alex is the one <u>who</u> came up with the idea.

What adjectives can you use to describe the objects shown here?

Words of *Describing:* Adjectives

An **adjective** describes, or modifies, a noun or pronoun. It answers one of these questions:

Which one? My supervisor wrote <u>that</u> report.

What kind? They bought some <u>peppermint</u> gum.

How many? Their sister has <u>several</u> goals in life.

How much? I bought <u>more</u> memory for my computer.

In a sentence, adjectives often appear just before the nouns (or pronouns) they modify. This is not always true, however. Adjectives can also appear after a *be* verb (*is, am, are, was, were, be, being,* or *been*):

> That grammatical error is <u>inexcusable</u>.

> They were <u>tired</u> but <u>happy</u>.

If you're ever unsure about whether a word is an adjective, try fitting it into the phrase, "_____ dog," as in "<u>tired</u> dog" or "<u>happy</u> dog." If it's an adjective, it will usually work in _____ dog or _____ dogs.

Words of *Doing:* Verbs and Adverbs

A **verb** expresses an action or a state of being. Think of verbs as words of *doing*.

Here are some important features of verbs:

- **Person.** Verb forms change slightly depending on the person(s) or thing(s) performing the action:

   I <u>walk</u>.
   He <u>walks</u>.

Verb Tenses

Tense	Description	Examples
Past	The action has already happened.	The technicians <u>inspected</u> the circuit breaker. The technicians <u>had inspected</u> the circuit breaker.
Present	The action is happening right now.	The technicians <u>inspect</u> the circuit breaker. The technicians <u>are inspecting</u> the circuit breaker.
Future	The action will happen at some point after right now.	The technicians <u>will inspect</u> the circuit breaker.

- **Tense.** The **verb tense** indicates the timing of the action. Verbs are grouped into past, present, and future tenses:

Helpers. Many verbs consist of multiple words that act together. In the chart at the bottom of the previous page, the words *had, are,* and *will* are part of the verbs *had inspected, are inspecting,* and *will inspect.* Some verbs contain multiple words that always appear together—for example, *work out* (exercise), *settle up* (pay a bill), and *put off* (postpone). This is called a **phrasal verb**.

An **adverb** modifies a verb, an adjective, or another adverb. It answers a question:

How? She read the textbook <u>slowly</u> and <u>extremely</u> <u>carefully</u>. (*Slowly, extremely,* and *carefully,* tell us *how.*)

When? The students will start their presentations <u>now</u>. (*Now* tells us *when.*)

Where? Josefa put her bags <u>down</u>. (*Down* tells us *where.*)

To what degree? I am <u>very</u> glad I got to work on time. (*Very* tells us *how much.*)

It helps to think of adverbs as words of *doing*, since they so often partner with verbs. Many adverbs are easy to identify because they end in *-ly*. Just remember that some adverbs do not have the *-ly* ending (*well, yesterday, never, sometimes,* and *fast* are some examples). Also, some words that end in *-ly* are not adverbs—for example, the words *friendly* and *lovely* are adjectives.

> ## Job Search **Tip**
>
> Your resume should be packed with verbs that show how active you are and help potential employers visualize you working for them. When describing your duties in past or current positions, use strong, descriptive verbs like these:
>
> | | | |
> |---|---|---|
> | designed | increased | trained |
> | managed | negotiated | updated |
> | expanded | planned | spearheaded |
> | presented | organized | purchased |
> | assembled | researched | provided |

What verbs describe what this person is doing?

Words of *Connecting:* Prepositions and Conjunctions

A **preposition** expresses the relationship between two words in a sentence. Think of prepositions as words that *connect*. Imagine that there are two objects in a room—an apple and a table. You can use prepositions to link the table and the apple in physical space:

> The apple is <u>on</u> the table.
>
> The apple is <u>below</u> the table.
>
> The apple is <u>near</u> the table.
>
> The apple is <u>by</u> the table.
>
> Please give the apple <u>on</u> the table <u>to</u> me.

Prepositions always come in prepositional phrases that begin with the preposition and end with a noun or pronoun. In the sentence "The apple is on the table," the prepositional phrase is *on the table.*

Here is a list of common prepositions:

about	during	since
above	for	through
across	from	throughout
after	in	till
against	inside	to
along	into	toward
among	like	under
around	near	underneath
as	next	unlike
at	of	until
before	off	unto
behind	on	up
below	onto	upon
beside	out	with
between	outside	within
by	over	without
despite	past	

Use prepositions to describe the relative positions of the objects shown here.

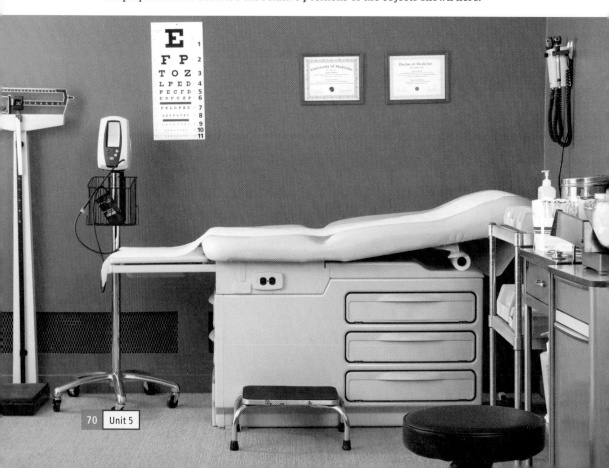

A **conjunction** is another word that connects. It joins two or more parts of a sentence—such as words or phrases—and expresses the relationship between those parts.

Rather than trying to identify conjunctions based on what they look or sound like, it's generally best to memorize them. Study the chart below.

Conjunctions

Type of Conjunction	Examples	Sentences
single conjunctions that connect two equivalent elements (words or groups of words)	and, or, nor, for, but, so, yet	We are ready <u>and</u> willing to go. You can hang your coat in the closet <u>or</u> on the hook.
pairs of conjunctions that connect two equivalent elements	both/and, either/or, neither/nor, as/as, not only/but also, not/but, whether/or	They will <u>either</u> sit <u>or</u> stand. Academic strategies are <u>not only</u> helpful <u>but also</u> necessary.
conjunctions that show the relationship between two phrases	because, when, if, now that, once, wherever, as if, in order that, although, so that, unless, rather than, furthermore, as a result, however, finally, therefore, similarly	<u>Because</u> the proposal is due tomorrow, we need to finish it as soon as possible. Please hand me the bill <u>so that</u> I can record it. I called twice to follow up; <u>however</u>, I never got a response.

Words of *Reacting:* Interjections

An **interjection** is a sudden word or phrase that expresses surprise or emotion. It often stands alone as a sentence. Think of interjections as words of *reacting*. They are usually followed by an exclamation point:

- Hey!
- Hooray!
- Look out!
- Ouch!

Practice
Critical Thinking

People use words differently depending on their culture—where they live, their ethnic background, their primary language, and even their government. For example, English speakers generally place an adjective before the noun it modifies, while speakers of Spanish place the adjective after the noun:

English: the red book

Spanish: el libro rojo (directly translated: "the book red")

1. What are some examples of how your use of language reflects your cultural background?

2. What differences do you notice in the way people write from culture to culture?

Roadblocks: Common Language Arts Errors

Grammar rules regulate communication the way traffic lights regulate the flow of vehicles; without them, you would have chaos. In this section, we'll discuss common errors in grammar and **mechanics**—conventions of writing in areas such as spelling, punctuation, and capitalization. The goal is to identify both the rules and the mistakes so that you'll be able to catch and correct problems with your own writing—and thus avoid sending the wrong message or making a negative impression.

Grammatical Roadblocks

You've already read about the parts of speech, so you're well on your way when it comes to grammar rules. Here are some common grammatical errors to avoid:

Sentence fragments. Avoid using incomplete sentences in formal writing.
Incorrect: Because English is a difficult language. Have to study every day.
Correct: Because English is a difficult language, we have to study every day.

How can you tell if you have a fragment or a sentence? You can check quickly if you remember that every complete sentence has a subject (main noun, the actor) and a verb. If you are missing one or the other, you have a fragment. For example, "Have to study every day" has a verb (*have*), but it doesn't have a subject. Who have? Oh, *we have*. The second sentence is correct because it has a subject to go with the verb.

Misusing pronouns.
Incorrect: We split the tips between <u>he</u> and <u>I</u>.
Correct: We split the tips between <u>him</u> and <u>me</u>.
Incorrect: <u>Her</u> and <u>him</u> came in first and second.
Correct: <u>She</u> and <u>he</u> came in first and second.

How can you tell if you have the right pronoun? Try repeating the sentence twice, once with each pronoun. For example, say, "Her came in first and second." That doesn't sound right, does it? How about, "Him came in first and second"? No, that's not right either. However, "She came in first and second" sounds much better, doesn't it?

Confusing adverbs and adjectives. To avoid these errors, remember that adjectives modify nouns or pronouns, while adverbs modify verbs, adjectives, and other adverbs.
Incorrect: Come here <u>real quick</u>. (*Real* and *quick* are adjectives used incorrectly as adverbs.)
Correct: Come here <u>really quickly</u>. (*Quickly* modifies the verb *come; really* modifies the adverb *quickly*.)

What's the method for checking an adverb? Try asking the question "How?" Come here how? "Come here real" doesn't sound right, does it? But "Come here really" sounds a bit better. Another trick: If it answers the question "How?" the word will probably end in *-ly*. This trick doesn't always work, but it's a good guideline if you're unsure and do not have access to a style guide.

Confusing past tenses of verbs. There are hundreds of irregular verbs in the English language. To avoid using the wrong tense, either memorize the irregulars or consult a dictionary. Here are some common errors:

Verb	Incorrect	Correct
blow	blowed	blew
break	breaked	broke
bring	brang	brought
cling	clinged	clung
cost	costed	cost
drag	drug	dragged
forgive	forgived	forgave
go	goed	went
grow	growed	grew
lay (to place)	lay	laid
lie (to lie down)	lied	lay

Noun/verb agreement. A verb must match, or agree with, the noun that is performing the action.

Incorrect: The <u>group</u> of doctors <u>do</u> rounds every morning.

Correct: The <u>group</u> of doctors <u>does</u> rounds every morning. (The verb *does* applies to *group*, not to *doctors*.)

Agreement is a difficult concept. (News anchors frequently make agreement errors on the air because they are talking quickly.) Look for the subject and the verb, and try to ignore the words in between. Agreement errors are usually caused by prepositional phrases (like *of doctors*) that mislead the writer. It sounds as if it should be *doctors do*, but the real subject is *group*, and it must agree with *does*.

Themselves/theirselves.

Incorrect: They baked the bread <u>theirselves</u>.

Correct: They baked the bread <u>themselves</u>.

Words with *-self/selves* are strange in that some (*himself*, *herself*, and *themselves*) contain pronouns that refer to specific people or things, while others (*myself*, *yourself*, and *ourselves*) contain pronouns that indicate ownership.

Confusion with helping verbs.

Incorrect: You should <u>of</u> told me sooner.

Correct: You should <u>have</u> told me sooner.

In this case, "of" is a preposition, not a verb. These errors are subtle and require that you learn your parts of speech. Learn the list of prepositions, and make sure that your prepositions always have an object (like "of speech" or "of water"). The preposition above doesn't have an object, which is a clue that something is wrong in the sentence.

Spelling Roadblocks

Spelling is one of the greatest roadblocks on the journey toward language arts perfection. Spelling mistakes can cause communication problems and extreme embarrassment. The English language has few hard-and-fast rules, and most of the rules have exceptions. If you struggle with spelling, follow the number one rule: When in doubt, look it up!

Here are some especially pesky spelling errors:

Homophones. Words that sound the same but have different meanings—and are often spelled differently—are called **homophones.** These word pairs are notorious spelling pitfalls because you have to know their meanings in order to spell them correctly:

accept/except	principle/principal
all ready/already	right/write
altogether/all together	road/rode
assistance/assistants	sell/cell
bare/bear	sent/cent/scent
brake/break	sight/site/cite
buy/by/bye	than/then
compliment/complement	there/their/they're
effect/affect	through/threw
everyday/every day	too/two/to
it's/its	vein/vane/vain
lets/let's	week/weak
meet/meat	wheeled/wield
muscle/mussel	whether/weather
not/knot/naught	whose/who's
patients/patience	your/you're
precede/proceed	

Near-homophones. These words sound *almost* the same, which makes them easy to confuse:

advice/advise	ensure/insure
desert/dessert	incidence/incident
emigrate/immigrate	loose/lose

Forming verb tenses or plurals. The spelling of a base word often changes—sometimes in an irregular way—when you add an ending to form a new verb tense or a plural noun.

Word	Incorrect New Tense	Correct New Tense
hop	hoped	hopped
hope	hopped	hoped
panic	paniced	panicked
live	liveing	living

Word	Incorrect Plural	Correct Plural
pony	ponys	ponies
vertebra	vertebras	vertebrae
hypothesis	hypothesises	hypotheses
criterion	criterions	criteria
mother-in-law	mother-in-laws	mothers-in-law

Other commonly misspelled words. Read this list, identify the examples that give you trouble, and memorize the correct spelling.

Correct	Incorrect
definitely	definately
judgment	judgement
duct tape	duck tape
receive	recieve
weird	wierd
pronunciation	pronounciation
acceptable	acceptible
believe	beleive
conscious	consious/concious
gauge	guage/gage
independent	independant
maintenance	maintainence
privilege	priviledge
schedule	skedule
supposedly	supposably
tomorrow	tommorrow
a lot	alot
truly	truely
cannot	can not
argument	arguement
acquit	aquit
committed	commited
embarrass	embarass
harass	harrass
license	licence
personnel	personel
recommend	recomend
until	untill

Punctuation Roadblocks

Punctuation can seem complicated and even intimidating. Use the chart below as a reference for the most common punctuation marks and their correct uses.

Name	Symbol	Common Use(s)	Examples
period	.	• to end a sentence • to abbreviate a word or phrase	• My resume is attached. • Mr., Jr., Dr., lb., etc., e.g.
question mark	?	• to end a sentence that is a direct question	• Where is the power switch?
exclamation point	!	• to end a sentence that expresses a strong emotion or a forceful command • to follow an interjection	• This is the most exciting day of my life! • Oh!
apostrophe	'	• to form a contraction • to show possession	• she's, they're, can't • Kira's job, dogs' leashes
comma	,	• to separate items in a list • to join whole, separate ideas within a sentence • to separate adjectives modifying the same noun • to set off introductory phrases • to set off mid-sentence phrases • to set off quotations, dates, addresses, and titles	• Write the day, time and date. • He left for Spain, but she went to Mexico. • The tall, elderly witness spoke. • For once, the sun came out on my birthday. • Rhonda, Jack's wife, works at the bank. • She said, "I agree." • August 25, 2012 • Sandra Alvarez, medical secretary
colon	:	• to introduce quotations, lists, summaries, or explanations	• Steinholtz claims: "It's impossible to predict recovery time." • I need three tools: calipers, a screwdriver, and wire cutters.
semicolon	;	• to separate two related ideas that are complete sentences	• They packed their bags; it was time to go.
dash	—	• to set off elements of a sentence	• Her new car—the blue convertible—gets her plenty of attention.
hyphen	-	• to form some numbers and fractions • to form some compound words	• thirty-six, one-fourth • pinch-hitter, self-care
quotation marks	" "	• to enclose direct quotations • to enclose titles of poems, short stories, chapters, and other short works	• "The deadline is Tuesday," he announced. • I'm reading the last chapter, "Recovery."
ellipsis	. . .	• to indicate that words in a quotation have been deleted • to show hesitation, interruption, or unfinished thought	• Kennedy said, "Ask . . . what you can do for your country." • "I'm not really sure . . . it's complicated," she said.
parentheses	( )	• to set off a tangential part of a sentence • to set off a person's life span	• It isn't raining (it rarely does in the desert), but I won't go backpacking. • Indira Gandhi (1917–1984) was prime minister of India.

Now, carefully review these common punctuation errors:

Run-on sentences/lack of end punctuation. Run-on sentences are formed when two or more complete sentences are joined together incorrectly.

Incorrect: I had to write the memo my computer was broken.

Correct: I had to write the memo. My computer was broken. **OR** I had to write the memo, but my computer was broken.

What's the hint that you have a run-on sentence? When you see a second subject (main noun), you know that you need some kind of a joiner. In the example above, the first subject is *I* ("I had to write the memo") and the second subject is *computer* ("my computer was broken"). You have some choices for punctuation: (a) you can end the first sentence with a period and start a second sentence (the first correction above), (b) you can join the sentences with a comma conjunction like , *but* (the second correction above), or (c) if the sentences have the right kind of relationship, you can join them with a semicolon or colon. (The semicolon should be used to join two sentences when you feel like saying "and furthermore" between them.) What you can't do is allow the sentence to keep going after the second subject appears.

Overusing exclamation points. Don't overuse the exclamation point, especially in academic or business writing. This punctuation mark is generally considered informal, and overuse will reduce the impact of true exclamations.

Inappropriate: I would like to apply for this position!

Appropriate: I would like to apply for this position.

Using contractions in formal writing. Since contractions (*they're, aren't,* and so on) are considered casual, they are out of place in formal academic and business writing. For instance, keep them out of essays or cover letters.

Using apostrophes to form plurals.

Incorrect: The machine weighs two <u>ton's</u>. <u>Thank's</u> for your help.

Correct: The machine weighs two <u>tons</u>. <u>Thanks</u> for your help.

Leaving out apostrophes when forming possessives.

Incorrect: The <u>keyboards</u> number keys are sticking.

Correct: The <u>keyboard's</u> number keys are sticking.

Misplacing or leaving out commas. Misuse of commas can confuse meaning and create sloppy writing.

Incorrect: <u>Laughing</u> she turned to her co-worker.

Correct: <u>Laughing</u>, she turned to her co-worker.

Incorrect: Tylenol which, is a brand name contains acetaminophen.

Correct: Tylenol, which is a brand name, contains acetaminophen.

Incorrect: Anyone, who wants to buy a ticket, should stand in line.

Correct: Anyone who wants to buy a ticket should stand in line.

There are many rules about the use of commas. ("Put them where it feels right" isn't one of them.) In order to become a comma expert, you will need to put in some practice time with a grammar textbook or grammar software. If you have trouble with commas, it's worth the investment of your time.

Using a comma instead of a period or semicolon.

Incorrect: I'd better start studying, my test is next week.

Correct: I'd better start studying. My test is next week. **OR** I'd better start studying; my test is next week.

A comma cannot join two sentences. Remember, your joining options are a period, a comma conjunction (like *and*), a semicolon, and, in some rare cases, a colon.

Incorrectly leaving out or inserting hyphens in compound words.

When in doubt, look up compound words in the dictionary.

Incorrect	Correct
self image	self-image
brother in law	brother-in-law
ex boyfriend	ex-boyfriend
cross examination	cross-examination
room-mate	roommate
sun-light	sunlight
health-care	health care

Using semicolons as commas.

Incorrect: I usually fix clients' computer issues within 24 hours; but today I'm backlogged.

Correct: I usually fix clients' computer issues within 24 hours, but today I'm backlogged.

The semicolon may be used as a "super comma" when you have a long series and there are commas within one or more items in the series.

Using dashes as periods or as phrase separators. This is a common error in casual writing such as email messages. Avoid transferring it to your formal writing.

Incorrect: That's all—see you soon—take care, Linda

Correct: That's all. See you soon, and take care.
Sincerely,
Linda

Using ellipses as phrase separators. This error often appears in text messages. Again, do not let this habit creep into your academic or professional writing.

Incorrect: That's all… see you soon… Linda

Correct: That's all. See you soon.
Sincerely,
Linda

Ellipses have one formal use: to show that you have removed something from a direct quotation. This is an advanced use that occurs in research papers or news reports. Otherwise, don't use ellipses in formal writing.

Capitalization Roadblocks

The use of capital letters is also governed by rules. Some are flexible depending on context, but as with all rules, be certain you know them before you bend them.

Use an initial capital letter for the following:

1. The first word of a sentence

   The book is on the shelf.

2. The pronoun *I*, and any contractions made with it

   Despite the rain, I'm going to the store. I hope I don't get wet.

3. The first word of a complete and direct quotation

   John asked, "Why are we going?"

4. Proper nouns and adjectives derived from them—including

   • **Personal names** (John Smith)
   • **Companies and other organizations** (the Library of Congress)
   • **Days of the week** (Wednesday) **and months** (May)

- **Trademarked products** (<u>M</u>icrosoft <u>W</u>ord)
- **Languages** (<u>S</u>wahili)**, countries** (<u>G</u>reenland)**, and nationalities** (<u>F</u>rench)
- **Holidays** (<u>T</u>hanksgiving)**, and major historical events** (the <u>R</u>evolutionary <u>W</u>ar)

5. A title that goes before a name (referring to someone specific)

> <u>D</u>r. Jones didn't have time to see <u>M</u>r. Jeni today.

6. The first, last, and any other important words of a title of a book, play, television program, periodical, or a shorter work such as an article, short story, or song.

> I read the novel <u>*W*</u>*ater for* <u>*E*</u>*lephants* last year.

> We couldn't get tickets to <u>*W*</u>*icked*.

7. In a letter, the first word and all nouns in the salutation, and the first word in the closing

> Dear <u>M</u>r. President:

> <u>V</u>ery truly yours,

Here are some common capitalization pitfalls:

Using capital letters to be fancy or to emphasize words.
Incorrect: Our special for today is Roast Duck with Berry Sauce.
Correct: Our special for today is roast duck with berry sauce.

This error may not seem like a big deal, but people who take grammar seriously will definitely notice this error and will consider you a poor writer.

Using capital letters when referring generally to a category of people.
Incorrect: My Aunt picked me up from the airport.
Correct: My aunt picked me up from the airport. **OR** Aunt Silvia picked me up from the airport.

This rule can be confusing. If you are talking about a specific person, then you capitalize (*Aunt Silvia* or *Mom*). If you are discussing a general category, then you don't (*my aunt, aunts, my mom,* or *moms*).

Using capital letters for academic subjects that are not proper nouns.
Incorrect: My courses this fall were Human Anatomy and Spanish.
Correct: My courses this fall were human anatomy and Spanish.

The easy rule on this is that if there is a number associated with the course, you capitalize it (*Human Anatomy 101*), and if there is no number, you do not (*human anatomy*). However, if there's some other reason to capitalize the course name, then that rule must be followed. (For example, Spanish is a language, so it would be capitalized anyway, regardless of whether you were referring to a course.)

Typing emails in all capital letters for emphasis.
This practice makes your writing look unprofessional and casual, and it makes text difficult to read. Also, when you type in uppercase (all capital letters), your writing appears more aggressive. Many people refer to it as "yelling" when emails are typed in all uppercase.

Around the Block:
The Proofreading Process

So, you've finally finished writing your report. You are done, right? Wrong! Now it's time to proofread your writing. This section provides you with helpful tips for catching your own mistakes.

I Have to Look at This *Again?*

Proofreading is a necessary, reputation-saving step in the writing process. The goal of **proofreading** is to eliminate errors in grammar and mechanics, such as the roadblocks outlined above. Proofreading can seem like a pain—especially when you're reviewing your own writing for the fourth or fifth time—but it's the single best way to make a positive impression on your reader.

The Proofreading Process

When it comes time to proofread your writing, examine it one sentence at a time. Mark problems with a pencil as you find them. As you examine the mechanics of your writing, check for one type of error at a time. That means that for each of the following questions, you will read through your entire piece. This method helps you maintain focus and catch more mistakes than trying to keep all of the issues in mind at once.

In addition to reviewing the common errors in the previous section of this unit, ask each of these questions while you proofread:

- Are all words used correctly?
- Are there too many or too few commas?
- Do all subjects and verbs agree?
- Are there any sentence fragments or run-on sentences?
- Are there any unnecessary verb tense shifts?
- Are all pronoun references clear—that is, is it obvious which noun(s) they replace?

ON THE JOB:

Proofreading is crucial in any industry. In medicine and pharmacology, the stakes are especially high. If a medical assistant doesn't proofread and double-check a doctor's notes, a pharmacy technician might prescribe the wrong medication or dosage. For example, a patient could end up taking Atacand—which is used to treat high blood pressure—instead of a simple antacid. Here are some other examples of medicines with similar names:

Advicor/Altocor	Amicar/Omacor
Anzemet/Avandamet	Matulane/Materna
rifaximin/rifampin	Folex/Foltx
Denavir/indinavir	HumaLOG/HumuLIN
Asacol/Os-Cal	

- Are apostrophes and other punctuation marks used correctly?
- Have all hyphenated and compound words been used correctly?

Here are some other proofreading tips:

Wait at least a few minutes before proofreading. This gives you some much-needed distance from the text you've just spent hours creating. You'll be able to look at it with fresher eyes.

Read the text aloud. Many people, especially auditory learners, are more likely to catch errors if they actually hear what they've written.

Read slowly. Consider every word carefully. If you read too quickly, you will miss errors.

Print it out. Hard copy is generally easier to read than words on a computer screen.

Read backward. When you read abnormally, from right to left, your brain is less likely to see what it expects to see—correct writing. Reading backward helps you catch spelling and punctuation errors.

Have a friend, family member, or co-worker take a turn. Don't be too proud to ask for help. Even the most accomplished writers—*especially* the most accomplished writers—have their writing edited and proofread, often by multiple people. Just remind your readers that proofreading is about catching errors, not making sweeping changes.

Practice Now: Engaged

It can be very difficult to see errors in your own writing, which is why it is great to use teamwork for proofreading. Find a friend or mentor who is great at language arts, and ask for some help with proofreading. Or, team up with a classmate, and you can proofread one another's writing. If neither of you is an expert, you may not catch everything, but you will catch more errors than if you work alone.

Use reference tools. Whenever you proofread, keep a dictionary and a grammar guide by your side. These tools can be physical or electronic.

Spell and Grammar Checkers: Your Best Friends and Worst Enemies

Some people's version of proofreading is a quick run of their computer's grammar checker and spell checker. While those programs do find errors, they aren't foolproof; it is a big mistake to rely on them completely. A recent university study showed that students with strong language skills, relying on these programs, made almost as many errors as students with weaker skills who proofread without grammar and spell checkers. Do your own proofreading, and then carefully use your grammar checker and spell checker to search for errors you may have missed.

Here is a paragraph that contains numerous errors, none of which were caught by a grammar checker or spell checker.

The problems with my patience mussels began a weak ago. I rode a report and ran a blood test. The red sells wear low.

Here's the proofread version, with corrections in **boldface** text:

*The problems with my **patient's muscles** began a **week** ago. I **wrote** a report and ran a blood test. The red **cells were** low.*

It's still a good idea to use grammar and spell checkers, but run them as a skeptic. Don't automatically make every change they suggest, and don't assume that they're always right. In the end, you'll need to use your brain.

TrueStory

"I worked for a company called Butcher, and our big competitor was our rival company, Cate. I got a cover letter from a candidate that said, 'I have wanted to work for your company my whole life because I think your approach is so sophistibutcherd.' We laughed about it for weeks. Clearly, the candidate had applied to our competitor first with the same letter and then used the 'find and replace' feature to change it to a letter for our company. If you trust your computer to do the proofreading, you're taking a risk!"

Blocks of Meaning: Using Prefixes and Suffixes to Unlock Words

If you're entering a field such as medicine or information technology, you'll come across tens or even hundreds of complicated new words—and you won't always have the time to run to the nearest dictionary. Now is the time to learn an academic skill that you can use on the fly.

Words and Their Parts

Just as you can break down sentences into words, you can break down words into their building blocks. Once you know the meanings of common word parts, you can use them as keys to unlock the meanings of unfamiliar words. This strategy applies to any word that stumps you, whether you're reading a prescription, a patient's chart, a manual for an electrical component, a newspaper, or an email.

The main part of a word is called its **root.** A root word, such as *do*, stands alone and has its own meaning—in this case, "to act or to make something happen." The meaning or function of a root word changes when you attach a word part called an **affix,** or attachment, to the beginning or the end. There are two main kinds of affixes: prefixes and suffixes. Using prefixes and suffixes to determine word meaning is an invaluable academic and professional strategy.

At the Beginning: Prefixes

A **prefix** is an attachment to the beginning of a word. Because every prefix has its own meaning or function, it changes the meaning or function of the root word. For example, the prefix *un-* means "not" or "opposite." If you add this prefix to the root *do,* the resulting word is *undo.* The addition of two little letters changes the meaning of the word dramatically. When you do a puzzle, you put it together; when you *undo* a puzzle, you do exactly the opposite: take it apart.

Study this chart of prefixes.

Selected Prefixes

Prefix	Meaning	Example Words
un-	not; opposite	**unhappy:** *not* happy **unconstitutional:** *not* allowed by the Constitution
pre-	before	**preview:** a short summary that you watch *before* a movie is released **preoperative:** happening *before* surgery
post-	after; behind	**postpone:** to delay until *after* more time has passed **postmortem:** occurring *after* death
over-	above; too much	**overtired:** *too* tired **overdo:** do something *too much*
under-	below; underneath; not enough	**underdone:** *not* cooked *enough* **underage:** *not* old *enough*
anti-	against	**anti-inflammatory:** a drug that fights *against* inflammation, or swelling **antibiotic:** a drug that fights *against* infection
hyper-	more than normal; beyond	**hyperactive:** *abnormally* active **hypertension:** *abnormally* high blood pressure
inter-	between or among	**interview:** a conversation *between* two people **interorgan:** existing *between or among* multiple organs
auto-	self	**automatic:** running by it*self* **autoimmune:** involving the immune system of one*self*
peri-	around	**perimeter:** the distance *around* an area or a figure **pericardium:** the membrane *around* the heart
bi-	two	**bimonthly:** happening every *two* months **bilateral:** having *two* sides

At the End: Suffixes

A **suffix** is attached to the end of a word. As with prefixes, every suffix has its own meaning or function and therefore changes the meaning or function of the root word. For example, the suffix -*able* means "capable of being." When you add -*able* to a word, the word becomes an adjective. Let's return to the root do, which is a verb. When you attach -*able*, you get *doable*. The verb is transformed into an adjective meaning "capable of being done."

As you'll see in the chart below, most suffixes are associated with a specific part of speech.

Selected Suffixes

Suffix	Part of Speech Created	Meaning	Example Words
-ness	noun	state of being	**happiness:** the *state of being* happy **wetness:** the *state of being* wet
-ist	noun	one who	**pharmacist:** *one who* practices pharmacy **dental hygienist:** *one who* practices dental hygiene
-ship	noun	position held	**internship:** the *position held* by an intern **relationship:** the relative *positions* of two or more objects or people
-logy	noun	study; science	**biology:** the *science* of organisms **oncology:** the *study* of tumors
-ate	verb	become	**dictate:** to *become* spoken **dilate:** to *become* enlarged
-fy	verb	make or become	**rectify:** to *make* right **calcify:** to *become* filled with calcium
-al	adjective	pertaining to; involving	**logical:** *involving* logic **abdominal:** *pertaining* to the abdomen
-less	adjective	without	**endless:** *without* end **penniless:** *without* money
-ous	adjective	full of; pertaining to	**famous:** *full of* fame **venous:** *pertaining to* veins

Putting It All Together

Now that you've looked at some examples of prefixes and suffixes, guess what the following words mean, based on their building blocks. Then look them up in a dictionary to check your guesses.

prefabricate	bilingual	underappreciate
craniology	binomial	professorship
fibrous	internal	hypertext

Closer to Correctness

The capacity to create and communicate in a spoken and written language is uniquely human. Many people spend their lives studying language arts. Whether or not the complexities of grammar and mechanics interest you, learning to express yourself correctly and appropriately is central to your education and your career.

Unit Summary

- Language arts skills are essential to educational and professional success.
- Eight parts of speech form the foundation of English grammar: nouns, pronouns, adjectives, verbs, adverbs, prepositions, conjunctions, and interjections.
- Mechanics are language rules that govern spelling, punctuation, and capitalization.
- Studying common grammatical and mechanical errors is an effective way to avoid making mistakes in your own writing.
- Proofreading, or reviewing a piece of writing to fix errors, is a critical part of the writing process.
- Breaking down a word into prefixes, roots, and suffixes can help you determine the word's meaning.

Important Terms

How well do you know these terms? Look them up in the glossary if you need help remembering them.

grammar	verb tense	homophones
parts of speech	phrasal verb	proofreading
noun	adverb	root
articles	preposition	affix
pronoun	conjunction	prefix
adjective	interjection	suffix
verb	mechanics	

Exercises

1. Choose three random sentences in this unit of the textbook. Identify the part of speech of each word in each sentence.

2. Choose an article in your favorite newspaper or magazine, a page in a book you're reading, or a letter you received in the mail. Look for the eight parts of speech you reviewed in this unit. Are any parts of speech missing? If so, why might that be the case?

3. Study the list of homophones and near-homophones on p. 73. Look up every word whose spelling *or* meaning you don't already know. Notice how the homophone pairs differ in meaning and, in some cases, part of speech.

4. Choose a magazine, book, or website and look for examples of each type of punctuation covered in this unit. Is each punctuation mark used correctly? If not, how would you change it?

5. Use the Internet to find a list of terms that apply to your industry or job. Look up any unfamiliar prefixes and suffixes that appear on the list. Circle words that you need to study and memorize.

UNIT 6

English Fundamentals: Writing Process

Identifying the stages of the writing process

Setting audience- and task-based goals for each piece of writing

Planning a piece of writing thoroughly

Drafting a piece of writing successfully

Revising a piece of writing effectively

Applying the writing process and rules of etiquette to email and IM communication

have you ever stared at a blank piece of paper—or a blank computer screen—and found yourself unable to write even one word? This is called writer's block, and it plagues even the most seasoned professional writers. One of the biggest myths about good writers is that they sit down, write a piece from beginning to end, and mysteriously emerge with a finished product.

Writing is a complex process that requires the application of several skills. It's like building a house. Builders must create a blueprint, build the foundation and framework, add internal and external features, and finish every small detail. If they skip a step, or if they complete the steps out of order, the house will be weak or unstable. This unit takes the mystery out of the writing process by breaking it down into clear steps and explaining the skills needed to complete them.

It Takes Three Stages

You're not alone if you find writing difficult. It *can* be intimidating, and even overwhelming, to commit ideas to paper. In a live conversation, you can see your audience. You receive constant feedback, and there is always something to react to. Writing is a more solitary activity, and it often feels one-sided.

But writing doesn't have to be hard. It can even be pretty easy if you break down the parts and then build them back up methodically. The advantage of following a consistent process is that it provides a sequence. Somehow the complexity melts away when you take it step by step. Another benefit is that a process gives you something to repeat every time you approach a writing assignment or task. And, as with any activity, practice makes perfect. The nature of your writing task may change, but the process itself always stays the same.

The Big Three: Planning, Drafting, and Revising

Here are the three stages of the writing process:

1. **Planning.** This stage is also called prewriting. It's like creating a builder's blueprint. You set goals, gather ideas and information, and organize the contents of your piece.

2. **Drafting.** During this stage, you implement your plan. You convert your blueprint into sentences and paragraphs, often through multiple versions (drafts).

3. **Revising.** This is the fine-tuning stage. You rewrite, revise, and proofread your work until you have a polished final product ready for your reader.

Practice
Critical Thinking

As you continue learning about the writing process, consider these questions:

1. How will you apply the steps of the writing process to your schooling?
2. How will you apply the writing process to day-to-day tasks in your chosen career?

From Concept to Communication: Planning, Drafting, and Revising

You want to get your message just right, and you want to focus on the reader. Doing it right can take time. If you're faced with writer's block, or if you find yourself going back over and over to delete what you've written, you might want to pull back for a few moments and consider a more methodical approach. Remember that writing isn't just one single task; it's a process, made up of three distinct stages.

Stage One: Planning

If you want to complete a writing task successfully—whether it is an essay, a technical manual, or an email message to a co-worker—you'll need to invest some preparation time. It might be tempting to jump right into the first draft, but that will actually make you less efficient. Let's take a look at each skill involved in planning a piece of writing.

Writing with a specific purpose. Every piece of writing needs a purpose or a goal. Ask yourself, "What result do I want to bring about by writing this? What is the main message I want to leave with my readers?" For example, do you intend to provide information, persuade someone to agree with your opinion, or request a favor? Every aspect of your piece—each sentence, paragraph, and detail—must contribute to the purpose you have set. Post your writing goal on your computer screen or desk as a reminder throughout the writing process. It's fine to have multiple goals, but focus on the most important one. For many writing tasks, an instructor or a manager will provide a clear purpose for you.

Building **Background**

This chart lists three traditional purposes of writing, along with some examples of writing products that achieve each purpose.

Purpose for Writing	Products That Fulfill the Purpose
to inform	essay, textbook, nonfiction book, technical manual, report, instructions, memo, newspaper article, magazine article, email message
to persuade	persuasive essay, editorial, persuasive letter, advertisement
to entertain	novel, story, poem, comic strip, play, movie script, blog

Writing to a specific audience. Another important writing skill is playing to your audience. Who is your ultimate reader? Your instructor? Several classmates? Your boss? A customer or vendor? Knowing your audience and purpose will help you establish the appropriate **tone,** or attitude toward your subject and reader. If you're writing a paper for school, your tone should be formal. Avoid jokes and informal language such as slang. An interoffice memo or email should be cordial, but not too familiar. A technical report should be precise, factual, and free of opinions. Put yourself in your readers' shoes, and remind yourself that they are spending valuable time processing what you have to say.

Choosing a topic. Your topic may already be provided—for example, "Write a user guide training new employees to access email remotely." You may have a limited list of choices—for instance, "Write a journal entry applying one of the topics in this unit to your career." Or perhaps your options are endless: "Write a research paper, using at least five online sources." In any case, there are two keys to selecting a topic:

1. When possible, write about something that interests you. If none of your options thrill you, try to choose a topic you already know something about.

2. Choose a topic that is neither too general nor too narrow. Let's say your assignment is to write a five-page research paper about a current topic in dentistry. "Dental practices around the world" would be too general a topic; you could write an entire book about it! On the other hand, "supplying reading materials in the waiting room" would probably be too narrow; few readers will stay interested long enough to make it through five pages of material on this topic. A topic

such as "improvements in root canal therapy" might be more suitable.

Gathering ideas. Your brain is absolutely filled with ideas worthy of communicating. All you need to do is access them, but this takes skill and practice. Here are a few methods for gathering ideas for your writing task:

Brainstorming. Brainstorming is an active, energetic way to get your ideas on paper. The idea behind brainstorming is that, even if you feel hesitant or nervous about tackling your topic, chances are you've already got some good ideas about how to approach it. Take 15 minutes to list every thought and idea that comes to mind. Don't judge or edit what comes out, and don't worry about spelling or grammar. Write quickly, and feel free to use abbreviations. When the 15 minutes are up, put a check mark next to the most promising ideas, and carry them to the next step in your planning. Brainstorming is especially effective in groups, since people's thoughts tend to feed on each other.

Mind mapping. A mind map is a diagram that begins with a central idea—your topic or purpose—and grows supporting ideas around it, much like a spider web. It is used both to generate ideas and to organize them. Below is a mind map for an essay on customer service skills.

Figure 6.1 Mind map

The five Ws. There is a reason journalists rely so heavily on the five W questions—*Who? What? When? Where?* and *Why?* You'll be surprised how many ideas rise to the surface when you ask these questions about your topic. Here is a sample 5W chart, written by a security guard gathering ideas for an incident report:

Who?	2 white males in 20s—1 about 5'7" w/brown hair & 1 about 6'2" w/ black hair, both in black clothing.
What?	– approached rear of bldg. from eastern parking lot – blocked camera A4 w/dark, gummy substance – call to police made – broke glass of right double door w/blunt object – alarm went off – perpetrators fled in car; drove north on Industrial Ave. – police arrived
When?	1:20 a.m. to 1:29 a.m., 11/24/11
Where?	Building A, 222 Industrial Ave., rear employee entrance
Why?	Suspected motive: theft of lab equipment

Talking it out. Having a conversation with a friend, classmate, or co-worker is a great way to access and clarify your thoughts. Just be sure to use your own ideas, not the ideas of others.

Research: gathering information. For some writing tasks, you will rely completely on your own knowledge and experience. For many others, however, you will have to gather information from external sources. The planning stage is when you do most of your research if your task requires it. The sources you find may help you gather your own thoughts, in addition

to providing valuable new information. We'll talk more about using research sources later in this course (and online research skills are covered in Unit 7), but here are a few preliminary tips:

- Use a variety of sources, both online and physical.
- Use only the most helpful sources; weed out sources with limited or unrelated information.
- Take thorough notes on each source, and record the citation details needed (author, title, date, URL, and so on).
- Make sure your sources are credible and reliable. For example, Wikipedia and many websites ending in *.com* are generally not considered reliable. Instead, look for websites managed by schools (*.edu*), research organizations (*.org*), and government agencies (*.gov*).

Organizing ideas and information. Now that you have gathered your ideas and information, you've come to perhaps the most crucial part of the planning process: organization. This is where you create your blueprint. The writing version of a blueprint is called a **graphic organizer.** It's a visual tool that presents ideas in a connected, clear way. Examples of graphic organizers include outlines, mind maps, charts, Venn diagrams, and time lines. You can also invent an original graphic organizer that fits your specific writing task.

Once you have a good number of ideas kicking around, you should organize them into an outline. Following a strict format isn't necessary; what matters is that you put your information and ideas into a logical order that will make it easy for both you and your reader to follow. On the following page is a sample outline for the essay on customer service skills. You'll notice that the writer used the mind map on page 90 to develop his or her outline.

I.

   A.

   B.

      1.

      2.

         a.

         b.

            i.

            ii.

I. Listening
  A. Don't interrupt
  B. Ask clarifying questions
    1. Can you please repeat that?
    2. How would you like your issue to be resolved?
      a. possible compensation/refund
      b. repair
      c. replacement
      d. other solution
  C. Take notes
II. Getting the facts
  A. 5 Ws: Who? What? Where? When? Why?
  B. Model number, part(s) involved
III. Staying calm and professional
  A. Even tone of voice
  B. Think before you speak
  C. Don't take complaints personally

Figure 6.2 Sample Outline

Stage Two: Drafting

Although this step in the writing process is considered the most intimidating, it doesn't have to be. Simply follow your blueprint—you did all that planning and organizing to make the rest of your work easier. The important thing during drafting is not to get caught up in the other two stages. If you've done a thorough job of planning, then all you have to do is trust your blueprint. Likewise, don't get bogged down revising your work as you go. There's no point in tinkering endlessly with your sentences at this point, because in the revising stage you may decide to delete them entirely. With practice, you'll discover that writing flows better if you count on writing two or more drafts.

Even though you have your blueprint as a guide, you can't cruise on autopilot while drafting. Here are some critical skills for conquering stage two of the writing process.

Drafting three distinct parts. Any good story has a beginning, a middle, and an end. It's the structure we learn to expect from childhood. Likewise, most pieces of academic and professional writing should contain three basic parts: an **introduction,** a **body,** and a **conclusion.**

Good introductions do two things: They announce your subject, and they grab (or hook) the reader's attention. Depending on your writing task, you might need to focus more on the announcement and less on the hook—or the other way around. For example,

a business memo should have a direct, brief introduction. But a cover letter for a job application is different. You'll need a hook that distinguishes your letter from the rest of the applications on the hiring manager's desk.

The body of a piece of writing contains the bulk of your message. It follows the introduction and presents the main ideas, along with details, examples, and evidence to support those ideas. The body is separated into paragraphs. Crafting an effective paragraph is one of the most important writing skills you can master. Every paragraph should include only one main idea, and each supporting detail should relate directly to that main idea. Here is the test of a good paragraph: If it's only two sentences long, you almost certainly haven't included enough detail to support your main idea. If the paragraph gets to be more than seven or eight sentences long, you've probably started discussing a new main idea, and it's time to start a new paragraph.

Your conclusion is the last paragraph or two of your product. It's your final chance to show your reader why everything you've said is important. Your conclusion should answer the question, "So what?" Here are a few ways to leave a lasting impression on your reader:

Look to the future. What do you anticipate doing or accomplishing? What outcome do you hope for?
Example: *If we implement this plan, by next quarter we should triple our sales.*

Ask a question.
Example: *What can our clinic do to improve our policies and procedures?*

Issue a call to action. Tell your readers what they should do.
Example: *Improve customer relations today by contacting each of your account holders.*

Remind your readers why your topic is important to them.
Example: *If we are going to enjoy a clean environment tomorrow, we must take action today.*

Refer to the hook you used in the introduction.
Example: *While there is no simple answer to the question of why the market has been slow to show signs of recovery, ...*

Using transitions. Always remember that there are readers on the receiving end of what you write. It's important to guide the reader through your piece, using key words and phrases that will help keep them on track. **Transitions** are words or phrases that connect ideas or indicate a change in topic. When you use transitions skillfully, you lead your readers seamlessly from one idea to another.

Study this chart of common transitions, and refer to it during your drafting process.

Citing sources to avoid plagiarism. No matter what your purpose, audience, or task, you must always **cite,** or give credit to, the outside sources you use in your writing. You need a citation when you use any of the following:

- Someone else's words (direct quotations) or ideas
- Ideas or information given to you in a conversation, an interview, or an email
- Pictures, diagrams, illustrations, or charts created by someone else

You do *not* need a citation when you use the following:

- Your own words that describe your experiences, thoughts, observations, or insights
- Information that qualifies as common knowledge (facts that appear in many sources and are widely known, such as the birth and death dates of a famous person)

Purpose	Transitions
to show addition	and, also, again, in addition, furthermore, moreover, besides, next, too
to introduce an example	for example, for instance, such as, in particular, in fact, that is, specifically, on the one hand/other hand, to illustrate
to indicate the passage of time	before, after, afterward, next, during, meanwhile, later, eventually, immediately, suddenly, finally
to indicate rank or importance	first, second, third, first and foremost, most importantly, more importantly, above all
to indicate cause	because, since, for this reason
to indicate effect	as a result, consequently, therefore, hence
to indicate comparison	similarly, likewise, like, just as, in the same manner
to indicate contrast	but, however, on the other hand, on the contrary, in contrast, yet, instead, rather, while, although, though, despite
to add emphasis	in fact, indeed, certainly, above all
to summarize or conclude	in sum, in summary, in short, in conclusion, to conclude, to sum up, that is, therefore, in the end

Failure to cite outside sources in your writing is called **plagiarism**—an act that can get you expelled from school, fired, or even sued. Today, one of the most common forms of plagiarism is to cut and paste text or graphics from a website into an "original" piece of writing. If you find this practice tempting, be warned that these few keystrokes could cost you your education or your job. It's simply not worth it. There are several computer programs that are used by instructors and employers to check to see if written work is original, and they work very well. If you fail to cite your sources, chances are very high that you will be caught and will suffer painful consequences.

The way to avoid plagiarism is to take good notes during your research. As you write down ideas, facts, and quotes, make a note of where you found them. Write down all identifying details: author(s), title, publisher, date, and page number(s).

There are several different formats to use for citations within your writing. Psychologists, for example, use the **APA citation format** (American Psychological Association), while literature scholars typically use the **MLA citation format** (Modern Language Association). While the citation formats differ, the information in them does not. In most cases, you can simply mention the source's author and year (in parentheses) within your text and include a bibliography or list of sources at the end. Remember to give credit for other people's information, ideas, and words. Here is an example of an in-text citation:

> Phillip Marsden (2010) argues that the IT industry has spawned a new generation of customer service practices.

The APA citation format is the easiest to use, and you can easily find rules for its use in the APA handbook—or just Google "APA citation" and you can find simplified rules for APA citation format on one of many college websites.

Other drafting tips. Here are some other pointers to keep in mind while you draft:

- If you have trouble getting started, try free-writing. For ten minutes, just type (or write) without stopping, even if you're typing non-sense some of the time. With a little luck, you'll gain momentum and begin to see ideas and paragraphs starting to take shape.
- If you've typed your outline on a computer, save it as a new file, and type your draft directly into it. Your blueprint will be right in front of you; all you have to do is fill it in.
- If you get stuck—or even if you don't—revisit your main goal. Make sure minor points or tangents aren't distracting you.
- Save, copy, or back up your work periodically. Every sentence you write is precious. One machine malfunction, and your work could be lost forever. Avoid learning this lesson the hard way.
- Discuss your draft with someone. It will help you keep ideas flowing. You can even record your conversation and then transfer key points from it to your writing.

Stage Three: Revising

Once you have a complete draft, it's time to go back and fine-tune your piece. If possible, take some time away from it so that you can come back to it with fresh eyes and a new perspective. Stage three actually consists of three tasks: **revising, editing,** and **proofreading.**

Revise literally means "to see again." Revising means looking at your rough draft with fresh eyes and making bold changes. Return to the big picture, and ask yourself the following questions:

- Have I achieved my purpose or goal? Do I stay focused on this goal throughout the piece?
- Have I followed the instructions of the assignment or project?
- Have I covered every aspect of my writing plan? If not, why not?
- Are my ideas expressed clearly? Is my argument logical?
- Do I have a distinct introduction, body, and conclusion?
- Does each paragraph have only one main idea and at least two supporting details?

- Have I used transitions between sections and paragraphs?
- Have I repeated the same idea or concept too many times?
- Does the tone support the nature of my writing (formal, casual, business, etc.)?

The revision process generally sends you back into the drafting stage, as you make big-picture improvements and reorganize whole sections and paragraphs. Once you're satisfied with the answers to the above revision questions, you can move on to editing. In this phase, you focus on sentences and words. On this pass through your draft, ask these questions:

- Are all of my sentences clear? Will every reader understand the point I am making, or is there any room for misinterpretation?
- Have I varied the length of my sentences?

- Have I varied the way my sentences begin?
- Have I used appropriate vocabulary, considering my purpose and audience?
- Have I avoided unnecessarily repeating certain words?
- Have I avoided or fixed all grammatical errors?

Once editing is done, you're on the home stretch: proofreading. During this final run-through, your goal is to correct errors in **mechanics** (spelling, punctuation, and capitalization) and **formatting** (details about how the text is arranged, such as margins, type size, and line spacing). Read your piece slowly and out loud, word by word, and apply the grammar and mechanics rules outlined in Unit 5 of this book. As your last step, perform a spell and grammar check with your word processor. Remember, however, that a spell checker is just a brainless computer script. It won't catch misspellings that happen to be real words, such as *roll* instead of *role* or *on and of* instead of *on and off*—and it won't tell you if you've left out important words. Nothing can take the place of proofreading by a human being.

As you revise, edit, and proofread, remember that you are not working alone. Throughout stage three of the writing process, consult these trusty tools (you can find them online or in hard copy):

- dictionary
- thesaurus
- grammar guide
- list of common language arts errors (see Unit 5)
- a copy of your writing assignment or instructions (if applicable)

Taking the Writing Process Online: Email

Email is one of the most common forms of online communication. In a school setting, students and instructors use email to communicate about assignments, attendance, course registration, and financial aid. At work, email is one of the most frequently used forms of contact both within and between organizations. Finally, people use email for social communication and management of their personal lives. Even if you use email already, it's important to become familiar with **email etiquette:** guidelines for using email professionally and courteously, regardless of your audience.

Planning: An Introduction to Formal Email

When you write an email, use an abbreviated version of the writing process. As with any piece of writing, start the planning process by identifying your purpose and audience. Are you writing to an instructor to discuss or submit an assignment? Are you addressing a question about your employee benefits to the human resources department of your company? Are you emailing three classmates to set up a time for a study session? Are you contacting a customer to request feedback on your company's services? Are you registering a complaint about a product you bought?

In emails like these, your tone should be conversational yet formal, polite, and respectful. Follow the rules of standard written English. Never use texting shortcuts, such as *u* for *you* or *thnx* for *thanks*. Because email is so impersonal—in many cases you've never met the person on the other end—it can be easy to be harsh or distant. Give your message the tone test: If you hesitate before sending it, don't send it. Sleep on it first.

Drafting: The Parts of an Email Message

Most email messages are brief—no more than a few paragraphs—so they generally require fewer drafts than other forms of writing. They are structured a lot like business memos, with short chunks of information placed in distinct locations for easy access. Let's review each section of an email message.

"From" field. This is where your own email address appears. For anything but the most casual email messages to close friends and family, your address should be appropriate and tasteful. Stick to something straightforward, like mjones@gmail.com, instead of a silly address like cheekymonkey@yahoo.com.

To, Cc, and Bcc fields. In the *To* field, type the email address(es) of the person or people for whom your message is intended. Next to *Cc*—an abbreviation for *carbon copy*—place the addresses of people who are not direct recipients of the message but ought to read it for some reason. For example, if you're submitting a group presentation to your instructor, you might want to cc: the other members of

your group so that they know you've completed that task. This is an efficient practice because you don't have to send a separate email to your group members to tell them what you've done; they've already received the original email.

The etiquette for the *Cc* field in work settings is complicated. If you send a message to a co-worker and cc: his supervisor, then your co-worker may think that you are exposing him to his boss for not doing his job. People can be very sensitive about who is in the *Cc* field in an email message, so make sure that you include on the email only the people who need to see the message. Also, be very careful about forwarding a message from one person to another person or group of people. Your co-worker might phrase things differently to you than she would if she were writing to your supervisor or a large group of people. Don't surprise her by changing the audience without her permission. Finally, organizations have different rules about how quickly email messages need to be answered. In some companies, all messages need to be answered by the end of the day, while other organizations are more casual, and it can be fine to leave a message unanswered for a week or more. If you have questions, you can always ask your supervisor for guidelines about email etiquette at your organization.

Bcc—which stands for *blind carbon copy*—is usually not appropriate for use in professional and academic contexts. When you put email addresses in this field, the recipients in the *To* and *Cc* fields do not see the names of the people you have blind carbon copied. It is generally best, and certainly more honest, for all recipients of an email message to be aware of each other. One exception is when the first line of a message clearly announces that it is being sent to a large group—for example, "Dear Students of CS102"—and placing all the email addresses

in the *Bcc* field prevents the top of the message from getting clogged.

Subject line. Reducing the topic of your email to a brief, clear subject line is an important skill to develop. Imagine sitting down to review your own email inbox. Look at the messages on the next page. When you scan the subject lines of your new messages, would you rather see version 1 or version 2?

The subject lines in version 2 pass the effectiveness test: You know exactly what the email is about without having to open it. That way you can prioritize your messages and open the most important ones first.

Always fill in the subject line of an email address—never leave it blank. If you're writing to an instructor, include the abbreviated course title. If you're writing to a colleague about a topic with an associated account number or billing code, include that reference. Subject lines are about saving time.

TrueStory

"One day at work, a few of my co-workers and I were talking about our department's strict dress code. I decided to send a formal complaint about the dress code to my boss. I sent her an email and bcc:ed my co-workers so they would know I was pushing for them. One of my friends replied to the message, so my boss could see that a lot of other people had been copied! She asked to meet with me and said that my blind copying was inappropriate and unprofessional. It's going to take me a while to earn back her trust."

```
Version 1:                          Version 2:
  Do you want to come                 Dinner invitation:
  over here for d...                  Fri. 5/23

  An overview of this                 CS102 week 4
  week's assignm...                   assignments

  Regarding the estimate              Dishwasher repair
  of your broke...                    estimate
```

Figure 6.3 Sample subject lines

Salutation. The salutation is the greeting at the beginning of your message. Follow email etiquette by always including a salutation, followed by a colon (for formal business communication) or a comma (for less formal messages to people you already know). When in doubt about using first or last names, err on the side of formality and use a title followed by a last name. If you are writing to a co-worker or classmate you know well, it is usually acceptable to omit the word *Dear* or to use a slightly different greeting. Here are some examples of salutations:

> Dear Dr. Rodriguez:
>
> Dear Ms. Albertson,
>
> Good morning, Nina,

Body. The body of your message should be in paragraph form. Your message should be as short as possible; keep in mind that many people receive 50 or more emails per day. Some people in large companies receive more than 1,000. Also, keep your paragraphs short—just a few sentences each—and separate each one from the next with a blank line.

Closing. In your concluding paragraph, include any action items or follow-ups you are requesting from your audience. Thank your reader for taking his or her time and for considering your request (if applicable).

Signature. Always include a signature at the end of your message. Depending on your audience and the level of formality, use one of these words or phrases before your name:

> Sincerely,
>
> Best wishes,
>
> Talk with you soon,

If you know your audience very well, just your name is often sufficient.

Many people use an automatic signature that appears at the end of every email they send. In a business setting, it is common (and appropriate) to include your name, title, department, company name, mailing address, phone number, and other contact information. Sometimes your company will provide a standard signature to use with a logo. If you use an automatic signature, keep it tasteful. Do not use silly quotations, slogans, moving icons or emoticons, or brightly colored text or backgrounds. Remember that every aspect of your communication reflects on you as a student or professional.

Attachment(s). Be sparing and judicial when attaching documents, such as Word files or images. Reduce images to the smallest reasonable size. Always announce attachments and their purposes within the text of your message so that your reader is aware of them.

Revising: Polishing an Email Message

When fine-tuning your email messages, ask yourself the same revision and editing questions introduced earlier. If you don't have time for multiple drafts and revisions, at least do one round each of editing and proofreading. All rules of standard written English apply to email messages. Use spell and grammar checkers, but as always, don't rely on these tools to catch all errors.

As you edit and proofread, eliminate any of the following breaches of email etiquette:

- casual acronyms and jargon (LOL, IMHO, OMG, TTFN, etc.)
- the use of ALL CAPS for emphasis or drama
- overuse of formatting features such as **boldface,** *italics,* or bright colors
- overuse of exclamation points

Instant Messaging (IM)

At many schools—and within a growing number of workplaces—**instant messaging (IM),** a real-time form of electronic communication, is now common. You can use IM to reach your instructors during office hours, to chat with fellow classmates or co-workers, and to work on group projects. The following are general etiquette guidelines when using IM:

Choose an appropriate screen name. Be sure that your screen name conveys a professional image. "HaleyR" is a better choice than "Luvs2Dance."

Give the recipient a chance to say no. When you IM someone, you don't know if he or she is sitting alone at the computer, sitting next to his or her boss, or presenting to a large group. Always start your IM with something short, like "Hi" or "ping," that does not provide information. This gives your recipient a chance to reply with "not now" or "I'm busy," sparing both of you some embarrassment.

Respond in a timely manner. An IM conversation should be a series of short, quick responses. Long pauses or lapses in time can be rude or frustrating for your recipient. If you initiate or engage in a chat on IM, it is courteous to give that person your full attention.

Use abbreviations and emoticons appropriately. Many people are not completely familiar with all the abbreviations, acronyms, and emoticons used in IM. Use them sparingly—if at all.

Use proper spelling and grammar. Put your best foot forward by using standard written English. With so many messages flying back and forth, you don't want to be misunderstood. As with email, avoid using ALL CAPITAL LETTERS; it's the online equivalent of screaming.

End conversations prior to leaving IM. It is polite to let your audience know that you are leaving the conversation. Simply type, "I have to go now. See you later."

ON THE **JOB:**

Because email is so immediate, it's easy to forget that electronic communication has permanence. It's not the same as an offhand remark or a quick phone call to a friend. Don't write anything in an email that you don't want a large audience to read. In a business setting, nothing is truly private; your company leadership can access every message on the server. Emails can be stored, printed, and even used against you in a court of law. Also be aware that the recipients of your message can forward it as widely as they wish. Don't make the mistake of treating email too casually.

One Last Word

As you practice the writing process with all forms of written communication, you will grow to trust and appreciate it. Some additional skills for strengthening workplace communications will be discussed in a later unit. Even if writing has never been one of your talents, you can develop the skills and habits of a professional writer and use them to your advantage. Your readers will thank you for it.

TrueStory

"I was in a really big business meeting and my friend was presenting to the CEO. It was a tense meeting and was running late—it was already 7:00 p.m. Suddenly, her husband's IM popped up on the screen as 'DowntownDingus'! He typed, 'Are you ever coming home?' and 'So much for tennis tonight.' The whole room roared with laughter. It really didn't help her professional image."

Unit Summary

- Writing is a complex process that involves three stages: planning, drafting, and revising.

- During the planning stage, gather and organize ideas for your writing product.

- During the drafting stage, use your writing plan to create an introduction, a body, and a conclusion.

- During the revising stage, restructure, edit, and proofread your work.

- When writing an email message, use an abbreviated version of the writing process and follow the rules of email etiquette.

- For any piece of writing, always keep your purpose and audience at the forefront of your mind.

Important Terms

How well do you know these terms? Look them up in the glossary if you need help remembering them.

planning	body	revising
drafting	conclusion	editing
revising	transitions	proofreading
tone	cite	mechanics
brainstorming	plagiarism	formatting
graphic organizer	APA citation format	email etiquette
introduction	MLA citation format	instant messaging (IM)

Exercises

1. In a notebook, write two to three paragraphs about your attitude toward writing. Do you enjoy writing? Why or why not? What are your strengths as a writer? What are your challenges?

2. Take 15 minutes to brainstorm ideas for the following assignment: Write an essay about how to balance school with other aspects of life.

3. Find a newspaper article, magazine article, or letter. Identify the start and end points of its introduction, body, and conclusion. Then determine two revisions you would apply to the piece if you had to write another draft of it.

4. Use the writing process to craft an email message to your instructor for this course. Your purpose is to summarize what you have learned in this unit.

Internet
Applications

Utilizing Web browsers and search engines effectively

Choosing and refining specific research questions and keywords

Identifying reliable, credible online research sources

Defining plagiarism and identifying its consequences

Citing online sources properly

Sometimes when you do a search on Google or Yahoo, you get millions of entries. A search on the words *medical assistant* gives you more than 28,000,000 results, and a search on *criminal justice* yields more than 43,000,000! Thanks to the online revolution, there is much more information available to the average person than at any other time in history. All you need is a computer and an Internet connection. But wading into that sea of digital data can be overwhelming. When you are looking at thousands or millions of possible references, where do you begin, and how do you tell what's relevant? Once you find a source, how do you know if it's a good one? In this unit, we will discuss tools and strategies that will help you sift through all the information to help you get the answers you need.

Getting onto the
Information Superhighway

Let's start with reviewing some definitions. **Research** is an investigation into a specific topic. It is a focused collection of facts. Any time you ask a question and then search for an answer, you are conducting research. Research tasks can be simple, or they can be very complex.

For example, you might ask, "What bus connections are available at the Broad Street and Eighth Avenue stop?" To find the answer, you can utilize one of several strategies. You could walk three miles to the Broad and Eighth stop and look at the sign, but that might take hours. You could call a friend who lives near the stop, but you might not reach her, or she might be unable to check because she is not at home. You could call the city bus company, but you'd have to follow several automated prompts before even speaking to a person. Or, you could walk down the hall to your computer, type NYC bus connections at broad st eighth ave into Google, click a few links, and have your answer within 30 seconds.

The Internet is a worldwide network of computers. It's called the information superhighway because it puts you on the fast track to answering your questions. The Internet is essentially an enormous research tool. Yes, you may also use it for communication and entertainment, but chances are that you've gone online to find a specific nugget of information at some point in the past week. In this section, we'll review basic Internet use and explain some general online search strategies.

Using Your Browser

To do an online search, you must first open a **browser.** This is a computer program that gives you access to the **World Wide Web**— the Internet's collection of **websites,** or specific electronic locations. Three of the most common browsers are Internet Explorer, Mozilla Firefox, and Safari (which is used on Apple computers). To review basic browser use and bookmarking, see Unit 4.

Every website has a unique URL (uniform resource locator), or electronic address. To visit a website, type the URL into the main field (rectangle for entering text) and press ENTER. The website will appear on the screen. Most websites consist of several pages. To navigate between different pages, you click your mouse or trackpad button on **links**—blocks of text or images that lead to another location on the Web. When people "surf" the Web, they go from page to page, or site to site, by clicking links.

Build **Background**

- At the time of Netcraft's April 2011 Web Server Survey, there were more than 300 million websites on the World Wide Web.

- According to the National Center for Educational Statistics, 35 percent of American public schools had access to the Internet in 1994. By fall 2005, that percentage had reached nearly 100 percent.

- According to Google, in 2010, the Internet contained about 5 million terabytes (5 billion gigabytes) of data. Google has indexed only about 0.004 percent of that data, or 200 terabytes. A single human brain can hold approximately 1 to 10 terabytes of data.

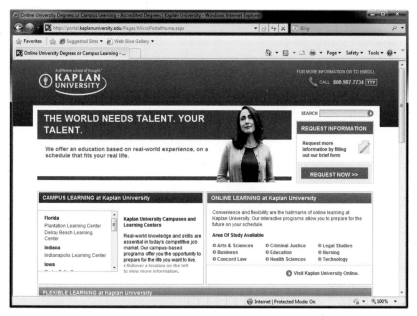

Figure 7.1

Along the top of a browser window like the one shown in Figure 7.1, you will find several navigation command buttons. The most important commands have the following functions:

Back. Use this button to go to the Web page you were on previously. If you continue to click on it, you will eventually reach the first page you visited when you opened your browser.

Forward. Use this button to return to the page(s) you were on before clicking Back.

Stop. Use this button if you want a Web page to stop loading—for example, if it's taking a long time or you change your mind about navigating to it.

Refresh. Imagine that you visited a favorite news site yesterday and then left the Web page open on your computer. Today you want to see the updated content, or information, on the site. Press Refresh to reload the Web page that currently appears on your browser. You'll still be looking at the same site, but the content will be refreshed. If the content hasn't been updated, the page will look exactly the same.

Home. Click this button to return to the default, or home, Web page. To customize this page in Internet Explorer, click on Tools in the top menu bar. Click on Internet Options. Click the General tab. In the Address box, type the URL of the website you want to set as your home page. (This process is similar in other browsers.) The website you entered will appear any time you open your browser.

History. This command shows you the list—sometimes a very *long* list—of websites you have visited over the past few hours and days. If you want to go to a previous location quickly, it is often faster to select from the sites on this list rather than clicking the Back button repeatedly.

Search. Many browsers have a search engine field built into the upper right-hand corner. If you want to do a quick search, you can use this field rather than typing in the URL of your preferred search engine first.

Figure 7.2

Search Engine Savvy

You've got a question to research, you've started up your Web browser, and you know how to use the browser's command buttons. But there's one problem: You have no idea where to go within the enormity of the World Wide Web. You don't have any specific URLs to visit.

Your go-to place to start any hunt for information is a **search engine.** This is a website that searches the entire Web for pages that contain the **keywords,** or main search terms, that you type in. Here are some examples of popular search engines:

- Google (www.google.com)
- Yahoo! (www.yahoo.com)
- Bing (www.bing.com)
- Ask.com (www.ask.com)

To do a basic search on any of these sites, follow these instructions:

1. In the top center field, type the URL of the search engine (for example, www.google.com) and press ENTER. The main search page will appear. Figure 7.2 shows what Google's looks like.

2. In the large search field at the center of the screen, type your question. You can use keywords, or you can just type in a question. Press ENTER.

3. A new page will pop up with the results of your search: a list of Web pages that contain the words you typed in the search box. At the bottom of the page, you can click page number links to see additional pages of results.

4. Click on the link of any Web page that looks as if it will answer your research question.

5. To get back to your search results, click Back as many times as necessary.

Let's look at an example using this research question: What is insulin?

1. You navigate to www.google.com.

2. You decide to use the whole question as your keyword entry, as shown in Figure 7.3.

3. Figure 7.4 shows the results.

4. You decide to click on the second link: Introduction to Insulin. As you continue navigating between the Google results screen and the links it provided, you take notes about the definition and functions of insulin. Before long, you are satisfied; your question is answered.

Figure 7.3

Search engines are very "smart." They have algorithms that prioritize which of the thousands of search results are likely to be most useful to you. For instance, the pages that seemed most relevant to the question "What is insulin?" appeared at the top of the search results. However, online searching isn't always this easy. If your first search—or your second or third one—doesn't yield any promising results, don't give up! Try these strategies for getting better results out of a search engine:

Figure 7.4

Do the right kind of search. Remember that the World Wide Web contains a lot more than just text. Let's say that after reading various sources about insulin, a new question occurs to you: What does an insulin molecule look like? To answer this question, words will get you only so far; you want to *see* the structure of the molecule. For this question you'll want to conduct an image search. With search engines such as Google, you can limit your search results to the following types of content:

- Images (images.google.com): See insulin molecules. What does an insulin molecule look like?

- News (news.google.com): Read recent articles on insulin research.

- Videos (video.google.com): Watch videos about insulin medication.

- Maps (maps.google.com): Find local facilities that conduct insulin research.

- Journal/scholarly articles (scholar.google.com): Read the latest discoveries about insulin.

- Online stores (www.google.com/products): Find retailers that sell insulin-related products.

To limit your search, you can either type in the specific URL or you can click on a filter link on the search engine page. To see how this works, go to Google and type in "what is insulin?" Then click on the Images link in the Google window. The search will be filtered to show just images. Don't be surprised if you find some odd or irrelevant images—the Internet is full of information, and not all of it is useful. You will need to browse through the images until you find one from a reputable source that shows an insulin molecule.

Join the quest for the perfect keywords.
If your keywords are generic, your results will show the most general and popular information—or they'll be completely unrelated to your topic. For example, let's say you want to know what types of stones to use for a gravel patio. You type stones into a search engine, and several of the results are websites about the Rolling Stones (a rock band), kidney stones, and a pizza restaurant called Hearth Stones. The more specific your keywords are, the closer—and faster—you'll get to what you really want. Follow these steps:

1. State your research goal in a phrase, sentence, or question.

   What types of stones should I use for a gravel patio?

2. Identify keywords by circling the most important words.

   What types of stones should I use for a gravel patio?

3. List synonyms, different spellings, and other forms of your keywords.

   types: type, kind, kinds, variety, varieties
   stones: stone, rock, rocks, material, materials
   gravel: (none)
   patio: patios, courtyard, courtyards

4. Type your original keywords—or some combination of the variations on your list—into a search engine. You'll be much happier with the results. type stone gravel patio

It may take several tries to find the right keywords. You will know you are doing well when your search results are small (fewer than 50 results) and most of the entries are relevant. It takes practice to choose the right keywords, so keep trying!

Use keyword qualifiers. Additional words or characters that help you refine or limit a keyword search are called **keyword qualifiers.** Here are a few helpful examples:

Quotation marks. Placing a phrase in quotation marks gets you only websites containing that exact phrase. For the patio stones search, you might consider using this method: "types of stone" gravel patio. That way there will be little chance that the word *stone* will get misinterpreted.

Plus sign or *and*. Put a plus sign (+) or the word *and* before a word to return only results that contain that word. For example, to find out what types of stone could be used for a patio *and* a sidewalk, use these search terms: "types of stone" patio + sidewalk.

Minus sign or *and not*. Put a hyphen (-) or the phrase *and not* before a word to return only results that do *not* contain that word. For instance, if you want to research the use of the word *stone* but do not want to include the band Rolling Stones, try this: usage word stone -"rolling stones".

Or. Use the word *or* to get results that include all the words in your list of synonyms and alternative forms. That way you don't have to retype keywords each time you want to try a new synonym; you can cover them all in one search: types or kinds or varieties stone.

Ask for help. If you're having a hard time, you're not alone. Online searches can be deceptively difficult. Ask your instructor, a librarian, a classmate, your boss, a co-worker, or a friend or family member for tips. Or, ask an online librarian at the Internet Public Library (www.ipl.org).

Research: Using Online Sources

At school and on the job, you will often need to do very intense, specific research. Your success will depend on how good you are at finding the best, most useful, and most accurate information and applying it to the task at hand. You're not looking for just any source, or for just the first source that answers your question. You're looking for a **reliable** source—a dependable, trustworthy website with a tested reputation. In this section, we will discuss how to find and use the best possible research sources.

Serious Investigations: General Tips

The stakes are a little bit higher now. Your grade, or your professional reputation, is on the line. Here are some tips for finding the information you need.

Establish your questions. As with any type of research, start with a question:

> *How much will it cost to upgrade our desktop computers?*

Then break your question down into more specific ones:

> *Which upgrades will make the biggest difference in performance?*

> *Which upgrades will be compatible with our printers, copy machines, and other peripherals?*

> *Which vendor can give us the lowest price on flat-panel monitors?*

These questions will end up driving your research.

Practice Now: Engaged

One of the best ways to build your teamwork skills is to ask questions. You can build relationships with classmates and co-workers by asking for their advice, which provides an entrée to future conversations. When you are having difficulty finding information on the Internet, find a classmate or co-worker and ask what keywords he or she might use. Not only will you find better information, but you will also be building an important connection.

Further specialize your search. The websites of most companies, organizations, and publications have their own search engines. They work just like Yahoo! or Google, but they search only within their own site or, in some cases, closely related sites. For example, if you're looking for information about childhood vaccinations, try visiting the website of the American Academy of Pediatrics—one of the most reliable organizations in the field of medicine—and searching the site for vaccinations. By using a trusted site within your field, you limit your results to medical information. You won't have to sift through news articles, opinion pieces, and millions of message-board posts by parents telling stories from the doctor's office. If you don't know what your topic or field's reputable organizations are, ask your instructor or boss for advice. It might be the most valuable step you take in the research process.

Think for yourself. Online sources only provide information. They can't *synthesize* anything; that's your job. If you're writing a paper for a course, your instructor will expect you to do more than just explain what other sources say about your topic; he or she will want you to analyze, evaluate, and compare other people's ideas, and then explain how you came to your own conclusion. If your boss puts you in charge of solving a problem or improving a process, he or she wants you to make recommendations. Always remember that the point of research is to help *you* make decisions.

Back it up. When you make your recommendation or state your conclusion, you want to be able to give some good, logical reasons for it. Gut instinct has its place, but the reason you're doing research is to be able to point to something solid to back up your decisions and to show why other people should agree with you. There is a significant difference between opinion and informed opinion. Opinions that are supported by facts or reputable research carry greater weight.

Types of Online Research Sources

Just as you can find numerous kinds of sources in a library—books, magazines, journals, encyclopedias, and so on—the Internet also houses many kinds of sources for researchers. Here are just a few:

Your online library. One of the best tools available to you while you are a student at a Kaplan Higher Education campus is your online library. Just go to Kaplan Quad and click on the library link. You will have access to the best and most reputable research databases in the world. If you don't know where to start, click on the Find Articles and E-Books tab and scroll down to click on the Academic Search Premier link. This connects you to Ebscohost, one of the largest research databases available. Unlike Google, it is filtered to contain reputable articles. If you want to ensure that your research is top drawer, click in the Scholarly (Peer Reviewed) Journals box. This will limit your search to scholarly journals that have peer review boards to ensure that every article meets rigorous research standards. This is how doctoral students do their research.

Archives. Many newspapers, magazines, and journals have put decades of their content on the World Wide Web. You can usually search these archives for free, and you can often read the articles at little or no cost. Either at a library or at home, you can search, download, and print an article in minutes.

Specialized information. If you're looking for information on a narrow or unusual topic—such as high-level electrical equipment, rare diseases, or a brand-new dental procedure in Australia—the Web gives you access to journals with small subscriber lists, local newspapers from around the world, and other resources that may not be available to you in print.

Original sources. Because the Internet has fewer size restrictions than printed publications, many authors, publishers, and organizations take advantage of the opportunity to post supplementary material along with main articles. An online newspaper might pair a short article about a presidential speech with a complete transcript or video of the original speech. Scientists might share the complete results of studies that they only provide a summary of in print form. If you want to dig more deeply into a story or topic, you'll find a wealth of bonus material online.

Reading Critically

There is, unfortunately, a big disadvantage to online research, and it's the same thing that makes the Internet so great: Anyone can post something on the World Wide Web, from experts and professionals to criminals and

hobbyists. To put it mildly, sources are not all equal. With most print sources, such as newspapers and magazines, you know that editors and publishers have signed off on the information. If it is a reputable print source, then the information is reasonably reliable. If it is a peer-reviewed journal, then the research has been validated by a review board and is even more credible. However, online sources are often backed by private agendas and may consist of opinions that are not substantiated by facts or research. Online, you'll want to seek out sources that carry an assurance of reliability, such as the websites of reliable print newspapers, magazines, and journals.

For every site you find, you need to conduct an **evaluation**—a judgment process that determines the quality and reliability of your source. Don't use any source until you are confident that it provides accurate, trustworthy information on your topic. If you're not careful, you could wind up basing your conclusions on a source that is entirely made up.

Like research, the evaluation process consists of asking and answering questions. If you ask the following questions about your source and can answer them in a satisfactory way, you can be assured that it is reliable:

What is the website's extension? A **domain extension** is the series of letters at the end of a URL. Generally speaking, websites that end in *.gov* (government), *.org* (organization), or *.edu* (school, university, or other educational institution) are more reliable than sites that end in *.com* or *.biz* (private companies). That said, a site that ends in *.com* might still be the best source to answer your question. If you need to recommend a laser printer to your boss, or if you need to know the correct spelling of *Hewlett-Packard,* it's best to go straight to the company's website. Some reliable news sites also end in *.com.*

Does the site have ads and other distractions? If you see several advertisements, flashing or moving graphics, neon colors, and other signs of messy design, proceed with caution. The website should look professional and appropriate for *any* viewer.

Does the source provide a name and contact information? Legitimate websites have authority. At the bottom of most home pages, you can find the contact information for the person, organization, or institution that is responsible for the content. A full name or names, an address, a phone number, and an email address should be provided—or the company's corporate address. If you can't find the

information, shorten the URL in the top center field by deleting everything to the right of the first slash, and then press ENTER. This will take you to the main page. Is a responsible author identified? Is the contact information correct? Don't rely on information from the site unless you can determine who claims responsibility for its content.

Is the author reputable? Once you've found the author of the site, ask some new questions. Do you know if the person or group is qualified to write about the topic? What are those qualifications? Look up the authors or the organization. Do they exist as they say they do?

Can you confirm the information in other sources? This is one of the best ways to test a website's reliability. Verify the information—test its truth—by putting the information *itself* into a search engine and seeing if it comes up in other reputable sources. Try to find similar information on three other websites that have not copied the information from the original site you visited.

Do the links work? If your source has links to pages that no longer exist, the source is probably either unreliable or outdated.

Does the source seem biased? Always be on the lookout for signs of **bias,** a preference or inclination that prevents impartial judgment. For instance, don't rely on air-quality data if it comes from a website in the commercial coal industry. Another example: If you're researching insulin pumps, consulting a site with reviews of many products, such as www.consumerreports.org, would be a better choice than believing a single company's online claim that its pump "beats the competition hands-down." Unless you understand the bias of the publisher, you risk using skewed statistics and other unreliable information.

Is the source timely? What we know about many subjects changes over time. Scientific research, court rulings, and even shifting public opinion can make information outdated. Look for the published date for news articles or journal articles. Relying on a six-month-old resource when you're dealing with an ever-changing subject such as pharmaceuticals is risky. What if the recommended dosage or proven side effects of a drug have changed? To find out if a source is outdated, look for "current" references to old material. (For example, is the 1996 presidential election referred to as the most recent?) Check the bottom of the page for the date when the site was last updated. If there is no date, or if it's been several months or longer, question the information. Most reliable sites are updated frequently.

Does the source cite its own information? Check out the statements that sources make. Do they tell you where their information comes from? If not, then it could be completely fabricated. If they do provide references, take a quick look at the source's source. Does it seem reliable? If your website includes links to its sources, click on the links to verify that the information is reliable. Sometimes it's just a link to another page on the same website—or to a different website with the same agenda.

Is it a personal website? Sites created by individuals often contain the most unreliable information. Individuals do not have to pass any test of accuracy or reliability before posting content on their own website. That's not to say that all personal pages are bad sources, but you should evaluate them more carefully. First, check the URL for clues. A personal website's URL often has one or more of the following: their first and last name, a tilde (~), a percent sign (%), the word *member*, or the word *user*.

Is it a blog? Your search results may yield entries from weblogs, or **blogs**—online diaries

> ## True Story
>
> "I was doing medical research and came across a website for an organization that called itself a Medical Center. At first it looked okay, and I started taking notes. But then I clicked on a few links, and I started getting suspicious. The site prompted me to download the latest Flash Player application, and the graphics looked really strange. Finally, on one page, I saw a video claiming to be about 'male pregnancy.' Needless to say, I didn't cite the information in my paper!"

that are usually casual in tone and focused heavily on commentary. Steer clear of blogs, unless you find the blog of a respected expert. Even then, be aware that blog entries carry much less weight than thoroughly researched and edited articles.

Does the URL start with the letters *wiki*? Do not necessarily trust information on "user-edited" or "community-edited" sites such as Wikipedia. You should verify any fact you find on such a site by checking at least two additional, reputable sources. The best use of wiki sites is to help you get a quick overview and find your way to some other, more reliable sources.

Does it ask you to spend money? Some research databases charge you a small amount of money to download an article—perhaps one or two dollars. But if a source prompts you to enter your credit card information for a high (or unstated) charge, navigate away from it immediately, and certainly don't use it as a source. If it is a reputable source, chances are that you can acquire it free through your online library on Kaplan Quad.

While this list of questions is rather long, checking your sources could not be more important, especially when other people are counting on you to conduct responsible research. If you make a decision based on false or biased information, you could be jeopardizing your career, your reputation, or even someone else's well being. With practice, evaluating your sources will eventually become second nature.

Research-Friendly URLs: Some Reliable Sources

Figure 7.5 shows a list of reliable online resources. When you have a research question, consider starting here.

General	• Library of Congress: www.loc.gov	• EBSCOHost: search.ebscohost.com
	• Internet Public Library: www.ipl.org	• Smithsonian: www.si.edu
	• Google Books: books.google.com	• U.S. Census Bureau: www.census.gov
Medical/ Pharmacy	• American Medical Association: www.ama-assn.org	
	• National Institutes of Health: www.nih.gov	
	• Mayo Clinic: www.mayoclinic.com	
	• JAMA (Journal of the American Medical Association): jama.ama-assn.org	
Electrical	• National Electrical Contractors Association: www.necanet.org	
	• Electric Utility Industry Data Finder: http://ewp.rpi.edu/hartford/library/industry/elecutil.htm	
Information Technology	• Information Technology Industry Council: www.itic.org	
Criminal Justice	• Academy of Criminal Justice Sciences: www.acjs.org	
Online Safety/ Fraud	• National Criminal Justice Reference Service: www.ncjrs.gov	
	• Federal Trade Commission Complaint Assistant (for cases of online fraud and identity theft): https://www.ftccomplaintassistant.gov/	

Figure 7.5 Sampling of reliable online resources

Give Credit Where It Is Due

You've reached the final step in your research. You've asked the right questions, found reliable sources, digested those sources, and taken careful notes. You're just about ready to communicate your research findings to others. Before you do so, your final task is to give credit to your sources. Remember, a lot of this information—perhaps most of it—did not come from you.

Plagiarism

Anytime you use someone else's information, ideas, or words, you have to say so. Partly, this is to give proper credit to the authors and researchers who've done the hard work. It's also to let your audience know the credibility of your statements. Identifying your sources actually makes your arguments stronger, because you're backing them up.

When you fail to identify the source of a piece of information, an idea, or a direct quotation, you are committing plagiarism. This is one of the most serious academic offenses you can commit. In essence, it is dishonest—and the consequences are dire. If you are caught plagiarizing, you will almost certainly fail your assignment. You may also fail an entire class or be expelled from your program or school.

Employers are also very concerned about plagiarism. Content published in print or online is protected by **copyright**—a body of law that gives authors control over their work and guarantees their right to be paid for its use. If you sell or even release a plagiarized document to the public, your employer could be publicly embarrassed or sued.

Computer technology makes it very easy for people to commit plagiarism. All you have to do is copy text from a website, paste it into a document, and reformat it, in order to pass it off as your own. On the other hand, the Internet also makes it very easy for people to *catch* plagiarism. All your instructor or employer has to do is take a direct quotation from a student's or an employee's work, enter it into a search engine, and see if the same exact phrase appears on a website—*any* website. Plagiarism is very risky.

Citing Online Materials

Citing a source—or giving proper credit—is easy. You just need to do two things:

1. **Cite it within the text,** where you use it. You can use footnotes if you want, but it's usually easiest to work the citation into a sentence:

   King and Associates' 2008 survey of Midwestern agriculture found a steady rise in corn acreage after 2005.

   OR

   According to King and Associates (2008), the Midwest experienced a steady rise in corn acreage after 2005.

Now your reader knows exactly where you acquired your information.

2. **Provide full publication information** for the source, generally in a list at the end of your document.

Practice
Critical Thinking

Once you have written a paper or report, read through it with a critical eye and ask yourself these questions:

- Is this my idea, opinion, or fact?
- Where did I get this information?
- Is this common knowledge, or is it a statistic established by a specific study?
- Am I being manipulative if I take credit for this?

There are several different formats for citations and reference lists, including popular formats from the American Psychological Association (APA) and the Modern Language Association (MLA). Your Kaplan Higher Education campus prefers the APA format. As you take notes on your online sources, write down these basics:

- Author(s)—first and last names
- Date/time of publication
- Article title
- Website name
- URL
- Date you accessed the website
- Any other details that seem relevant

You can find detailed information on how to use APA format at websites devoted to research and writing, such as Purdue University's Online Writing Lab (owl.english.purdue.edu).

The Internet has revolutionized the way we conduct research. With the abundance of information now immediately available to us, we must remember to stop and verify that this information is still credible and upholds the same standards that are required in our own reports and essays.

Unit Summary

- Online research usually consists of using a browser and one or more search engines to locate websites on the World Wide Web.

- To use a search engine effectively, you need to search for the appropriate medium (text, images, video) and use specific keywords and qualifiers.

- When conducting research in an academic or a professional environment, seek specialized sources.

- It is critical to evaluate every online source to make sure it is accurate and reliable.

- You must give credit to your sources by citing them in an appropriate format.

TO-DO List

- ✔ Check out the library link on the Kaplan Quad. Practice researching articles here first!

- ✔ After choosing a topic for your next **research** project or paper, write down as many possible search **keywords** as you can think of to get started on your research.

- ✔ Find out if your local library has a **website,** and explore it. Can you access the catalog from home?

- ✔ The next time you disagree with a friend about a fact, try using one of the **search engines** mentioned in this unit.

- ✔ Take a look at your local newspaper's opinion page. Are the arguments backed up with evidence and sources? How **reliable** do the sources seem?

Important Terms

How well do you know these terms? Look them up in the glossary if you need help remembering them.

bias	keywords
blog	links
browser	reliable
copyright	research
domain extension	search engine
evaluation	websites
keyword qualifiers	World Wide Web

Online Resources

Learn to Use Internet Explorer
www.newbie.org/internet_explorer/

The Online Writing Lab (OWL) at Purdue University
owl.english.purdue.edu

How to Evaluate the Credibility of a Source
www.wikihow.com/Evaluate-the-Credibility-of-a-Source

Exercises

1. Perform some online searches on one or more search engines to find out about recycling in your area. Keep refining your keywords and using qualifiers until you find specific, useful information.

2. Evaluate three of the websites that came up in your search for exercise 1. Rate each website's reliability on a scale of 1 (unreliable) to 5 (very reliable).

3. Choose a specific fact stated by one of your online sources from exercises 1 and 2, and try to trace it to its original source. Does the author of the page you found say where the fact came from? If so, try to find that source. If no source is identified, try using a search engine to find something that backs up the claim.

4. For one of your online sources, write a complete reference entry in APA style. See the Purdue OWL website for additional format information.

UNIT

8

Applying Communication Techniques in the Workplace

Identifying the best strategies for active communication at work

Practicing listening techniques for identifying and meeting co-worker and customer needs

Adopting best practices for handling disagreements to prevent conflicts

Developing a professional approach to diversity in the workplace

S ome of engineering's biggest mistakes have come as a result of poor communication. For example, two teams dug from opposite sides to create the Saltersford tunnel in England, but when they got to the middle, their tunnels didn't meet. To this day, the tunnel has a kink in it because the two teams did not communicate effectively. Also, analyses of airplane crashes and disasters like the space shuttle *Challenger* explosion have often identified poor communication between crew members or ground support teams as root causes.[1] Poor communication in the workplace is not always fatal, but it can still cause unhappiness or interfere with team goals. You might do something for a co-worker, thinking you're doing him a favor, and then have him snap at you for interfering. An unexpected turn like this could ruin your day at work or damage a relationship with a colleague. In this unit, you will practice practical skills for improving workplace communication, so you can improve the probability that you will understand and be understood.

[1] Maier, M. (1993). Teaching from tragedy: An interdisciplinary module on the space shuttle Challenger. *T H E Journal, 21*(2), 91. Retrieved from EBSCOhost; and Gladwell, M. (2008). *Outliers: The story of success*. New York: Little, Brown and Co.

Communication Every Day

Each day at work, we interact with other people who approach issues from differing perspectives, or points of view. Diversity of experience is part of what makes teams stronger, and good communication is key to achieving positive results. Healthy team members can approach tension and conflict directly, support one another through discord, and use differences of opinion to find creative solutions to problems. However, not all teams function in this optimal way. When disagreements escalate into conflicts, co-workers can become emotional and take the discord personally. Often, the difference between healthy conflict and destructive conflict comes not in what is said, but in *how* it is said. Learning effective communication skills is largely a matter of developing the ability to deliver a message in the way the audience can best receive it.

Miscommunications can arise when co-workers do not understand one another's intentions. Consider an example: Marta walks into the office knowing that her co-worker Paul is going to be stressed out today. She knows that he has too much to do and too little time. Marta, thinking she is being thoughtful and helpful, takes initiative and completes the first few tasks on Paul's typical "To-Do" list before he arrives. When Paul arrives, Marta tells him about the tasks that she has already handled for him. However, instead of being grateful, Paul is furious: "Do you think I can't do my job?" he hollers at Marta. "If I wanted your help, I'd ask for it!" he snaps and storms away.

Marta clearly had the best of intentions; she genuinely wanted to help Paul. But her approach backfired. She did not communicate with Paul before acting; and when she did speak with him, she did not consider how he might react. For his part, Paul could have received Marta's comments less defensively. Each missed the opportunity to practice pre-communication behaviors—listening and thinking carefully before speaking, and respecting each other's individual differences. A thoughtful and respectful mindset is the foundation of active communication, which can prevent or resolve disagreements before they become conflicts. *How* you communicate dramatically affects your ability to work well with others.

Making a Good First Impression Every Day

You've learned about types of communication in Unit 3, so you know the difference between expression and communication. You know that you are always communicating, either verbally or nonverbally. In the workplace, that knowledge about communication can help you do your job well. At work, you must send information to another person so that person understands it and can act upon it if necessary. Effective communication at work also builds positive relationships with your co-workers. The way you communicate makes an impression on others. Your co-workers, therefore, will form opinions about you based on how they feel about you. How can you be sure you make a good impression? It can be as simple as being aware of how you communicate verbally and nonverbally. To help you make a good impression on others at work, recall what you learned in Unit 3 about the elements of verbal communication, and apply the following tips:

Verbal Communication

- Choose professional words. Remember that at work, you are in a professional setting. Use formal words in complete sentences. Avoid slang or overly casual terms. There's a big difference between "Yes, the doctor will see you at two o'clock," and "Yeah, he'll check ya at two."

- Check your speed and volume. Make sure you don't speak too quickly or too quietly. People need to hear you and understand you, especially in an urgent situation. But don't speak too loudly either—you are in a professional setting, so use an appropriate volume.

- Monitor your tone and inflection. You know from Unit 3 that tone sends a message on its own, regardless of the words you say. "You need help again?" said in a friendly tone and "You need help *again?*" said in a sarcastic tone send two very different messages. Make sure the *way* you speak matches the words so that your message is received correctly.

Nonverbal Communication

- Use professional posture. Standing straight and sitting upright make you look authoritative and attentive. Good posture may also help people take you more seriously at work.

- Do a face check. You know that eye contact is important in effective communication. But the expression on your face can communicate as much as the words you say. Make sure your facial expression matches your verbal message.

You can say all the right words, but if you don't believe what you're saying, you may be unwittingly conveying that too. Have you ever been in a group where people have just given up and will agree with the leader just to finish the meeting? Their words may be the right ones, but the way they act, listen, and react to others conveys a different message entirely. Even worse, it might convey a negative attitude. Does that mean you should always pretend to be cheerful? Not at all. What it does mean is

that you should always be aware of what message you are sending to those around you. You can control the impressions that you make, communicating in a positive way that develops relationships and helps you do your job.

And speaking of your job, it may help you communicate better if you think about why you are communicating in the first place. At work, you have tasks that you must complete; these tasks may change daily or over time, but you are there to complete them. When you communicate at work, your purpose for communication is to get the job done. So, it makes sense to always listen and speak with those tasks in mind. Consider Tami, who is a medical office receptionist whose main job is to make patient appointments with the doctors. Sometimes the doctors need to take care of emergencies, so Tami has to let a patient know about changes to appointments. She uses a friendly tone and speaks clearly when rescheduling a patient's appointment, doing her best to fit the patient in as soon as possible. Her friendly manner and efficiency help patients feel that their time is important. When Tami notices problems with patient appointments and a doctor's schedule, Tami professionally asks the doctor about it. Her professionalism shows respect for the doctors and reminds them that Tami cares about her job and the patients. Tami has to make sure the appointments are accurate, so she communicates in order to do her job well.

The Basics of Good Communication at Work

In Unit 3, you learned that active listening involves paying attention to the speaker and working to understand what he or she is communicating. Applying active listening strategies at work can be a first step toward successful communication. Active listening not only shows respect, a valuable trait in the workplace, it also ensures your understanding of the message, which can help you do your job well. The following are key strategies for active listening in the workplace:

Give a speaker your full attention. No matter what the work situation—an informal conversation in the hallway, a small meeting around a table, or a staff meeting in a large room—your full attention is required for active listening. Full attention ensures that you hear what is said and also that you understand it.

Pay attention to nonverbal cues. Just as you monitor your own nonverbal communication, you need to monitor how the speaker says words and what he or she looks like when saying them. If a speaker emphasizes certain words, for instance, you know those words are important. If a speaker stands tall and smiles, it may mean that the speaker is confident in the message being communicated.

Ask questions for clarification. Your role as an active listener is to understand the message. So, this is perhaps the most important strategy for active listening. Ask questions about parts of the message you don't understand, or ask for clarification if you are unsure about the message's meaning.

Consider the following scenarios, and think about how using active listening strategies could have made a difference:

- Marco, an IT help specialist, does not give his full attention to Josie, a caller whose computer is not working. Josie tries to explain that certain applications won't run properly. Marco isn't paying attention and orders new software. But that won't solve Josie's problem, and if Marco had been practicing active listening, he would have known that. At the very least, he would have known to ask follow-up questions.

- Alex works as a dental assistant. He asks his patient routine questions about her dental care. "Do you floss every day?" he asks, looking down at the patient's chart. "Oh, *sure*," she replies, rolling her eyes and smirking. Alex records *yes* but then becomes concerned when during cleaning he notices several troubling areas along the patient's gums. He tells the doctor he suspects gum disease. But if Alex had been practicing active listening and paying attention to non-verbal cues, he would have realized that the patient was being sarcastic and that all she needs is flossing advice.

- Carla is a nurse's assistant whose office is using a new charting system. She attended the meeting where the new system was explained, but she didn't understand parts of it very well. At the end, when her manager asked if there were questions, Carla stayed silent, thinking she would figure it out later. But later is now, and her charts are incomplete, and her supervisor is wondering why. If Carla had practiced active listening, she would have asked questions to make sure she understood.

TrueStory

"I had been in my new job for a couple of months as foreman of a construction site, when my boss showed up at the site. He held up his mobile phone and played a voicemail that he had received from one of my female employees. She and another female employee from a different worksite were hollering into the phone. They were both clearly drunk, slurring, and swearing. They left a 5-minute voicemail rant about one of the men on our team, talking about how rude he was, calling him some choice names, and accusing him of stealing from the company. Not a great way to express your opinion to the boss."

Of course, listening is only half of communication. At work, you speak in formal conversations and informal conversations, with individuals, in groups, and on the phone. In Unit 3, you learned that speaking is more than just talking. In the workplace, you can apply the speaking strategies listed earlier in this unit: using professional words, watching tone, volume, and inflection, and controlling your nonverbal cues. When you speak, it is evident to others whether or not you know what you are talking about. It is much better to ask for information if there is something that you don't know than to pretend. Honesty and clarity are components of effective communication.

We communicate all the time at work, and opportunities for communicating are both small, such as telling a co-worker about a new sitcom, and large, such as giving a presentation to inform patients about a new process or system. These conversations help you and your co-workers form relationships and do your jobs. It is important to get to the point quickly and stay on topic. Know what you need to cover before initiating a conversation, and provide the details that support your position when you need to be persuasive.

It is good to be cheerful, friendly, and sociable with work peers. Not every conversation in the workplace is formal and strictly task-related. However, it is important to maintain a level of professionalism at all times. When you speak with others at work, keep in mind that even though you see them every day, you do not necessarily know or share their views about what constitutes comfortable and appropriate conversation. For example, some people share with co-workers personal details about their lives, such as health issues they experience, family problems, or detailed stories about what they did last Saturday night. Not everyone considers surgery, family fights, or partying appropriate work topics. Many people also prefer not to discuss religion and politics in the workplace. Remember to look for nonverbal cues, and if you notice someone become uncomfortable with a topic or joke, change the subject. You can always go back to talking about work.

Keep in mind that you may also communicate in writing. Emails, memos, reports, charts, or presentations may be part of your workplace. You can apply some of the same strategies for verbal communication to written communication. The following tips apply specifically to written communication.

Pay careful attention to tone. Because there isn't any nonverbal communication accompanying writing, it is often more difficult to interpret tone. Choose your words very carefully to make sure your message is clear.

Stay on topic. In conversations, it's natural for topics to veer off for a while and then get back on track. In writing, it's important to state the main idea and stick with the topic. If you have a lot to say, consider different formats or separate documents.

Be professional. Use complete sentences and formal words. Keep the emoticons and jokes for personal communication. If you feel a sentence needs a smiley face at the end so it reads as friendly, consider revising it so it conveys what you want to say.

Check spelling and grammar. Take the time to check your writing for errors, and then correct them. Error-free written communication sends a positive impression to others.

Understanding Your Audience: Internal and External Customers

Of course, it is important to use speaking and listening strategies with your supervisors. But you don't communicate with just supervisors at work. You communicate with co-workers—your peers either on your team or in another department or division. You may communicate with people outside your workplace, such as customers or patients. You can think of everyone you interact with at work as an internal or external customer. An **internal customer** is a person or department within your organization that

receives support from something that you do. An **external customer** is an outside party doing business with your company.

It is critical to understand and do your best to meet external customer needs, because the external customers are the reason your organization exists. Without external customers using your organization's goods or services, the organization ceases to exist, and so do your team and your job. Most likely, you will communicate with external customers in a specific way. For example, a nurse asks a patient about allergies before giving a shot; a security guard asks residents of an apartment building if he can see some identification before opening the gate; a receptionist calls a patient about setting up an appointment with the dentist to fill a cavity. In each case, the communication should be friendly but also professional.

Communication with your internal customers, often your co-workers, may not be as clearly defined in your job. It is helpful to remember that *you* are an internal customer to your co-workers as well. Even if the people at your workplace perform different tasks, their efforts are related and contribute to the same bigger picture. For example, Liz works in the pediatric ward in a hospital. Sometimes she must transfer a patient to the intensive care unit. Before she can do that, she must contact the patient's doctor. Liz professionally and clearly explains the patient's situation to the doctor, who then contacts the ICU and requests a transfer. When the ICU is informed, they request paperwork from Liz. If Liz had not communicated effectively with the doctor, the doctor wouldn't have contacted the ICU. If the doctor had not communicated effectively with the ICU, Liz would still be waiting for the transfer. Liz, the ICU staff, and the doctor are all internal customers. They are communicating so that the patient, the external customer, gets the best care.

Using the word *customer* to describe people you work with may seem strange, but it is a helpful reminder to treat co-workers with the same professionalism and respect that you give customers. Often, work can be a busy, stressful place. In the rush of work, it can be easy for co-workers to forget to treat each other as internal customers. If your own needs as an internal customer are ignored, it likely makes you feel as if others don't value your work or respect your efforts. If you don't listen and respond to the needs of your internal customers, you can expect them to feel resentful toward you. A workplace where feelings of disrespect and resentment develop is an ineffective and often unpleasant place to work.

Even if you practice active listening and use effective speaking strategies, communication mishaps can occur in the workplace. Bosses give unclear directions, co-workers misinterpret information, questions go unasked or unanswered, feelings get hurt, and conflicts arise. Disagreements need not be tense, but they do often lead to conflict. Even people who listen and speak well can encounter communication barriers, or things that prevent effective communication. Active communication involves anticipating communication barriers and working every day to overcome them.

Practice Now: Dependable

Your internal and external customers will be much more comfortable and cooperative if they trust you. This is why employers say that they want employees who are dependable—people who are consistent and predictable. Practice now by thinking about the things you have said you will do. Dependable people follow through on their commitments on time, every time. If you have told a customer that you will follow up, make a note in your calendar to ensure that you do follow up. If a co-worker is depending on your part of the project to do her part of the project, make sure you get your part done on time.

How to Get Through the Rough Patches

It is better to prevent problems that can stem from communication barriers, but when conflicts do occur, it becomes necessary to practice conflict resolution. Conflict resolution is the process of arriving at solutions while taking the interests of all parties into account. The process involves listening, evaluating, prioritizing, and compromising. The key strategy in conflict resolution is negotiation. **Negotiation** is a process of discussion and compromise.

So, how do you put the negotiation strategy into action? In a one-on-one misunderstanding, two people can listen carefully and speak respectfully with each other to resolve their problem. If you find yourself in such a situation, following these guidelines can help you reach a positive outcome:

Listen. Listen to the other person without interrupting. It's important for both sides to share their points of view.

Try to control your emotions. It is a human reaction to feel upset or angry or nervous during conflict. Keeping those emotions to yourself as much as possible may help you communicate more clearly.

Compromise. Make reaching a compromise the goal of the discussion. The purpose of negotiation is to find a solution that is reasonable to both parties.

Remember that working through disagreements can build stronger relationships. Once you've resolved a disagreement, you have a better understanding of the other person, and they have a better understanding of you. You can use this understanding to develop your relationship in the future.

Sometimes one or both people lack the patience and trust to find common ground. Then it becomes necessary to involve a third party and a more deliberate, formal process, which you will read about in the next section of this unit.

The workplace gathers many people, both internally (co-workers) and externally (customers, patients, clients). Gathering so many unique points of view and personalities can lead to conflict. Sometimes at work you will encounter people who you find difficult to deal with or to please. It is important to treat difficult people with as much respect and professionalism as possible. Keep in mind that the conflict may be a result of a simple misunderstanding, a bad day, or a negative situation that has nothing to do with you. Remember that you have the power to control the impression you give in your communication; professional, effective communication could resolve the conflict right away. If not, practice active listening and effective speaking strategies to resolve conflict. Many organizations have established policies about how both internal and external conflicts will be resolved. Knowing these policies will give you a framework for dealing with disagreements. One bonus of negotiating conflict to a compromise is that it will help you become a better communicator.

When All Else Fails

At times, you may encounter a conflict with someone outside the company that you cannot resolve on your own. If you have done your best but are unable to negotiate a compromise, you can refer that person to the next level up in the chain of command. For example, remember Tami, the receptionist at a busy doctor's office. If a patient calls to schedule an appointment for that week, but there are no appointments available, Tami can ask the doctors if one of them can fit the patient in. It is important to rely on supervisors and managers for help when conflicts that you cannot resolve arise with external customers, such as patients, consumers, or clients. What if you are a supervisor and someone who reports to you has a conflict that cannot be resolved? You may have the power to resolve the issue. However, if you aren't able to resolve it, you can then go to your manager.

What about conflicts among co-workers? We mentioned what to do if you have a conflict with a peer. But if you have tried to have a patient and honest conversation to solve a problem between you and a peer, and the problem persists, you can again rely on help from a manager or supervisor. Part of a supervisor's role is to ensure effective teamwork, so he or she may be able to help you negotiate a compromise and come to a better understanding of each other. Present your issues to your manager calmly. Be prepared to suggest a solution and give your reasons for it. Offer your ideas efficiently; get to the point. Also, remember that it is your boss's duty to maintain a productive working environment, and that involves solving problems. Finally, be prepared to accept the outcome. Remember that the goal of negotiation is to reach a compromise in which both parties can agree to a solution. The solution may not be exactly what you want, but if it leads to a better working relationship or environment, it is a good one.

If you are a supervisor and you need to help the people who report to you resolve disagreements, you can use the same active listening and effective speaking strategies that you apply to other areas at work. Your role should be that of an unbiased listener, making sure you understand both sides and have a clear sense of the issue. As a supervisor, your job is to make sure the work gets done correctly and on time, and that should guide you as you help your reports reach a compromise. And unless the issue involves a violation of company policies or legal issues, know that your role should be helping your reports find a solution, not solving the problem for them. Frame the disagreement in terms of the work as you help reports come to a compromise.

What should you do if the person you are in a conflict with *is* your boss? Remember everything you have learned about professional and respectful communication. You may not always agree with your boss, but it is usually in your best interest to be professional. Set up a meeting with your boss to talk about the issues. Make sure you have enough time for the discussion. Preparing what you want to say on note cards can help you keep your thoughts clear and your emotions controlled. Listen to what your boss has to say; remember that there are two sides to the conflict and that both sides must be represented to reach a compromise. As with any conflict resolution, bring possible solutions to the meeting. If you have talked with your boss and you haven't found a solution, or if you feel the solution is not a true compromise, you can contact your human resources department. Schedule a meeting with an HR representative. Bring your notes and any documentation you may have that relates to the issues of the conflict. Make sure you are professional and respectful when speaking about your boss. Your HR representative can help you identify the issues, inform you of any formal company policies that may address the issues, and guide you in arriving at a compromise. The HR person may invite you and your boss to a meeting where the three of you can work out a solution.

Practice
Critical Thinking

If you have a problem with a person at work, ask yourself these questions to help you reach a compromise:

- What is our work goal?
- What do I do to support that goal?
- What does the other person do to support that goal?
- Am I doing anything now that interferes with our achieving the goal? If so, what?
- Is the other person doing anything now that interferes with our achieving the goal? If so, what?
- What is *really* our problem?
- Whom does it affect? How?
- In a perfect world, how would I change the situation?
- How would that change affect everyone involved?
- How would that change help us achieve the work goal?
- What is my proposed solution?

You should have thoughtful answers to these questions before you meet to resolve a conflict.

If you have followed the steps above and you still have not found a solution, you can rely on your organization's grievance policy. A formal grievance policy typically requires documentation of issues and actions you collected that support or explain the conflict. If you have to rely on a grievance procedure, you can visit your organization's human resources department to learn more about it. Familiarizing yourself with your organization's HR department and understanding the grievance policy when you start your job can be helpful. Ideally, you won't need them, but knowing what resources are available can make a disagreement with a supervisor less stressful and help you resolve issues more quickly.

Understanding Diversity

As we learn new information, our brains often separate ideas and concepts into two categories: *same* and *different*. This ability to recognize similarities and differences helps us learn about all subjects. We understand ideas and information by how they compare and contrast with ideas we already know. In other words, we are mentally wired to classify information into groups. Information about people is no exception. When it comes to people, however, we need to classify and label carefully.

People are amazingly diverse. Put simply, **diversity** is variety, or a range of differences. Among many other things, each person brings his or her own different background, ideas, beliefs, and points of view to the world. Identifying the differences between two people is one way to understand them. Understanding a difference enables you to be mindful and respectful of it. But it is important to remember that people are complex. If you try too hard to label a difference, you may make a generalization, or an overly simplified statement, which can become a stereotype. A **stereotype** is a generalized assumption that is made about members of a particular group. For example, if you meet a person with red hair who enjoys reading mysteries, would you then assume that all redheads enjoy reading mysteries? Of course not. So, while it is good

to learn more about people in order to understand them and communicate effectively with them, avoid oversimplifying the traits that make them special.

Cultural Diversity

Culture is the particular customs, values, and shared beliefs among a group. Culture shapes the people in a group, and the people shape and pass on the culture. For example, in a culture in which a religion is highly valued, most of the families raise their children to practice the religion. The children become adults who value the religion, and they raise *their* children to practice the religion.

The culture a person comes from affects his or her worldview. When people receive new information, they see it within the context or framework of the values they learned from their culture. People interpret new information through their own personal filter, or way of seeing. Suppose a person comes from a culture in which it is common to work a 12-hour workday. Another person comes from a culture in which a 6-hour day is the norm. A third person proclaims, "I worked 8 hours today." The first thinks that sounds like an easy day; the second thinks it sounds like overtime. What does the third person think? Without knowing more about his or her background and values, you can't know even what the third person is likely to think, never mind what he or she actually does think.

Cultural diversity, which means the range of cultures represented, is increasing in the workplace. A culturally diverse workplace gathers people with many different customs, values, and beliefs. However, people at work always have at least one thing in common: They are there to do a job. You can remember this common goal when communicating with people from different cultural backgrounds. You can also use your brain's natural tendency to recognize the *same* and *different* categories to identify the many cultural backgrounds of your co-workers. Identifying these similarities and differences will help you understand people

better, as long as you avoid stereotyping. So, how can this diversity help you in the workplace? Well, you can use that diversity to learn new ways of solving problems, building relationships, and completing tasks. You know how you would solve a problem at work, based on your cultural background. But if your solution isn't working, you can draw from your workplace's cultural diversity and discover different solutions that may work better. Bouncing ideas off other people can help you learn more about yourself and how to be successful at work.

Of course, when you are working with a diverse group, keep in mind that everyone has his or her own personal filter, or way of seeing things. When people have two very different

worldviews, that can create communication barriers. It is important to remember that just because a co-worker thinks about the world in a different way from you, that doesn't make your way of thinking either right or wrong. Being open to new ideas or ways of thinking can help you communicate better. You don't have to agree, but you do have to be respectful. Remember that the job is the top priority, and communicate with that common goal of work in mind.

Language Diversity

An increase in cultural diversity is often paired with an increase in language diversity. You might work with people, or be a person, for whom English is not the native language. Of course, language differences can make communication difficult, but communication is still possible. When you have difficulty understanding someone who speaks with an accent, realize that you still need to communicate, especially at work. If you aren't able to communicate orally, you may be able to communicate with writing. People who speak English as their second language might have more difficulty reading and writing it, or they might actually find the written language easier to understand. If you practice the same level of attentive active listening in conversations with people of all language backgrounds, you will quickly note whether you are being understood. Using and paying attention to eye contact, facial expressions, and body language can help you convey and assess understanding, or lack of it, across language barriers.

Speaking of body language, spoken words are not the only ways in which languages from different cultures can differ. Body language differs, as well. For example, Americans tend to keep about three to four feet of space between themselves and others during casual and business conversation. People from Asian cultures tend to be comfortable standing more closely together, almost touching, while people in Scandinavian countries would likely feel their personal space was being invaded at that closeness. Intermittent eye contact is the comfort zone in the U.S.; more prolonged eye contact is normal in Middle Eastern countries; and eye contact in Japan is fleeting and can be regarded as almost invasive.

Keep these differences in mind when you practice active listening. As you observe body language, remember that customary differences such as these could easily cause misunderstandings if they are misinterpreted.

ON THE JOB

On a busy hospital floor, a Japanese woman approached the nurses' station. She told the nurse's assistant that she was very worried that her daughter was put in room number 4. She asked to be switched to another room over and over again, but the assistant assumed that she just wanted a better room. She politely and clearly explained to the Japanese woman that there was nothing that she could do. It was only after the doctor asked why she was so worried that the woman explained that the number 4 in Japanese culture is synonymous with death. She told the doctor that most hospitals in Japan don't even have a room 4, since it's considered unlucky. The assistant and doctor realized it was similar to why some hotels in the United States don't have a 13th floor. Once they understood, the hospital staff made the arrangements to move the woman's daughter to a different open room.

Age Diversity

Even when people grow up in the same community, if they grew up at different times, they might see the world very differently. **Age diversity,** or a range of individuals of different generations, is also common in the workplace. We think of generations within our families as groupings of grandparents, parents, children, grandchildren, and so on. In society, a generation is a group of people who grow up during roughly the same time period and who have many of the same life experiences. Generations overlap, but certain generations are identified with the historical conditions of their times.

The Silent Generation The label *Silent Generation* is used to refer to the generation born from 1925 through about 1945. They grew up during the Great Depression.

The Baby Boom In the prosperous period after World War II, the Silent Generation gave birth to the *Baby Boomers* from the mid-1940s to the mid-1960s. Baby Boomers grew up during the 1960s, a period that was perceived to represent significant social change and shifts in values.

Generation X Commonly referred to as Gen X, this is the generation born after the post-World War II baby boom, generally from the late 1960s to the early 1980s. Generation X grew up in times that were more economically secure than the Silent Generation's, but less so than the Baby Boomers'. Gen X grew up with technological advances such as the home computer, cable television, and the introduction of the Internet.

Generation Y Also labeled the *Millennials*, this generation was born from the late 1980s through the end of the 20th century (which was also the end of the last millennium, thus the name). Millennials, even more than Gen X, grew up during enormous acceptance of and advances in digital technology.

Generation Z Born from the 1990s through the first decade of the 21st century, Generation Z is also referred to as the *Internet Generation* or "digital natives." They have always lived in a world connected by the Internet.

Most of the Silent Generation has now left the workforce. Baby Boomers are moving toward and into retirement now, but they still represent a large segment of the workforce, alongside Gen X and Millennials. Digital natives are the wave of young workers now entering the workforce. You can see how you could easily work in a setting with individuals from four generations.

What does this mean for communication in the workplace? Age diversity can introduce as many different perspectives to a situation as cultural and language diversity can. Individuals who grew up in different social and political climates may have different values and may prioritize differently. They may also have very different comfort levels with technology.

Many Baby Boomers worked in the same jobs for large portions of their lives. Today, though, it is not uncommon for people to go back to school and start new careers in their 30s and 40s. When these people begin their new careers, they are likely to be surrounded by younger peers and report to younger supervisors. This may feel strange to both age groups, because it switches traditional roles. The oldest person is not necessarily the most experienced; the youngest person is not necessarily the one who needs the most help.

As with all types of diversity, it is important to avoid stereotypes and not make assumptions based on age. In every interaction you have with people at work, whether verbal or nonverbal, whether with internal or external customers, you will be most effective if you listen carefully and always speak with work goals in mind.

Unit Summary

- Active listening and always speaking with goals in mind are good strategies for effective workplace communication.

- Good communication can help co-workers prevent conflicts and handle disagreements.

- People encounter a variety of barriers to effective communication at work.

- Workplace diversity makes it important to use a thoughtful communication process.

TO-DO List

✔ Write your active listening strategy, and refer to it at least twice a week.

✔ Be an active listener in every conversation.

✔ Use best practices to resolve any existing conflicts instead of ignoring them.

✔ Do research to learn more about gender, **culture,** and **age diversity.**

Important Terms

How well do you know these terms? Look them up in the glossary if you need help remembering them.

age diversity

cultural diversity

culture

diversity

external customer

internal customer

negotiation

stereotype

Exercises

1. Think about the people with whom you communicate every day at work, at school, and even at home. Make a list of the people with whom you need to communicate—your "internal customers." Write what they need from you in order to be able to do their jobs, complete an assignment, or function happily at home. Then write a sentence or two about how well you meet each need.

2. Using the same list from the previous activity, consider what you need from people in order to be able to do your job, succeed in school, or be happy at home. Identify the person with whom you most need to improve communication. Write a strategy for improving your communication with that person.

3. Do an inventory of your classroom. Make a list of all the people you interact with at school during a typical day. Identify the most obvious way in which you differ from each person. Also identify something that you have in common with each person.

success

Adding, subtracting, multiplying, and dividing
to solve problems

Determining if a measurement is reasonable for a particular object

Converting U.S. Customary measurements to metric system

Performing operations on metric measurements to solve problems

n umbers are everywhere! Have you noticed how often you use numbers to find answers in your daily life? Even though some people like to say, "I'm no good at math" or "I never liked math," you use math and numbers every day.

Paying bills and having a checking account or a debit card involves the use of math. Knowing how much money you have and how much you need to pay means that you are adding or subtracting money, which is expressed in decimals. Grocery stores are filled with numbers. When shopping, you need to use math to figure out how much and how many items you can buy. Stores sell some items, such as deli meat, by the pound. To determine how much a $\frac{1}{2}$ pound of meat costs, you multiply the price by $\frac{1}{2}$, or 0.5. To find the cost of 4 of another item, you multiply the price by 4.

Being able to add, subtract, multiply, and divide numbers is an important part of knowing what's happening around you. It's even more critical on your job. You would not want faulty wiring in your home because the electrician didn't add correctly. If the pharmacy technician didn't multiply correctly, you could take the wrong dose of your medicine. You might receive a bill for the wrong amount because the medical clerk didn't subtract correctly. When you are on the job, you need to make accurate calculations and double-check your work. Mastering the mathematical operations of addition, subtraction, multiplication, and division will set you up to be successful in your job when opportunities to use math arise.

Applying Mathematical Operations to Different Types of Numbers

To solve problems, you perform mathematical operations on numbers. Addition, subtraction, multiplication, and division are the four basic operations in mathematics.

What is Addition?

When you add two numbers, you are combining the value of the numbers. The new value is the **total** of the two numbers. For example, when you add $7 + 8$, the total is 15. So, you say $7 + 8 = 15$. You can also add three or more numbers. The numbers you add are the **addends,** and the total is the **sum** of the numbers. The symbol denoting addition is the plus sign, $+$.

Building **Background**

These are common properties of numbers that make addition easier.

- Adding 0 to any number results in that number. (Identity Property)

- When you add two numbers, the order of the addition of the numbers does not matter. For example, both $4 + 5$ and $5 + 4$ result in the same answer, 9. (Commutative Property)

- When you add three or more numbers, you can group any two numbers to add first. The result will be the same. For example, $(16 + 9) + 11 = 25 + 11 = 36$ and $16 + (9 + 11) = 16 + 20 = 36$. (Associative Property)

Adding Whole Numbers

Place value shows the value of each digit in a number. For example, 425 is 4 hundreds, 2 tens, and 5 ones. When adding a group of numbers, writing the numbers in columns by aligning the place values may make the addition easier. Line up each number by the ones place and then add each column. Think of each digit as its place value.

> Add $231 + 517$.

231	$\rightarrow$	2 hundreds	3 tens	1 one
+ 517	$\rightarrow$	+ 5 hundreds	1 ten	7 ones
		7 hundreds	4 tens	8 ones $\rightarrow$ 748

$231 + 517 = 748$

If the result of a column is 10 or greater, you need to *regroup*, or *carry*, to the next place. Start on the right and regroup from right to left.

Points to **Remember**

When you *regroup,* you write a number using its place values. You *carry* one of the digits to the next place column in the addition problem.

For example, think of the number 14 as 1 ten and 4 ones. Write the 4 ones in the ones column in the answer, and "carry" the 1 ten to add with the other tens in the problem.

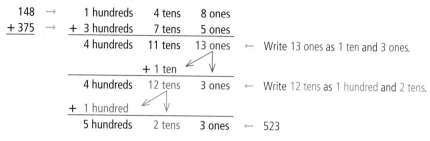

Add 148 + 375.

148	→	1 hundreds	4 tens	8 ones	
+ 375	→	+ 3 hundreds	7 tens	5 ones	
		4 hundreds	11 tens	13 ones	← Write 13 ones as 1 ten and 3 ones.
			+ 1 ten		
		4 hundreds	12 tens	3 ones	← Write 12 tens as 1 hundred and 2 tens.
		+ 1 hundred			
		5 hundreds	2 tens	3 ones	← 523

148 + 375 = 523

You can use a shortcut to show place-value addition. Write the regrouped amount above the next column on the left.

Add 162 + 317 + 425.

```
 11
 162   ←  Add the ones: 2 + 7 + 5 = 14. Write the 4 in the answer and carry the 1.
 317   ←  Add the tens: 1 + 6 + 1 + 2 = 10. Write the 0 in the answer and carry the 1.
+425   ←  Add the hundreds: 1 + 1 + 3 + 4 = 9. Write the 9 in the answer.
 904
```

162 + 317 + 425 = 904

Adding Decimals

You have seen operations on whole numbers. To indicate a *part* of a whole number, you use decimal form.

0.1	0.5	0.25	0.33	0.875

The decimal numbers above represent parts of a whole, and are therefore less than 1 in value. A decimal point is used to separate the whole number part from the decimal part of a number.

Decimal form is based on the powers of 10. Each place is 10 times the place to its right. For example, tenths are 10 equal parts of a whole number.

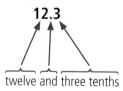

twelve and three tenths

You can extend the place value of whole numbers to include decimals. For example, 425.761 is: 4 hundreds, 2 tens, 5 ones, 7 tenths, 6 hundredths, 1 thousandth. Using place value will help you perform operations on decimals.

To add decimal numbers, follow these steps:

1. Line up the decimal points.
2. Insert trailing zeros, if necessary, so that all numbers have the same number decimal places. This will help avoid careless mistakes.
3. Add each column, and regroup if necessary.
4. Place the decimal point in the answer directly below the decimal point in the addends.

For example, to add 8.599 to 234.6, follow the four steps above.

Add 234.6 + 8.599.

Line up the decimal points.
Insert two trailing zeros
in 234.6.

$$234.600$$
$$+ \ \ 8.599$$

Add each column.
Regroup.
$6 + 5 = 11$
$1 + 4 + 8 = 13$

$$\overset{1\ 1}{234.600}$$
$$+ \ \ 8.599$$
$$\overline{243199}$$

Place the decimal
point in the answer.

$$\overset{1\ 1}{234.600}$$
$$+ \ \ 8.599$$
$$\overline{243.199}$$

$234.6 + 8.599 = 243.199$

Putting It **Together**

Estimating Your Answer

When adding many numbers, it often makes sense to find an estimate first to make sure your answer is reasonable. Round each number to the same place and then add the rounded numbers. Find the exact answer and compare it to the estimate.

Recall the rules for rounding.

- Identify the digit in the place to which you are rounding.
- Look at the digit in the place to its right.
- If that digit is 4 or less, keep the same digit in the place you're rounding.
- If that digit is 5 or greater, add 1 to the digit in the place you're rounding.
- Drop all digits to the right of the place to which you are rounding, and replace with zeros.

	Estimate. Round to hundreds, because the first two numbers start in the hundreds place.	Add to get exact answer.
$435.56	$400	$435.56
$250.99	$300	$250.99
$5,145.75	$5,100	$5,145.75
+ $1,962.01	+ $2,000	+ $1,962.01
	$7,800	$7,794.31

The exact answer 7,794.31 is about 7,800, the estimate. So, the answer $7,794.31 is reasonable.

What is Subtraction?

When you subtract, you remove one number amount from another number. The result is the **difference** of the numbers. The symbol denoting subtraction is the minus sign, $-$.

$$8 - 3 = 5 \qquad \text{The difference is 5.}$$

All the properties of addition do not apply to subtraction. The identity property does apply, because subtracting 0 from any number results in that number. However, you cannot change the order or the grouping of numbers being subtracted. The results of changing the order of the numbers in a subtraction problem will not be the same. For example, $10 - 6$ equals 4, but $6 - 10$ equals -4. So, subtraction does not follow the commutative and associative properties.

Subtracting Whole Numbers

As in addition of whole numbers, subtraction involves lining up the numbers on the ones place. Then subtract each column from right to left.

If a larger digit is being subtracted from a smaller digit, use regrouping, or borrowing, before you subtract. To regroup, you write a number by changing groups of digits from one place value to another.

$$
\begin{aligned}
74 &= \quad\ 7 \text{ tens} \quad 4 \text{ ones} \\
&= \quad 6 \text{ tens } 1 \text{ ten } 4 \text{ ones} \leftarrow \text{Write 7 tens as 6 tens and 1 ten.} \\
&= 6 \text{ tens } 10 \text{ ones } 4 \text{ ones} \leftarrow \text{Write 1 ten as 10 ones.} \\
&= \qquad 6 \text{ tens } 14 \text{ ones} \leftarrow \text{Add the ones.}
\end{aligned}
$$

When subtracting $74 - 38$, you cannot subtract 8 from 4. First write 74 as $60 + 14$. Then subtract.

Subtract 74 − 38.

After rewriting 74, subtract each place.

$14 - 8 = 6$

$6 - 3 = 3$

$$
\begin{array}{r}
{}^{6}\ {}^{14} \\
\cancel{7}\cancel{4} \\
-\ 38 \\
\hline
36
\end{array}
$$

$74 - 38 = 36$

Subtract 4,835 − 647.

1 Write 35 as $20 + 15$.
Subtract $15 - 7 = 8$.

$$
\begin{array}{r}
{}^{2}\ {}^{15} \\
4{,}8\cancel{3}\cancel{5} \\
-\ 647 \\
\hline
8
\end{array}
$$

2 Write 800 as $700 + 100$.
Add the 100 to the existing 20 and write 12 in the tens place.
Then subtract $12 - 4 = 8$.

$$
\begin{array}{r}
{}^{12} \\
{}^{7}\ \cancel{2}\ {}^{15} \\
4{,}\cancel{8}\cancel{3}\cancel{5} \\
-\ 647 \\
\hline
88
\end{array}
$$

3 Continue subtracting from right to left.
$7 - 6 = 1$

$$
\begin{array}{r}
{}^{12} \\
{}^{7}\ \cancel{2}\ {}^{15} \\
4{,}\cancel{8}\cancel{3}\cancel{5} \\
-\ 647 \\
\hline
188
\end{array}
$$

4 Continue subtracting from right to left.
$4 - 0 = 4$

$$
\begin{array}{r}
{}^{12} \\
{}^{7}\ \cancel{2}\ {}^{15} \\
4{,}\cancel{8}\cancel{3}\cancel{5} \\
-\ 647 \\
\hline
4188
\end{array}
$$

$4{,}835 - 647 = 4{,}188$

Subtracting Decimals

Subtracting decimals is similar to subtracting whole numbers, except that you have to line up the decimal points. In order to subtract two numbers, they must have the same number of decimals. Add zeros to a number after the last decimal place to increase the number of decimal places without changing the value of the number. Remember to place the decimal point in the answer directly below the decimal points in the numbers you are subtracting.

Subtract 5.398 – 3.76.

Write the problem vertically, and align the decimal points. Add a trailing zero in 3.76 so the number of decimal places are equal.

$$\begin{array}{r} 5.398 \\ -\ 3.760 \\ \hline \end{array}$$

Subtract from right to left.
$8 - 0 = 8$
$9 - 6 = 3$

$$\begin{array}{r} 5.398 \\ -\ 3.760 \\ \hline 38 \end{array}$$

Write 5.3 as 4 + 13 tenths.
Subtract $13 - 7 = 6$.
Subtract $4 - 3 = 1$.

$$\begin{array}{r} \overset{4\ \ 13}{5.398} \\ -\ 3.760 \\ \hline 1.638 \end{array}$$

$5.398 - 3.76 = 1.638$

Subtract 0.65 – 0.0275.

Insert two zeros at the end of 0.65.

$$\begin{array}{r} 0.6500 \\ -\ 0.0275 \\ \hline \end{array}$$

Regroup twice. Write 5 hundredths as 4 hundredths, 9 thousandths, 10 ten-thousandths. Then subtract each place.

$$\begin{array}{r} \overset{9}{\overset{4\ \ 10\ 10}{0.6500}} \\ -\ 0.0275 \\ \hline 0.6225 \end{array}$$

$0.65 - 0.0275 = 0.6225$

What is Multiplication?

You can think of multiplication as repeated addition. When you multiply, you combine groups of equal size. Because you are combining equal-sized groups, you add the groups a specific number of times. For example, think of 3×6 as finding the total of 3 groups of 6. You can add $6 + 6 + 6$ to get 18, or you can multiply 3×6 to get 18.

The numbers you multiply are the **factors,** and the result is the **product** of the numbers. Multiplication uses more than one operation symbol.

times sign	raised dot	asterisk	parentheses		
3×6	$3 \cdot 6$	$3 * 6$	3(6)	(6)3	(3)(6)

Multiply Whole Numbers

To multiply whole numbers, multiply each digit in one factor by the other factor. Each of these products is called a **partial product.** Then add the partial products to get the answer.

Multiply 43 × 7.

Use partial products.

Think of 43 as 40 + 3.

$$\begin{array}{r} 43 \\ \times\ 7 \\ \hline \end{array}$$

$7 \times 3 = 21 \quad \rightarrow \qquad 21$

$7 \times 40 = 280 \quad \rightarrow \quad +\ 280$

$$\begin{array}{r} \hline 301 \end{array}$$

> ## Building **Background**
>
> These are common properties of numbers that make multiplication easier.
>
> ■ Multiplying any number by 0 results in 0. (Property of Zero)
>
> ■ Multiplying any number by 1 results in that number. (Identity Property)
>
> ■ When you multiply two numbers, the order of the numbers does not matter. For example, both 4 × 5 and 5 × 4 result in the same answer, 20. (Commutative Property)
>
> ■ When you multiply three or more numbers, you can group any two numbers to multiply first. The result will be the same. For example, (8 × 6) × 5 = 48 × 5 = 240 and 8 × (6 × 5) = 8 × 30 = 240. (Associative Property)

You can use regrouping to multiply mentally. Instead of writing each partial product, you "carry" one of the digits to the next place column. Then add that digit to the next partial product.

Multiply 43 × 7 again, this time using regrouping.

Multiply 7 × 3 = 21.
Write the 1 in the answer. Carry the 2.

$$\begin{array}{r} {}^{2}\ \\ 43 \\ \times\ 7 \\ \hline 1 \end{array}$$

Multiply 7 × 4 = 28.
Add the 2 to 28 and write 30 in the answer.

$$\begin{array}{r} {}^{2}\ \\ 43 \\ \times\ 7 \\ \hline 301 \end{array}$$

When you multiply numbers with two or more digits, align each partial product under the digit being multiplied. You can do this because when you multiply a number by a multiple of 10 (such as 20 or 300), the final digits in the partial product are 0. You can avoid writing those final 0's if you align the partial product under the digit being multiplied.

For example, 20 × 241 is 4,820. In the problem below, you can write the second line as either 4,280 aligned at the right, or 482 aligned the number under the 2, as shown.

Multiply 241 × 326.

$$\begin{array}{r} 241 \\ \times\ 326 \\ \hline \end{array}$$

Multiply 6 × 241. Align under the 6. → 1446

Multiply 2 × 241. Align under the 2. → 482

Multiply 3 × 241. Align under the 3. → + 723

$$\begin{array}{r} \hline 78{,}566 \end{array}$$

If there are zeros in one factor, you can insert a single zero in the partial product instead of a complete row of zeros.

Multiply 241 × 306.

Write a line of 0's for the 0 factor.

```
                 241
            ×    306
              1446
```
Align under the 6. → 1446
Align under the 0. → 000
Align under the 3. → + 723
```
            73,746
```

Use a shortcut of writing only 1 zero.

```
                 241
            ×    306
              1446
```
Align under the 6. → 1446
Write one 0 under the 0. → + 7230
Align 723 under the 3.
```
            73,746
```

Multiply Decimals

Multiplying decimals is similar to multiplying whole numbers, except that in decimal multiplication, you need to place the decimal point in the answer.

To multiply decimal numbers, follow these steps:

1. Write the numbers in a column and align them at the right.
2. Multiply the numbers without regard to the decimal point and obtain a whole number product.
3. Count the number of digits that are to the right of the decimal point in *both* factors.
4. Place the decimal point in the whole number product so that it has the same number of digits to the right of the decimal point as counted in Step 3. Add leading zeros, if necessary.

For example, to multiply 12.9 by 0.07, first multiply 129 by 7, which equals 903. Next, count the number of digits to the right of both decimal points. There is one digit in 12.9 and two digits in 0.07: 1 + 2 = 3. Then, take the whole number product, 903, and place the decimal point so that it has 3 digits to the right of the decimal point. That makes the answer 0.903.

TrueStory

"As a medical billing specialist, I prepare customers' bills by determining how much a procedure or a service costs and how much of that cost the insurance company will pay. Because my work involves money amounts, I have to add, subtract, multiply, and divide decimals every day. It is very important that I am accurate in my calculations and that I double-check all my work before I send out any bills.

If I do send out a bill with an error, it causes a lot of problems. The patient will over- or under-pay, and the insurance company will not pay the correct amount. I will have to do more paperwork to fix my mistakes, and people may get angry at me for wasting their time. It is not good customer service for our company."

Multiply 4.002 × 8.3.

Multiply the numbers.

```
             4.002      ← 3 decimal places
        ×      8.3      ← 1 decimal place
           12006
        + 32016
           33.2166      ← 4 decimal places
```

Multiply the numbers.

$$
\begin{array}{r}
0.3095 \quad \leftarrow \text{4 decimal places} \\
\times \quad 0.25 \quad \leftarrow \text{2 decimal places} \\
\hline
15475 \\
+ \ 6190 \\
\hline
0.077375 \quad
\end{array}
$$

← 6 decimal places. Add a 0 after the point to make the 6 decimal places.

What is Division?

When you divide, you separate a quantity into smaller groups of equal size. The number you are dividing is the **dividend,** the number you divide by is the **divisor,** and the result is the **quotient.** Division uses more than one operation symbol.

division sign	slash	fraction bar	division house
$8 \div 2$	$8/2$	$\dfrac{8}{2}$	$2\overline{)8}$

In the problem $8 \div 2 = 4$, the dividend is 8, the divisor is 2, and the quotient is 4.

Divide Whole Numbers

The most common way to divide whole numbers is to use long division, which is represented by the division house symbol. Work from left to right to divide the divisor into each successive digit of the dividend. You repeat the steps of multiply, subtract, and bring down until there are no more digits of the dividend. Any number left over from the subtraction is the **remainder,** the amount that does not evenly divide into the dividend.

Building **Background**

These are common properties of numbers that make division easier.

- Dividing any number by 1 results in that number. (Identity Property)
- Dividing any number by itself results in 1. (Property of One)
- Dividing 0 by any number is 0. (Property of Zero)
- Dividing any number by 0 is undefined. (Property of Zero)
- When you divide two numbers, the order of the numbers <u>does</u> matter. The results will not be the same. For example, $10 \div 5$ equals 2 but $5 \div 10$ equals $\frac{1}{2}$.

Since 23 does not divide into 7, divide 23 into 70. Multiply $23 \times 3 = 69$. Write 3 in the answer. Subtract $70 - 69$.

$$
\begin{array}{r}
3 \\
23\overline{)7,061} \\
\underline{69} \\
1
\end{array}
$$

$7,061 \div 23 = 307$

Bring down the 6. 23 does not divide into 16. Write 0 in the answer. Bring down the 1.

$$
\begin{array}{r}
30 \\
23\overline{)7,061} \\
\underline{69} \\
161
\end{array}
$$

Multiply $23 \times 7 = 161$. Write 7 in the answer. Subtract $161 - 161$. There is no remainder.

$$
\begin{array}{r}
307 \\
23\overline{)7,061} \\
\underline{69} \\
161 \\
\underline{161} \\
0
\end{array}
$$

Instead of having a remainder in the answer, you can continue dividing to get a decimal answer. Put a decimal point at the end of the whole number dividend, and then add trailing zeros. Place a decimal point in the answer directly above the decimal point in the dividend.

Divide 210 ÷ 4. Write the answer with a remainder.

$$
\begin{array}{r}
52R2 \\
4\overline{)210} \\
20 \\
\overline{10} \\
8 \\
\overline{2}
\end{array}
$$

Multiply $4 \times 5 = 20$. Write 5 in the answer. →
Subtract $21 - 20 = 1$. Bring down the 0. →
Multiply $4 \times 2 = 8$. Write 2 in the answer. →
Subtract $10 - 8 = 2$. The remainder is 2. →

$210 \div 4 = 52R2$

Divide 210 ÷ 4 again. Write the answer as a decimal.

$$
\begin{array}{r}
52.5 \\
4\overline{)210.0} \\
20 \\
\overline{10} \\
8 \\
\overline{20} \\
20 \\
\overline{0}
\end{array}
$$

← Place the decimal point in the answer above the point in the dividend.

Insert a decimal point in the dividend. →
Add a trailing zero. Divide.

Bring down the new 0. →
Multiply $4 \times 5 = 20$. Write 5 in the answer. →
Subtract $20 - 20$. The remainder is 0. →

$210 \div 4 = 52.5$

Divide Decimals

Dividing decimals is similar to dividing whole numbers, except that you have to be careful where you place the decimal point in the quotient.

To divide decimals, follow these steps:

1. Set up the long division problem.
2. Count the number of digits to the right of the decimal point in the divisor.
3. Move the decimal point in the dividend the number of places found in Step 2.
4. Place the decimal point in the quotient directly above the newly placed decimal point in the dividend.
5. Divide as if there were no decimal points.
6. Add trailing zeros in the dividend, if necessary, to find the answer.

To divide 0.39 by 2.6, look at the divisor 2.6. It has one digit to the right of the decimal point. So, move the decimal point one place to the right in the dividend. Place the decimal point in the quotient directly above this new point position.

Move the decimal points. Place the point in the answer.	Multiply $26 \times 1 = 26$. Write 1 in the answer. Subtract $39 - 26 = 13$.	Since 26 does not divide into 13, insert a trailing zero after 9 in the dividend. Bring down the 0.	Multiply $26 \times 5 = 130$. Write 5 in the answer. Subtract. The remainder is 0.

$$2.6\overline{)0.39}$$

$$\begin{array}{r} .1 \\ 26\overline{)3.9} \\ \underline{26} \\ 13 \end{array}$$

$$\begin{array}{r} 0.15 \\ 26\overline{)3.90} \\ \underline{26} \\ 130 \end{array}$$

$$\begin{array}{r} 0.15 \\ 26\overline{)3.90} \\ \underline{26} \\ 130 \\ \underline{130} \\ 0 \end{array}$$

$0.39 \div 2.6 = 0.15$

Putting It **Together**

Checking Your Answer

To make sure that you have placed the decimal point in the correct position in the quotient, it is a good idea to estimate before dividing. Then compare your estimate to the exact answer.

To estimate division, use compatible numbers, which make division computation easier to perform. For example, to estimate $29.2 \div 4.3$, pick two numbers that divide easily. You can choose 4, which is close to 4.3, and 28, which is a multiple of 4 and close to 29.2. So, to estimate $29.2 \div 4.3$, write $28 \div 4 = 7$. The quotient $29.2 \div 4.3$ is about 7.

Another way to check your division is to multiply the quotient and the divisor to see whether your result is the dividend.

Divide 927.3 ÷ 28.1.

Estimate by choosing a number close to 28.1 that can be easily divided into a number close to 927.3.	Divide to find the exact answer.	Check your answer by multiplying.
$927.3 \div 28.1$	$\begin{array}{r} 33 \\ 28.1\overline{)927.3} \\ 843 \\ 843 \\ \underline{843} \\ 0 \end{array}$	$\begin{array}{r} 28.1 \\ \times\ \ \ 33 \\ \hline 843 \\ +\ 843 \\ \hline 927.3 \end{array}$
$900 \div 30 = 30$		

The exact answer 33 is about 30, the estimate. So the answer 33 is reasonable. The check using multiplication also confirms that the answer is 33.

Multiplying and Dividing by Powers of Ten

When you multiply by a power of ten, move the decimal point to the right the same number of places as there are zeros in the power-of-ten factor. Look at 2.5×10. There is 1 zero in 10. Move the decimal point in 2.5 one place to the right to get 25. So, $2.5 \times 10 = 25$. Here are some examples to show why moving the decimal point to the right works.

0.1755×10	68.034×100	$0.0875 \times 1,000$

$$
\begin{array}{r}
0.1755 \\
\times \quad 10 \\
\hline
0000 \\
1755 \\
\hline
1.7550
\end{array}
\qquad
\begin{array}{r}
68.034 \\
\times \quad 100 \\
\hline
00000 \\
00000 \\
68034 \\
\hline
6803.400
\end{array}
\qquad
\begin{array}{r}
0.0875 \\
\times \quad 1,000 \\
\hline
000 \\
000 \\
000 \\
875 \\
\hline
87.5000
\end{array}
$$

$0.1755 \times 10 = 1.755$ $68.034 \times 100 = 6,803.4$ $0.0875 \times 1,000 = 87.5$

1 place   2 places   3 places

When you divide by a power of ten, move the decimal point to the left the same number of places as there are zeros in the power-of-ten factor. Look at $22.5 \div 10$. There is 1 zero in 10. Move the decimal point in 22.5 one place to the left to get 2.25. So, $22.5 \div 10 = 2.25$. Here are some examples to show why moving the decimal point to the left works.

$1.65 \div 10$	$382.4 \div 100$	$57.6 \div 1000$

$$
\begin{array}{r}
0.165 \\
10\overline{)1.650} \\
\underline{10} \\
65 \\
\underline{60} \\
50 \\
\underline{50} \\
0
\end{array}
\qquad
\begin{array}{r}
3.824 \\
100\overline{)382.400} \\
\underline{300} \\
824 \\
\underline{800} \\
240 \\
\underline{200} \\
400 \\
\underline{400} \\
0
\end{array}
\qquad
\begin{array}{r}
0.0576 \\
1000\overline{)57.6000} \\
\underline{5000} \\
7600 \\
\underline{7000} \\
6000 \\
\underline{6000} \\
0
\end{array}
$$

$1.65 \div 10 = 0.165$ $382.4 \div 100 = 3.824$ $57.6 \div 1000 = 0.0576$

1 place   2 places   3 places

Notice that in the division $57.6 \div 1,000$, you had to insert a leading zero in order to get 3 decimal places.

What are Fractions?

A **fraction** is a rational number in the form $\frac{a}{b}$, where a and b are whole numbers. The number on top is called the **numerator,** and the number on the bottom is called the **denominator.** There is one restriction: The denominator cannot have the value of 0. This would be the same as division by zero, which is undefined.

Proper Fractions	One	Improper Fractions	Mixed Numbers
Numerator smaller than the denominator	Numerator equals denominator	Numerator greater than the denominator	Whole number and a fraction
(value: less than 1)	(value: 1)	(value: greater than 1)	(value: greater than 1)
$\frac{1}{2}, \frac{3}{4}, \frac{7}{8}, \frac{5}{12}$	$\frac{2}{2}, \frac{3}{3}, \frac{6}{6}, \frac{10}{10}$	$\frac{4}{3}, \frac{15}{6}, \frac{9}{7}, \frac{27}{20}$	$1\frac{1}{3}, 5\frac{3}{8}, 10\frac{5}{9}, 14\frac{11}{12}$

To write a mixed number as an improper fraction, multiply the denominator by the whole number, and then add the numerator to that sum. Put the total over the denominator. Use the formula: $A\frac{B}{C} = \frac{(C \cdot A) + B}{C}$. For example, look at $1\frac{2}{3}$. Multiply 3 by 1, and then add 2 to get 5. Put 5 over the denominator 3.

$$1\frac{2}{3} = 1\frac{2}{3} = \frac{(3 \times 1) + 2}{3} = \frac{5}{3}$$

To write an improper fraction as a mixed number, do the reverse. So, you divide. Use the formula: $\frac{A}{B} = A \div B = C\,R\,D = C\frac{D}{B}$, where C is the quotient without the remainder and D is the remainder. For example, to write $\frac{9}{4}$ as a mixed number, divide 9 by 4. You get 2 R1. That means there is the whole number 2 and 1 fourth remaining.

$$\frac{9}{4} = 2R1 = 2\frac{1}{4}.$$

Add Fractions

To add fractions, the fractions must have the same denominator. Add the numerators and put the sum over the denominator.

Add $\frac{2}{7} + \frac{3}{7}$.

$$\frac{2}{7} + \frac{3}{7} = \frac{2+3}{7} = \frac{5}{7}$$

One way to find a common denominator is to multiply all the denominators together. Another method of finding a common denominator may reduce the amount of computations you have to do. List all the *multiples* of the denominators. Then identify the multiples that the denominators have in common. Determine which multiple is the least number. That least common multiple of the denominators is called the **least common denominator (LCD)** of the fractions. Write each fraction so it has this LCD as its denominator.

Points to **Remember**

A *multiple* of a number is the product of that number and a nonzero whole number.

The multiples of 3 are

3, 6, 9, 12, 15, 18, …

To add fractions, follow these steps:

1. Write the fractions so they have the same denominators.
2. Add the numerators and keep the denominator.
3. Simplify the fraction if necessary.

For example, to add $\frac{13}{15}$ and $\frac{3}{5}$, find the LCD, which is 15, because 5 is a factor of 15. Rewrite the problem with denominators of 15 by multiplying both the numerator and the denominator of $\frac{3}{5}$ by 3. You can multiply the numerator and the denominator by the same number without changing the value of the fraction.

$$\frac{13}{15} + \frac{3}{5} = \frac{13}{15} + \frac{3 \times 3}{5 \times 3} = \frac{13}{15} + \frac{9}{15} \quad \leftarrow \quad \frac{9}{15} \text{ is equal to } \frac{3}{5}.$$

$$= \frac{13 + 9}{15} \quad \leftarrow \quad \text{Add the numerators and keep the denominator.}$$

$$= \frac{22}{15} = 1\frac{7}{15} \quad \leftarrow \quad \text{Write the final answer as a mixed number.}$$

Sometimes the LCD is not one of the denominators. In the problem below, both 6 and 10 are factors of 30. So, use 30 as the common denominator.

Add $\frac{7}{10} + \frac{1}{6}$.

$$\frac{7}{10} + \frac{1}{6} = \frac{7 \times 3}{10 \times 3} + \frac{1 \times 5}{6 \times 5} = \frac{21}{30} + \frac{5}{30} = \frac{21 + 5}{30} = \frac{26}{30}$$

Notice that the final answer is not in simplest form. A fraction is in **simplest form** when the only common factor of the numerator and denominator is 1. Divide the numerator and denominator of $\frac{26}{30}$ by 2 to simplify the fraction. As with multiplication, you can divide the numerator and denominator of a fraction by the same number without changing the value of the fraction.

$$\frac{26}{30} = \frac{26 \div 2}{30 \div 2} = \frac{13}{15}$$

Adding Mixed Numbers. When mixed numbers have the same denominators, first add the whole number parts. Then add the fraction parts. Simplify the result, if necessary. For example, in the problem below, add 1 and 3, and then add $\frac{2}{5}$ and $\frac{4}{5}$.

Add $1\frac{2}{5} + 3\frac{4}{5}$.

$$1\frac{2}{5} + 3\frac{4}{5} = 1 + \frac{2}{5} + 3 + \frac{4}{5} = 1 + 3 + \frac{2}{5} + \frac{4}{5}$$

$$= 4 + \frac{2 + 4}{5} = 4 + \frac{6}{5}$$

$$= 4 + 1\frac{1}{5} = 5\frac{1}{5} \quad \leftarrow \text{Write the improper fraction as a mixed number.}$$

To add mixed numbers with unlike denominators, first change the fraction parts to have the same denominators. Then add.

$$6\frac{2}{3} + 3\frac{1}{4} = 6\frac{2 \times 4}{3 \times 4} + 3\frac{1 \times 3}{4 \times 3}$$ ← The least common denominator is 12.

$$= 6\frac{8}{12} + 3\frac{3}{12} = 6 + 3 + \frac{8 + 3}{12} = 9\frac{11}{12}$$

Subtract Fractions

Subtracting fractions is similar to adding fractions. Write the fractions so they have the same denominators. Subtract the numerators and keep the denominator. Simplify the resulting fraction.

Subtract $\frac{9}{16} - \frac{3}{16}$.

$$\frac{9}{16} - \frac{3}{16} = \frac{9 - 3}{16} = \frac{6}{16}$$ ← Subtract the numerators.

$$= \frac{6 \div 2}{16 \div 2} = \frac{3}{8}$$ ← To simplify the result, divide both the numerator and the denominator by 2.

Subtract $\frac{4}{5} - \frac{7}{20}$.

$$\frac{4}{5} - \frac{7}{20} = \frac{4 \times 4}{5 \times 4} - \frac{7}{20} = \frac{16}{20} - \frac{7}{20}$$ ← Since 4 is a factor of 20, use 20 as the common denominator.

$$= 16 - \frac{7}{20} = \frac{9}{20}$$ ← Subtract the numerators.

Subtracting Mixed Numbers. Use a similar process as adding mixed numbers. Subtract the whole number parts and then the fraction parts. Make sure the fractions have the same denominator. Setting the problem vertically may make the subtraction easier to complete.

Subtract $6\frac{5}{6} - 2\frac{1}{8}$.

$$6\frac{5}{6} = 6\frac{5 \times 4}{6 \times 4} = 6\frac{20}{24}$$
$$-2\frac{1}{8} = -2\frac{1 \times 3}{8 \times 3} = -2\frac{3}{24}$$
$$4\frac{17}{24}$$

← The LCD is 24. Write each fraction part with a denominator of 24. Then subtract the whole numbers and the fraction parts.

If a larger fraction is being subtracted from a smaller fraction, use regrouping before you subtract. To regroup, rename one whole number as a fraction in the form $\frac{a}{a}$, where a is the denominator of the fraction. Then add that fraction to the fraction part.

Subtract $8\frac{1}{6} - 6\frac{3}{4}$.

$$8\frac{1}{4} = 7\frac{5}{4}$$
$$-6\frac{3}{4} = -6\frac{3}{4}$$
$$1\frac{2}{4} = 1\frac{1}{2}$$

← Since $\frac{1}{4}$ is less than $\frac{3}{4}$, regroup $8\frac{1}{4}$.

$8\frac{1}{4} = 7 + 1 + \frac{1}{4} = 7 + \frac{4}{4} + \frac{1}{4} = 7 + \frac{4+1}{4} = 7 + \frac{5}{4}$

Sometimes you have to subtract a mixed number from a whole number. You can also use regrouping with a whole number if you need a fraction part in order to subtract. Just take 1 whole from the number and write it as a fraction, as you did for mixed numbers in the example above.

Subtract $11 - 3\frac{5}{9}$.

$$11 = 10\frac{9}{9}$$
$$-3\frac{5}{9} = -3\frac{5}{9}$$
$$7\frac{4}{9}$$

← Regroup 11 to have a fraction with ninths.

$11 = 10 + 1 = 10 + \frac{9}{9} = 10\frac{9}{9}$

Sometimes a problem will contain multiple steps and incorporate several skills. The problem $4\frac{1}{3} - 2\frac{5}{6}$ includes finding a common denominator, regrouping when subtracting, and simplifying the answer. The first step is to write the fractions so they have the same denominator, in this case, 6. Then regroup, subtract, and simplify to find the answer.

$$4\frac{1}{3} = 4\frac{1 \times 2}{3 \times 2} = 4\frac{2}{6} = 3\frac{8}{6}$$
$$-2\frac{5}{6} = -2\frac{5}{6} = -2\frac{5}{6} = -2\frac{5}{6}$$
$$1\frac{3}{6} = 1\frac{3 \div 3}{6 \div 3} = 1\frac{1}{2}$$

← Since $\frac{2}{6}$ is less than $\frac{5}{6}$, regroup $4\frac{2}{6}$.

$4\frac{2}{6} = 3 + 1 + \frac{2}{6} = 3 + \frac{6}{6} + \frac{2}{6} = 3 + \frac{6+2}{6}$
$= 3 + \frac{8}{6}$

← Write the answer in simplest form.

Multiply Fractions

To multiply fractions, you do not need a common denominator as you did when adding and subtracting fractions. Simply multiply the numbers in the numerator, and then multiply the numbers in the denominator. For example, to multiply $\frac{1}{2} \times \frac{3}{4}$, multiply the numerators (1×3) and place that number over the product of the denominators (2×4): $\frac{1}{2} \times \frac{3}{4} = \frac{1 \times 3}{2 \times 4} = \frac{3}{8}$.

If the numerator and denominator have common factors, you can *simplify*, or *cancel*, before you multiply.

Another way to solve the problem is to simplify the fraction *after* multiplying by writing the resulting fraction in its simplest form. You get the same result with either method.

Multiply $\frac{7}{9} \times \frac{3}{16}$.

Simplify *before* multiplying: $\frac{7}{9} \times \frac{3}{16} = \frac{7}{\underset{3}{9}} \times \frac{\overset{1}{3}}{16} = \frac{7 \times 1}{3 \times 16} = \frac{7}{48}$ ← 3 and 9 have a common factor of 3.

Simplify *after* multiplying: $\frac{7}{9} \times \frac{3}{16} = \frac{7 \times 3}{9 \times 16} = \frac{21}{144} = \frac{21 \div 3}{144 \div 3} = \frac{7}{48}$ ← 21 and 144 have a common factor of 3.

Multiplying Mixed Numbers. To multiply mixed numbers, first write the mixed numbers as improper fractions. Then multiply the numerators and denominators.

Multiply $1\frac{5}{6} \times 2\frac{1}{2}$.

$$1\frac{5}{6} \times 2\frac{1}{2} = \frac{11}{6} \times \frac{5}{2}$$

← Recall how to write improper fractions:

$$1\frac{5}{6} = \frac{(6 \times 1) + 5}{6} = \frac{11}{6} \text{ and } 2\frac{1}{2} = \frac{(2 \times 2) + 1}{2} = \frac{5}{2}$$

$$= \frac{11 \times 5}{6 \times 2}$$

$$= \frac{55}{12} = 4\frac{7}{12}$$

← Write the answer as a mixed number.

A whole number can be written as a fraction with a denominator of 1. That is true because any number divided by 1 equals the same number. Writing the division as a fraction shows that the whole number A is the same as $\frac{A}{1} = A \div 1 = A$. So you can write any whole number A as $\frac{A}{1}$.

$$6 \times 2\frac{1}{4} = \frac{6}{1} \times \frac{9}{4}$$ ← Write 6 as $\frac{6}{1}$. Write $2\frac{1}{4}$ as $\frac{9}{4}$.

$$= \frac{\overset{3}{\cancel{6}}}{1} \times \frac{9}{\underset{2}{\cancel{4}}} = \frac{3 \times 9}{1 \times 2} = \frac{27}{2} = 13\frac{1}{2}$$ ← 6 and 4 have a common factor of 2.

Divide Fractions

Division is the inverse operation of multiplication. For example, you know that
$8 \div 2 = 4$. You also know that $8 \times \frac{1}{2} = \frac{8}{1} \times \frac{1}{2} = \frac{8 \times 1}{1 \times 2} = \frac{8}{2} = 4$. So, dividing by 2 is
the same as multiplying by $\frac{1}{2}$. The multiplicative inverse of a fraction is the **reciprocal,**
or "flip," of the fraction. To divide fractions, multiply the first fraction by the reciprocal
of the second fraction.

Divide $\frac{1}{6} \div \frac{1}{5}$.

$$\frac{1}{6} \div \frac{1}{5} = \frac{1}{6} \times \frac{5}{1} = \frac{1 \times 5}{6 \times 1} = \frac{5}{6}$$

Be sure to simplify. Remember that you can simplify by cancelling common factors
before performing the operation. You can also simplify after performing the operation
by writing the answer in simplest form.

Divide $\frac{1}{4} \div \frac{3}{8}$.

Simplify *before* multiplying: $\quad \frac{1}{4} \div \frac{3}{8} = \frac{1}{4} \times \frac{8}{3} = \frac{1}{\cancel{4}} \times \frac{\overset{2}{\cancel{8}}}{3} = \frac{1 \times 2}{1 \times 3} = \frac{2}{3}$

Simplify *after* multiplying: $\quad \frac{1}{4} \div \frac{3}{8} = \frac{1}{4} \times \frac{8}{3} = \frac{1 \times 8}{4 \times 3} = \frac{8}{12} = \frac{8 \div 4}{12 \div 4} = \frac{2}{3}$

Dividing Mixed Numbers. The first step in dividing mixed numbers is the same as
for multiplying mixed numbers—write the mixed numbers as improper fractions. Then
divide the fractions.

Divide $1\frac{5}{8} \div 2\frac{1}{2}$.

$$1\frac{5}{8} \div 2\frac{1}{2} = \frac{13}{8} \div \frac{5}{2}$$ ← Write the mixed numbers as improper fractions.

$$= \frac{13}{8} \times \frac{2}{5} = \frac{13}{\underset{4}{\cancel{8}}} \times \frac{\overset{1}{\cancel{2}}}{5} = \frac{13 \times 1}{4 \times 5} = \frac{13}{20}$$ ← Multiply by the reciprocal and simplify.

Complex Fractions. A **complex fraction** has fractions in its numerator or its denominator. Recall that a fraction bar indicates division. So, to simplify a complex fraction, you divide the numerator by the denominator.

Simplify $\dfrac{\frac{2}{3}}{\frac{1}{2}}$.

$$\frac{\frac{2}{3}}{\frac{1}{2}} = \frac{2}{3} \div \frac{1}{2} = \frac{2}{3} \times \frac{2}{1} = \frac{2 \times 2}{3 \times 1} = \frac{4}{3} = 1\frac{2}{3}$$

Exercises

Answers and explanations are located at the end of the unit.

1. $248 + 375 = $ __?__

2. $14.3 \div 2.2 = $ __?__

3. $431 \times 607 = $ __?__

4. $4 \times 3\frac{1}{8} = $ __?__

5. $\frac{3}{4} - \frac{3}{6} = $ __?__

6. $2\frac{1}{5} \div 1\frac{1}{15} = $ __?__

7. $25.3 + 10.75 + 6.4 = $ __?__

8. $3.9 - 0.685 = $ __?__

9. $3,843 \div 18 = $ __?__

10. $\frac{4}{9} + \frac{5}{6} = $ __?__

11. $10\frac{1}{10} - 3\frac{2}{5} = $ __?__

12. $12 \div \frac{8}{11} = $ __?__

13. $0.125 \times 0.15 = $ __?__

14. $1\frac{3}{4} + 2\frac{1}{2} = $ __?__

15. $8,065 - 2,725 = $ __?__

Defining Systems of Measure

You are probably familiar with the **U.S. Customary system** of measurement. This system is used in the United States and is based around measures such as feet and inches for length, fluid ounces and cups for liquid capacity, and pounds and ounces for weight.

The **metric system**, used worldwide, is known as the International System of Units (SI). The metric system is based on base 10, rather than other conversion factors. For example, in the U.S. Customary system 1 ft = 12 in. and 1 yd = 3 ft, but in the metric system 1 km = 1,000 m and 1 cm = 10 mm. The units in the metric system vary by a power of ten.

For each measure (length, capacity, mass), there is a base unit (meter, liter, gram) that relates to the number 1. Other units, such as kilometer, have prefixes with numerical meanings that indicate how large or small the measurement is compared to the base unit. Each unit increases or decreases by a power of ten.

Metric System

Unit	Meaning	A Way to Remember the Prefix Order
Kilo-	One thousand (1,000)	**K**ings
Hecto-	One hundred (100)	**H**ave
Deka-	One ten (10)	**D**iamonds
Base unit (meter, liter, gram)	One (1)	**B**ut
Deci-	One tenth (0.1)	**D**iamonds
Centi-	One hundredth (0.01)	**C**ost
Milli-	One thousandth (0.001)	**M**oney

All the measures in the metric system use the same prefixes. When you know the base unit of each measure, you can identify the other measurements related to that unit.

Length	Capacity	Mass	Area
Kilometer	Kiloliter	Kilogram	Square kilometer
Hectometer	Hectoliter	Hectogram	Square hectometer
Dekameter	Dekaliter	Dekagram	Square dekameter
Meter	**Liter**	**Gram**	**Square Meter**
Decimeter	Deciliter	Decigram	Square decimeter
Centimeter	Centiliter	Centigram	Square centimeter
Millimeter	Milliliter	Milligram	Square millimeter

Larger ↑   Smaller ↓

Determining the Reasonableness of a Measurement

Many jobs in the United States now use the metric system, because the work crosses national boundaries. For example, international trade and commerce companies use metric measurements because other countries may not accept goods weighed or measured in U.S. Customary units. Many scientists, especially in medicine, use the metric system so that their work can be shared with and understood by scientists in other countries. To get accustomed to thinking in metric terms, you can use visual examples of common objects to determine whether a metric measurement is reasonable.

Length

Length is the distance between two points. The base unit in the metric system for length is the **meter.** Other commonly used units are kilometer, centimeter, and millimeter. A yard in the U.S. Customary system is close in length to a meter.

Unit	Abbreviation	Visual Example
Kilometer	km	Length of 11 football fields
Meter	m	Width of a doorway
Centimeter	cm	Width of a fingernail
Millimeter	mm	Thickness of a dime

The table above gives some references for visually defining how large each measurement is. For example, a reasonable length of a charity run would be 5 kilometers, but it would not make sense if someone said that the race was 5 centimeters (or fingernails) long.

> An HDMI cable is one type of cable that connects electrical equipment, such as computers, TVs, and DVD players. What is a reasonable length for an HDMI cable: 3 mm or 3 m?

Think about the lengths: 3 mm is the width of about 3 dimes, and 3 m is the width of about 3 doorways. An electrical cable would be measured in meters, not millimeters, so 3 m is more reasonable.

Capacity

Capacity is the amount of liquid that a container can hold. The base unit in the metric system for capacity is the **liter.** Another commonly used unit is the milliliter. A quart (think of a quart bottle of milk) in the U.S. Customary system is close to a liter.

Unit	Abbreviation	Visual Example
Liter	L	Large bottle of water or juice Half of a 2-liter bottle of soda
Milliliter	mL	10 drops from an eye dropper

A milliliter of liquid takes up the same space, or volume, as a cubic centimeter. Most liquid medicines are measured in milliliters (mL) or cubic centimeters (abbreviated as cc or cm^3).

Think about the capacities: 60 L is about 60 quarts or large water bottles, and 60 mL is about 600 drops. A gas tank would be measured in liters, not milliliters, so 60 L is more reasonable.

What is a reasonable capacity for a syringe for a needle: 5 L or 5 mL?

Think about the capacities: 5 L is about 5 large water bottles, and 5 mL is about 50 drops. A syringe would be measured in milliliters, not liters, so 5 mL is more reasonable.

TrueStory

"One day, I was doing dosage calculations on a Friday. I was ready to go home, and I guess I wasn't paying as much attention as usual. We'd been crazy busy all day. I gave the finished syringe to the supervisor on duty, and she pointed out that I had 30 cc of the medication instead of 3 cc. It was for a baby boy, and it would definitely have killed him. I was so terrified. I could barely walk back to fix the error. Needless to say, I have never made a mistake since."

Mass

Mass is the amount of matter in an object. People often use both *weight* and *mass* to describe the same measure. Technically, mass is not affected by gravity but weight is. If you were standing on the moon, your mass would be the same but you would weigh less than on Earth. In everyday language, however, the terms *weight* and *mass* are used interchangeably.

The base unit in the metric system for mass is the **gram.** Other commonly used units are kilogram, milligram, and microgram, a much smaller measurement than the milligram. A pound in the U.S. Customary system is about a half of a kilogram, or, conversely, a kilogram is about 2.2 pounds.

Unit	Abbreviation	Visual Example
Kilogram	kg	A textbook
Gram	g	Two paper clips
Milligram	mg	An eyelash or very small insect
Microgram	mcg	0.001 of a milligram

Many medicines in tablet form are measured in milligrams. Some daily vitamin doses are given in micrograms.

What is a reasonable mass for an adult male: 80 g or 80 kg?

Think about the mass: 80 g is about 160 paper clips, and 80 kg is about a stack of 80 textbooks, or about 176 pounds (80 × 2.2). A person's weight would be measured in kilograms, not grams, so 80 kg is more reasonable.

Think about the mass: 100 g is about 200 paper clips, and 100 mg is about 100 eyelashes. Daily servings of food would be measured in grams, not milligrams, so 100 g is more reasonable.

Area

Area is the size of the interior of a flat figure. For example, the amount of wall-to-wall carpet you install in a room would equal the area of the floor of the room. A floor plan of a house shows the area of each room.

Area is measure in square units. You find the area of a rectangular figure by multiplying the length of the figure by the width of the figure.

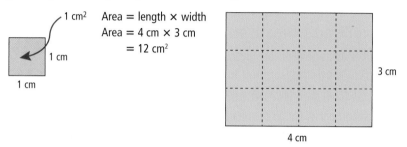

The base unit in the metric system for area is the **square meter.** Other commonly used units are square kilometer, square centimeter, and square millimeter. A square yard in the U.S. Customary system is close in area to a square meter.

Unit	Abbreviation	Visual Example
Square kilometer	km²	Washington D.C.: about 177 km²
Square meter	m²	Average bedroom: about 12 m²
Square centimeter	cm²	Index card: about 100 cm²
Square millimeter	mm²	Face of a dime: about 250 mm²

The sizes of cities and states are measured in square kilometers. So, a reasonable area for the city of Chicago is 600 km², but it would not make sense if someone said that the city had an area of 600 m² (50 bedrooms) or 600 cm² (6 index cards).

Think about the area: 8 m² is close to the size of an average bedroom in a house, and 8 cm² is much smaller than the size of an index card. Prison cells would be measured in square meters, not square centimeters, so 8 m² is more reasonable.

Answers and explanations are located at the end of the unit.

16. What is a reasonable length for an insulin syringe needle: 12.7 mm or 12.7 m?

17. What is a reasonable capacity for a container of dental mouth rinse: 0.5 L or 0.5 mL?

18. What is a reasonable length for a patrol circuit of one level of a mall: 0.8 m or 0.8 km?

19. What is a reasonable mass for a medication tablet: 600 g or 600 mg?

Solving Measurement Problems

Converting Measurements Within the Same System

Sometimes measurements are given in a different unit than what you need. You will have to convert the measurement to the correct unit. With the metric system, that means you multiply or divide by a power of ten.

The chart below shows the relationship between the units, and identifies how many of the base units (m, L, g) are equal to the other units. Because the metric system uses the same prefixes for length, capacity, and mass, you need to remember only one set of conversions.

Length	Capacity	Mass
1 km = 1,000 m	1 kL = 1,000 L	1 kg = 1,000 g
1 hm = 100 m	1 hL = 100 L	1 hg = 100 g
1 dam = 10 m	1 daL = 10 L	1 dag = 10 g
meter (1 m)	**liter (1 L)**	**gram (1 g)**
1 dm = 0.1 m	1 dL = 0.1 L	1 dg = 0.1 g
1 cm = 0.01 m	1 cL = 0.01 L	1 cg = 0.01 g
1 mm = 0.001 m	1 mL = 0.001 L	1 mg = 0.001 g

Another way to write these relationships is to show how many of the other units are in each of the base units (meter, liter, gram).

0.0001 km = 0.001 hm = 0.01 dam = **1 m** = 10 dm = 100 cm = 1,000 mm

0.0001 kL = 0.001 hL = 0.01 daL = **1 L** = 10 dL = 100 cL = 1,000 mL

0.0001 kg = 0.001 hg = 0.01 dag = **1 g** = 10 dg = 100 cg = 1,000 mg

1 mg = 1,000 mcg

Think of the metric system like the place value system. The value of each unit is 10 times greater than the value of the unit to its right. When you convert from one unit of measure to another unit, you multiply or divide by a power of ten. Counting the number of places between the units tells you which power of 10 to use.

Larger → Smaller

To convert, multiply by 10 for each place.

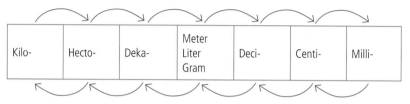

Kilo-	Hecto-	Deka-	Meter Liter Gram	Deci-	Centi-	Milli-

Larger ← Smaller

To convert, divide by 10 for each place.

When you convert from a *larger* unit to a *smaller* unit, you need more of the smaller units to equal one larger unit. So, you multiply. For example, the kilometer is larger than the meter. It takes 1,000 m to make 1 km. To convert 5 km to meters, multiply the 5 by 1,000 to get 5,000 m.

5 km = ___?___ m

To convert from kilometers to meters, you count 3 places to the right.

Move the decimal point 3 places to the right, which is the same as multiplying by 1,000.

5.000 × 1,000 = 5,000
3 places

A SATA cable to connect a hard drive inside a computer is 0.5 m. How long is the cable in millimeters?

0.5 m = ___?___ mm

Meters are larger than millimeters.

To convert, multiply by 1,000 because 1 m = 1,000 mm.

0.5 × 1,000 = 500   ← Move the decimal point 3 places to the right.

0.5 m = 500 mm   *Recall the rules for multiplying by powers of 10 presented earlier in this unit.*

0.25 g = ___?___ mg

Grams are larger than milligrams.

To convert, multiply by 1,000 because 1 g = 1,000 mg.

0.25 × 1,000 = 250   ← Move the decimal point 3 places to the right.

0.25 g = 250 mg   *Recall the rules for multiplying by powers of 10 presented earlier in this unit.*

When you convert from a *smaller* unit to a *larger* unit, you need fewer of the larger units to equal one smaller unit. So, you divide. For example, the milligram is smaller than the gram. It takes 1,000 mg to make 1 g. To convert 400 mg to grams, divide the 400 by 1,000 to get 0.4 g.

A package of dental floss contains 25 m of floss. The length of floss used on one patient was around 45 cm. Write the length of the patient's floss in meters.

45 cm = ___?___ m

Centimeters are smaller than meters.

To convert, divide by 100 because 100 cm = 1 m.

45 ÷ 100 = 0.45   ← Move the decimal
point 2 places to the left.

45 cm = 0.45 m   *Recall the rules for dividing by powers of 10 presented earlier in this unit.*

Points to Remember

When converting measurements, think of the prefixes and whether you are converting from a larger to a smaller unit or from a smaller to a larger unit.

- **Larger unit to smaller unit:** Multiply.
- **Smaller unit to larger unit:** Divide.

Adjusting Measurements

Sometimes you have to adjust a measurement because the measurement is not in the form that you need. For example, suppose a prescription needs to be filled, and you know the prescription order and the size of the available tablets. To determine how many tablets to place in the bottle, you divide the order amount by the tablet size. Adjust measurements by adding, subtracting, multiplying, or dividing by a number or another measurement.

A doctor orders an IV fluid of 1,000 mL every 8 hours for a patient. How many milliliters of fluids will the patient receive every hour?

Divide the total amount of the fluid by the number of hours.

1,000 ÷ 8 = 125

The patient receives 125 mL every hour.

A liquid medicine indicates that the correct dose is 30 mL, to be taken no sooner than every 4 hours. What is the maximum amount of medicine a person should take in one day?

First, determine how many times per day the person can take the medicine. There are 24 hours in a day. *Every 4 hours* means there are at most $24 \div 4 = 6$ doses per day.

Next, find the amount of liquid medicine the person can take. Multiply to find the total.

30 mL × 6 doses = 180 mL per day

The maximum amount is 180 mL per day.

A medication order is 1,250 mg per day. The tablets available are 500 mg each and 125 mg each. What is the fewest number of tablets the patient could take to get the correct dosage? Describe the number and size of the tablets.

To find the fewest number, start with the larger tablet. Subtract its dose (500 mg) from the medication order as many times as possible. When you can no longer subtract 500 mg, start subtracting the smaller tablet (125 mg) until you reach zero.

```
  1,250
−   500   ← one 500-mg tablet
    750
−   500   ← one 500-mg tablet
    250   ← less than 500, so subtract a 125-mg tablet
−   125   ← one 125-mg tablet
    125
−   125   ← one 125-mg tablet
      0
```

The fewest number of tablets is 4, with the patient taking two 500-mg tablets and two 125-mg tablets each day.

Practice
Critical Thinking

Have you ever heard the saying "measure twice, cut once"? Carpenters follow this rule to avoid making mistakes when cutting wood. Otherwise, they might have to cut again, which wastes time and materials.

How can you avoid making errors in your job? It doesn't matter if you are preparing customers' bills, administering medications, repairing equipment, or keeping people and property safe. Using the wrong numbers on your job can have serious consequences. How will you be sure that you have calculated correctly? What will you do to double-check your work?

Converting Measurements Between Systems

In the United States, household situations mainly use U.S. Customary measurements. Because many jobs that use weights and measures, such as medicine, science, and commerce, involve the use of metric measurements, you need to be able to convert from one system to the other. The systems are different, so these conversions are approximate values. Having a list of the key conversions will help you get the correct result.

Points to **Remember**

These relationships are an easy way for you to estimate conversions.
• A meter is about a yard.
• A liter is about a quart.
• An inch is about 2 and a half centimeters.
• A pound is about half of a kilogram.

Conversion Table

Metric to U.S. Customary			U.S. Customary to Metric		
1 cm	=	0.3937 in.	1 in.	=	2.54 cm
1 m	=	3.281 ft	1 ft	=	0.3048 m
1 m	=	1.094 yd	1 yd	=	0.914 m
1 km	=	0.621 mi	1 mi	=	1.609 km
1 mL	=	0.034 fl oz	1 fl oz	=	29.57 mL
1 L	=	33.81 fl oz	1 fl oz	=	0.0296 L
1 L	=	1.057 qt	1 qt	=	0.946 L
1 L	=	0.264 gal	1 gal	=	3.785 L
1 g	=	0.0353 oz	1 oz	=	28.35 g
1 kg	=	35.27 oz	1 oz	=	0.0284 kg
1 kg	=	2.21 lb	1 lb	=	0.454 kg

Each relationship is shown in two ways above, such as 1 cm = 0.3937 in. and
1 in. = 2.54 cm. Choose the appropriate column for the measurement you have. For
example, to convert from U.S. Customary to the metric system, use the second column.
Find the conversion that you need. Multiply the measurement you have by the number
of units in the measure you want to find.

> **An Ethernet cable may lose signal performance when it is longer than 100 meters.
> How many feet can a cable be before signal loss?**

You need to convert the cable length from meters to feet.

100 m = ___?___ ft

From the first column in the table, 1 m = 3.281 ft. To convert, multiply by 3.281.

$100 \times 3.281 = 328.10$

100 m = 328.10 ft

An Ethernet cable can be about 328 ft long before signal loss.

> **A child weighs 42 pounds, but his medicine has a dosage for kilograms.
> What is the child's weight in kilograms?**

You need to convert the child's weight from pounds to kilograms.

42 lb = ___?___ kg

From the second column in the table, 1 lb = 0.454 kg. To convert, multiply by 0.454.

$42 \times 0.454 = 19.068$

42 lb = 19.068 kg

The child weighs about 19.1 kilograms.

> A drinking glass holds 8 fluid ounces. A medication order indicates to dissolve the tablets in 200 mL of water. Will the glass hold enough water for the medication?

You can convert either the glass's capacity to mL or the water needed to fl oz.

Consider the drinking glass.

8 fl oz = ___?___ mL

From the second column in the table, 1 fl oz = 29.57 mL. To convert, multiply by 29.57.

$8 \times 29.57 = 236.56$

8 fl oz = 236.56 mL

The glass holds about 237 mL, so it is large enough for the 200 mL of water needed.

Instead, consider the water needed.

200 mL = ___?___ fl oz

From the first column in the table, 1 mL = 0.034 fl oz. To convert, multiply by 0.034.

$200 \times 0.034 = 6.8$

200 mL = 6.8 fl oz

The amount of water needed is about 6.8 fl oz, so it will fit in the 8-fl-oz drinking glass.

Exercises

Answers and explanations are located at the end of the unit.

20. 310 mcg = ___?___ g   **21.** 22.5 m = ___?___ cm   **22.** 87.5 mL = ___?___ L

23. 2.5 mi = ___?___ km   **24.** 300 g = ___?___ oz   **25.** 4.8 L = ___?___ qt

26. A medication order is 375 mg per day. The tablets are available in 100 mg and 25 mg doses. Describe three different ways the tablets can be grouped so that the patient receives the correct dosage. Identify the number and size of the tablets in each group.

27. A doctor orders an IV fluid drip of 1.8 L every 12 hours. The IV machine administers 10 drops per milliliter. Recall the conversion 1 hour = 60 minutes. What is the rate of the drip in milliliters per hour? How many drops per hour will the machine administer? How many drops per minute does the patient receive?

28. A Body Mass Index (BMI) score of 25 to 29.9 indicates that a person is considered overweight. A score above 30 indicates obesity. The formula for BMI is $BMI = \frac{w}{h \times h}$, where weight is in kilograms and height is in meters. A male patient is 6 feet tall and weighs 175 pounds. Is he considered overweight or obese? Explain your answer.

Unit Summary

- To solve problems involving quantities or measurements, you may have to add, subtract, multiply, or divide whole numbers, fractions, and decimals.

- In order to avoid mistakes in calculations, estimate whether a quantity or measurement is reasonable, and be sure to check your work and your answers.

- Because many jobs use the metric system, you may have to convert U.S. Customary measurements to metric measurements.

- When you encounter a metric measurement that is not the quantity you need, adjust your original measurement by multiplying or dividing.

Important Terms

How well do you know these terms? Define them in your journal, or look them up in the glossary to help you remember them.

total	quotient	simplest form
addends	remainder	reciprocal
sum	fraction	complex fraction
place value	numerator	U.S. Customary system
difference	denominator	metric system
factors	proper fraction	meter
product	improper fraction	liter
partial product	mixed number	gram
dividend	least common denominator (LCD)	
divisor		

Answer Solutions to Exercises

1. $248 + 375 = 623$

$$
\begin{array}{r}
\overset{1\,1}{248} \\
+\ 375 \\
\hline
623
\end{array}
$$

2. $14.3 \div 2.2 = 6.5$

$$
\begin{array}{r}
6.5 \\
2.2\overline{)14.30} \\
132 \\
\hline
110 \\
110 \\
\hline
0
\end{array}
$$

3. $431 \times 607 = 261{,}617$

$$
\begin{array}{r}
431 \\
\times\ 607 \\
\hline
3017 \\
+\ 25860 \\
\hline
261{,}617
\end{array}
$$

4. $4 \times 3\dfrac{1}{8} = \dfrac{4}{1} \times \dfrac{25}{8} = \dfrac{\overset{1}{\cancel{4}}}{1} \times \dfrac{25}{\underset{2}{\cancel{8}}} = \dfrac{1 \times 25}{1 \times 2}$

$$= \dfrac{25}{2} = 12\dfrac{1}{2}$$

5. $\dfrac{3}{4} - \dfrac{3}{6} = \dfrac{3 \times 3}{4 \times 3} - \dfrac{3 \times 2}{6 \times 2} = \dfrac{9}{12} - \dfrac{6}{12}$

$$= \dfrac{3}{12} = \dfrac{3 \div 3}{12 \div 3} = \dfrac{1}{4}$$

6. $2\dfrac{1}{5} \div 1\dfrac{1}{15} = \dfrac{11}{5} \div \dfrac{16}{15} = \dfrac{11}{5} \times \dfrac{15}{16} = \dfrac{11}{\cancel{5}} \times \dfrac{\overset{3}{\cancel{15}}}{16}$

$$= \dfrac{11 \times 3}{1 \times 16} = \dfrac{33}{16} = 2\dfrac{1}{16}$$

7. $25.3 + 10.75 + 6.4 = 42.45$

$$
\begin{array}{r}
\overset{1\,1}{25.30} \\
10.75 \\
+\ 6.40 \\
\hline
42.45
\end{array}
$$

8. $3.9 - 0.685 = 3.215$

$$
\begin{array}{r}
\overset{8\ \overset{9}{\cancel{10}}\ 10}{3.9\cancel{0}\cancel{0}} \\
-\ 0.685 \\
\hline
3.215
\end{array}
$$

9. $3{,}843 \div 18 = 213.5$

$$
\begin{array}{r}
213.5 \\
18\overline{)3843.0} \\
36 \\
\hline
24 \\
18 \\
\hline
63 \\
54 \\
\hline
90 \\
90 \\
\hline
0
\end{array}
$$

10. $\dfrac{4}{9} + \dfrac{5}{6} = \dfrac{4 \times 2}{9 \times 2} + \dfrac{5 \times 3}{6 \times 3} = \dfrac{8}{18} + \dfrac{15}{18}$

$$= \dfrac{8 + 15}{18} = \dfrac{23}{18} = 1\dfrac{5}{18}$$

11. $10\dfrac{1}{10} - 3\dfrac{2}{5} = 10\dfrac{1}{10} - 3\dfrac{2 \times 2}{5 \times 2} = 10\dfrac{1}{10} - 3\dfrac{4}{10}$

$$= 9\dfrac{11}{10} - 3\dfrac{4}{10} = 6\dfrac{7}{10}$$

12. $12 \div \dfrac{8}{11} = \dfrac{12}{1} \div \dfrac{8}{11} = \dfrac{12}{1} \times \dfrac{11}{8} = \dfrac{\cancel{12}^{3}}{1} \times \dfrac{11}{\cancel{8}_{2}}$

$= \dfrac{3 \times 11}{1 \times 2} = \dfrac{33}{2} = 16\dfrac{1}{2}$

13. $0.125 \times 0.15 = 0.01875$

$$
\begin{array}{r}
0.125 \quad \leftarrow \text{3 decimal places} \\
\times\ 0.15 \quad \leftarrow \text{2 decimal places} \\
\hline
625 \\
+\quad 125 \\
\hline
0.01875 \quad \leftarrow \text{5 decimal places}
\end{array}
$$

14. $1\dfrac{3}{4} + 2\dfrac{1}{2} = 1\dfrac{3}{4} + 2\dfrac{1 \times 2}{2 \times 2} = 1\dfrac{3}{4} + 2\dfrac{2}{4} = 3\dfrac{3+2}{4}$

$= 3\dfrac{5}{4} = 3 + 1\dfrac{1}{4} = 4\dfrac{1}{4}$

15. $8,065 - 2,725 = 5,339$

$$
\begin{array}{r}
{\scriptstyle 7\ 10\ 5\ 14} \\
8,\cancel{0}\cancel{6}\cancel{4} \\
-\ 2,725 \\
\hline
5,339
\end{array}
$$

16. Think about the lengths: 12.7 mm is the width of about 12 dimes, and 12.7 m is the width of about 12 doorways. So, 12.7 mm is more reasonable for the length of a syringe needle.

17. Think about the capacities: 0.5 L is about half of a large water bottle, and 0.5 mL is half of 10, or 5, eye drops. So, 0.5 L is more reasonable for a container of dental mouth rinse.

18. Think about the lengths: 0.8 m is less than the width of 1 doorway, and 0.8 km is a little less than the length of 11 football fields. So, 0.8 km is more reasonable for the distance around one level of a mall.

19. Think about the mass: 600 g is the weight of about 600 × 2, or 1200, paper clips, and 600 mg is the weight of about 600 eyelashes. So, 600 mg is more reasonable for the mass of a medication tablet.

20. Micrograms are smaller than grams. Divide by 1,000 because 1,000 mcg = 1 g. Divide: 310 ÷ 1,000 = 0.310. So, 310 mcg = 0.31 g.

21. Meters are larger than centimeters. Multiply by 100 because 1 m = 100 cm. Multiply: 22.5 × 100 = 2250. So, 22.5 m = 2,250 cm.

22. Milliliters are smaller than liters. Divide by 1,000 because 1,000 mL = 1 L. Divide: 87.5 ÷ 1,000 = 0.0875. So, 87.5 mL = 0.0875 L.

23. Use the conversion 1 mi = 1.609 km. Multiply 2.5 × 1.609 = 4.0225. So, 2.5 mi = 4.0225 km.

24. Use the conversion 1 g = 0.0353 oz. Multiply 300 × 0.0353 = 10.59. So, 300 g = 10.59 oz.

25. Use the conversion 1 L = 1.057 qt. Multiply 4.8 × 1.057 = 5.0736. So, 4.8 L = 5.0736 qt.

26. One way the tablets can be grouped is by finding the greatest number of the larger dosage tablets. Then find the number of smaller dosage tablets in the remaining amount.

375 − 100 = 275; 275 − 100 = 175; 175 − 100 = 75; 75 − 25 = 50; 50 − 25 = 25; 25 − 25 = 0

One dosage of tablets is three 100-mg tablets and three 25-mg tablets.

A second way to group the tablets is to change the first grouping by replacing one 100-mg tablet with four 25-g tablets (4 × 25 = 100). 100-mg tablets: 3 − 1 = 2, and 25-mg tablets: 3 + 4 = 7. The new group of tablets for the dosage is two 100-mg tablets and seven 25-mg tablets.

A third way is to use only 25-mg tablets. Divide 375 ÷ 25 = 15. The dosage can be filled with fifteen 25-mg tablets.

27. The first question asks for the drip in milliliters per hour. The order is for 1.8 L per 12 hours, so divide 1.8 ÷ 12 = 0.15 L per hour. Convert 0.15 L to mL by multiplying by 1,000: 0.15 × 1,000 = 150. The drip rate is 150 mL per hour.

The second question asks for the machine's drops per hour. You know the drip rate is 150 mL/hr. Each milliliter contains 10 drops. Multiply 150 × 10 = 1,500. The machine administers 1,500 drops of fluid every hour.

The third question asked for drops per minute. You know there are 1,500 drops per hour. Divide 1,500 ÷ 60 = 25. The patient receives 25 drops per minute.

28. Convert the man's height and weight to metric measurements (meters and kilograms).

6 feet = ___?___ m. Use the conversion 1 ft = 0.3048 m. Multiply 6 × 0.3048 = 1.8288. So, 6 ft = 1.8288 m.

175 pounds = ___?___ kg. Use the conversion 1 lb = 0.454 kg. Multiply 175 × 0.454 = 79.45. So, 175 lb = 79.45 kg.

Substitute the metric measurements into the formula. Use a calculator if you have one.

$$BMI = \frac{w}{h \times h} = \frac{79.45}{1.8288 \times 1.8288} = 23.8$$

(rounded to the nearest tenth)

The man's BMI is less than 25, so he is not considered either overweight or obese.

Identifying and applying problem solving strategies

Solving problems involving decimals, ratios, and proportions

how often does a computer network need backing up? Is this the same for all networks, or does it vary? If you know how many patients can be seen in 3 hours, can you find out how many can be seen in 8 hours?

Many math problems you need to solve in everyday life or on the job are stated in words, instead of with symbols. Some may not even look like math problems until you have read them closely. When working a word problem, a good strategy can help you organize the information, find a solution, and record your procedure. It may take several attempts and more than one approach to solve some complex problems. But you need to stick with it. An important part of any job is to be able to find the correct answers, not only to mathematical problems but also to all types of problems and situations you will encounter. Knowing how to understand what a problem asks, as well as the ability to use a variety of strategies to solve problems, will allow you to be successful in your job.

Identifying and Applying Problem Solving Strategies

Steps for Solving Problems

The **five-step problem-solving process** is a plan that you can use for many problems. The steps below give you an outline to follow when solving almost any problem. Using these steps is especially helpful for longer problems.

Solving Word Problems	
Step 1	State what the problem is asking for as a solution.
Step 2	Identify the information that is given.
Step 3	Make a plan.
Step 4	Carry out the plan.
Step 5	Answer the question and look back.

STEP 1: State what the problem is asking for as a solution.

Read the problem carefully. Are you asked to find a *sum*, a *difference*, a *product*, or a *quotient*? Be on the lookout for those words, and also for common terms that refer to these operations, as shown in the table below.

Addition	Subtraction	Multiplication	Division
sum	difference	product	quotient
total	fewer	times	divided by
more	less than	of	split
increase	decrease	twice	half

Check to see whether the result should be only a number, or whether it needs to be a unit of measurement. If you are asked to make a comparison, does the problem also request an explanation of your choice? Look for all those clues when beginning your solution.

STEP 2: Identify the information that is given.

What information is stated in the problem? Is it ready to use? You may have to perform some intermediate steps, such as finding a measurement or converting units, before solving the main problem. Sometimes organizing the information in a list or a diagram will help you identify what you have, as well as what you need. Also, check to see whether there is any information that is not needed for the solution.

Your plan might be as simple as, "Add all the hours worked this week to find the total." A multistep plan could be "Add all the hours for the week, multiply by the hourly wage, and subtract the fixed costs." For a more complex problem, one or more of the strategies in this unit, such as *Find a Pattern* or *Make a Diagram*, may be needed to solve the problem.

As you solve the problem, you might work a problem with pencil and paper, fill in a graph or chart, or use a calculator or computer. Make sure you are using the correct numbers. Check your work for accuracy and reasonableness as you go along. If the strategy doesn't work out, try a different one.

Re-read the question. Does your answer make sense? For example, if the question asks for a number of people, and your answer is a decimal or a fraction, you should round your answer to a whole number, since you cannot have fractions of people. If the problem asks for units of measurement, make sure your answer includes them. You should also check your work to be sure that you made no mistakes. If you do the problem a different way or with a different strategy, do you get the same answer?

You may not need to use the five-step problem-solving process for every problem you solve, but it is a good framework and very useful if you ever get "stuck" on a problem.

The strategies in this unit will give you many useful ways to solve problems. You can probably think of other strategies you have used in the past, or find other strategies to try for some problems. Use any strategy you can to solve a problem.

Some problems can be solved with more than one strategy. You may need to use another strategy if the first one you choose does not work. It is important to continue to try to solve a problem, even if it means using multiple approaches or strategies, because when you are on the job, you'll be expected to find the answer.

Practice Now: Empowered

Many people lack confidence in their math skills, but employers favor confident employees who believe in themselves. Practice now by expressing confidence in your ability with calculations. People often say, "Oh, I'm bad at math," but that diminishes their credibility. Find an area of math in which you have confidence, and reassure yourself that math is a skill, and you can be good at it.

Find a Pattern

To use the strategy of finding a pattern, look at given information such as numbers, shapes, or words. Observe each element or characteristic and see whether any patterns emerge. You can also look for the difference between pairs of elements, or the quotient of two consecutive numbers in a list or a chart.

State what the problem is asking for as a solution. The amount of weight a patient lost after 12 weeks on a weight-loss plan.

Identify what is given. The weight of the patient every two weeks. Organizing the information in a table makes it easier to see the given information.

Number of Weeks Passed	Patient's Weight (lb)
0	211
2	205
4	200
6	196

Make a plan. Because the weight loss "continues in the same way," filling in more parts of the table will help you find a pattern you can use.

Carry out the plan. Look at the numbers in the column labeled "Patient's weight." Use them to find how much weight the patient lost in each two-week period. For example, after 2 weeks, the patient lost $211 - 205 = 6$ pounds.

Number of Weeks Passed	Patient's Weight (lb)	Weight Lost (lb)
0	211	—
2	205	6
4	200	5
6	196	4
8		
10		
12		

Notice that in each two-week period, the patient loses one less pound than he did during the previous period. Because you know that the weight loss continues in the same way, you can complete the table by filling in the "Weight lost" column first. Next complete the "Patient's weight" column by subtracting the weight lost.

Number of Weeks Passed	Patient's Weight (lb)	Weight Lost (lb)
0	211	—
2	205	6
4	200	5
6	196	4
8	$196 - 3 = 193$	3
10	$193 - 2 = 191$	2
12	$191 - 1 = 190$	1

Finally, find the total amount of weight lost by subtracting the final weight from the original weight: $211 - 190 = 21$.

Answer the problem and look back. After 12 weeks, the patient has lost 21 lb.

Check your work by adding all the weight lost shown in the third column:
$6 + 5 + 4 + 3 + 2 + 1 = 21$. ✓

Make a Picture or Diagram

Many problems are easier to understand if you sketch the situation. Your diagrams can be simple. Use circles to represent people, for example. This strategy is a good one when the problem is about geometric figures, lengths, and other measures, but it can also be handy for other types of problems.

> An electrician plans to install a wire around the perimeter of a rectangular room. If the room is 18 ft wide and 24 ft long, and has one door that is 3 ft wide, how many feet of wire are needed?

State what the problem is asking for as a solution. The number of feet of wire needed for a room.

Identify what is given. The dimensions of the room; the size of a door.

Make a plan. Because the information is about the dimensions of a room, draw a diagram of the room and label it. Use the diagram to find the room's perimeter.

Carry out the plan. Sketch the room. Even though you don't know where the door is, include it in the sketch. Its position will not affect the total length of wire needed.

Add the lengths of the walls and subtract the width of the door to find the amount of wire needed.

$18 + 24 + 18 + 24 - 3 = 81$

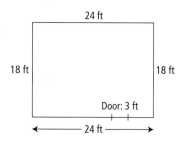

(continued on next page)

Answer the problem and look back. **The electrician needs 81 ft of wire.**

Check by starting with the answer, adding in the length of the door, and then subtracting the room dimensions. Door: $81 + 3 = 84$; Lengths: $84 - 2 \cdot 24 = 36$; Widths: $36 - 2 \cdot 18 = 0$. ✓

Work Backward

If you have ever planned to save a particular amount of money, you may have used the strategy of working backward. You know the amount you want to end up with, and working backward from the end tells you how much to save now. This strategy can be used whenever you are given an end result and asked for the starting value.

> **A security officer's shift is over at 2:00 P.M. He needs to make two patrols of his area and watch the security cameras for 30 minutes after each patrol. If each patrol lasts 45 minutes, what time should he start the first patrol?**

State what the problem is asking for as a solution. **The starting time for two patrols and two periods of watching security cameras.**

Identify what is given. **The time it takes for a patrol; the time spent watching security cameras; the end time.**

Make a plan. **Work backward from the end time to find the starting time. Subtract the time that each event takes from the end time.**

Carry out the plan. **You might find it helpful to keep track of the times in a table.**

Activity	Time Needed	Time
End time		2:00 P.M.
Start watching security cameras	30 min	$2:00 - 0:30 = 1:30$ P.M.
Start second patrol	45 min	$1:30 - 0:45 = 12:45$ P.M.
Start watching security cameras	30 min	$12:45 - 0:30 = 12:15$ P.M.
Start first patrol	45 min	$12:15 - 0:45 = 11:30$ A.M.

Answer the problem and look back. **The officer should start the first patrol at 11:30 A.M.**

Read the problem again. To check, start with 11:30 A.M. Add the times for the patrols and the camera watching sessions: $2 \times 30 + 2 \times 45 = 150$ minutes. Write 150 min as 2.5 hours. Add to the starting time. 11:30 A.M. $+ 2.5$ hours $= 2:00$ P.M. ✓

Use a Formula or Rule

Many problems can be solved by applying a formula or rule. The formula may come from geometry, such as the formula for the area of a figure; or from measurement, such as a conversion formula; or from a topic specific to a career.

> **A computer technician has 50 meters of cable. How many feet is this?**

State what the problem is asking for as a solution. The length in feet of 50 meters of cable.

Identify what is given. The cable length in meters. A formula is not always given in a problem of this type. You may have to look up a conversion formula.

Make a plan. Use the conversion formula to convert meters to feet.

Carry out the plan. Convert the cable length from meters to feet.

$50 \text{ m} = \underline{?} \text{ ft}$

The conversion formula is 1 m = 3.281 ft. To convert, multiply by 3.281.

$50 \times 3.281 = 164.05$

Answer the problem and look back. **50 meters is about the same as 164 feet.**

Check by using the other conversion formula 1 ft = 0.3048 m and dividing: 50 m ÷ 0.3048 = 164.04, which is close to 164. So the answer is reasonable. ✓

> **True**Story
>
> "When I'm at work, I try to anticipate the reports and figures that my boss is going to need. One day, as I was flying to our corporate office for a meeting with the CEO, I thought of a new way to measure our progress. I didn't have anything to write on, so I did my calculations on a newspaper that I found in the seatback pocket. In the meeting, the CEO asked me how I would measure progress, so I pulled out my newspaper and explained my idea. He was really impressed! Having my calculations ready at that meeting made a huge difference in my career."

Make a List or a Table

If a problem supplies a large amount of information, putting it in a list or a table can be a very helpful strategy. As you saw earlier, this strategy is often used in combination with the strategy of finding a pattern, but it may be used on its own.

> **A client needs an air conditioner that will cool four rooms and a hallway. The rooms are 12 ft by 13 ft, 12 ft by 11 ft, 13 ft by 18 ft, and 8 ft by 10 ft, and the hallway is 6 ft by 25 ft. A multiple-room air conditioner can cool an area of up to 800 square feet. Will this air conditioner be powerful enough to cool the client's space?**

State what the problem is asking for as a solution. **Whether an air conditioner is the right size for a space.**

Identify what is given. **The dimensions of the space that needs air conditioning; the area that the air conditioner can cool.**

(continued on next page)

Make a plan. Because the information is about several rooms, organize the dimensions and areas in a list or table. Then find the total area. If the total area is less than or equal to 800 square feet, the air conditioner will work. If it is greater than 800 square feet, the air conditioner is not powerful enough for the space.

Carry out the plan. List each room in a table. Number the rooms to help you keep track of the information. Record the dimensions of each room and find its area. Then find the sum of the areas.

Room or Hallway	Dimensions	Area (Length × Width)
1	13 ft by 12 ft	13 × 12 = 156
2	12 ft by 11 ft	12 × 11 = 132
3	18 ft by 13 ft	18 × 13 = 234
4	10 ft by 8 ft	10 × 8 = 80
5	25 ft by 6 ft	25 × 6 = 150
		Total: 752

752 < 800, the space that an air conditioner can cool.

Answer the problem and look back. The total area of the space is 752 sq ft, so the air conditioner will cool the entire space.

Check whether your answer is reasonable by sketching each room, including the dimensions. Be sure that you don't miss one of the rooms listed in the original problem. Although they are probably connected in the actual building, draw a separate rectangle for each room. Then find the area of each room and add the areas to find the total.

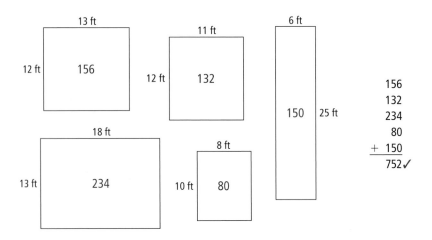

In looking back on this problem, you may have found that you prefer to make the sketch before writing the table, or that you prefer to make the sketch but did not need the table. Many of the problem-solving strategies overlap, and you can choose the strategy that works best for you as well as for the given information.

Solve a Simpler Problem

Some problems may involve very large numbers or numbers with several decimal places. If so, using smaller numbers or an estimate is an effective strategy. If a problem has many different conditions, perhaps you can look at just a few of them to start with. A simpler version of the problem may tell you what process to use or help you know what to expect as a solution.

> A help desk specialist has 4 different requests for service to answer. In how many different orders can she answer them?

State what the problem is asking for as a solution. The number of different ways that 4 requests can be ordered.

Identify what is given. There are 4 requests. It might help to label them A, B, C, and D.

Make a plan. This problem might seem confusing at first. Try looking at a simpler version of the problem. Test the number of possible orders for only 1, 2, or 3 requests, and see whether that can help. Keep a list of the results for the smaller numbers and look for a pattern.

Carry out the plan. If there is only one request for service, there is only one possible order. If there are two requests, there are two possible orders. It seems that the number of orders <u>could</u> be the same as the number of requests, but test the number of orders for 3 requests to see whether that is true.

Number of Requests	Possible Orders	Number of Possible Orders
1	A	1
2	AB, BA	2
3	ABC, ACB, BAC, BCA, CAB, CBA	6

The number of orders does <u>not</u> equal the number of items. Notice that adding the third request has the effect of multiplying the previous number of possible orders by 3 (2 × 3 = 6). A good guess is that adding the fourth request will multiply the number of possible orders by 4. Since 6 × 4 = 24, the number of possible orders is 24.

Answer the problem and look back. The help desk specialist can answer 4 requests in 24 different orders.

Check your answer by writing out all the ways to order the 4 requests, starting with ABCD, ABDC, BACD, BADC, etc. Count the ways to see that 24 is correct. ✓

Guess and Check

Sometimes you don't see a straightforward way to solve a problem, and there is no pattern in the given information, either. This is a good time to take a guess at an answer and see whether it works. If it doesn't, adjust your guess and try again.

> The area of a rectangular room is 216 sq ft and its perimeter is 60 ft. What are the dimensions of the room?

State what the problem is asking for as a solution. **The dimensions of a room.**

Identify what is given. **The area of the room; the perimeter of the room.**

Make a plan. **Make a sketch to help understand the given information.**

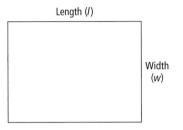

Length (*l*)

Width (*w*)

The area is $lw = 216$.

The perimeter is $2l + 2w = 60$.

Since there are two dimensions that you don't know, guessing some values and checking to see whether they work in both equations is a good strategy.

Carry out the plan. **Organize your guesses in a table. Because you know the product of the dimensions is 216, your guesses for the length and width should be factors of 216. Choose one factor for the length, and then find the corresponding width.**

Guess	Length	Width	Perimeter	Comments
1	108	$216 \div 108 = 2$	$2 \times 108 + 2 \times 2 = 220$	Too high, and strange shape for a room.
2	24	$216 \div 24 = 9$	$2 \times 24 + 2 \times 9 = 66$	Too high
3	18	$216 \div 18 = 12$	$2 \times 18 + 2 \times 12 = 60$	Just right

Answer the problem and look back. **The dimensions of the room are 18 ft by 12 ft.**

In looking back, notice that both a sketch and a table were used in the solution. It is very common to use more than one strategy for a single problem. Check your answers by multiplying the dimensions to verify the area: $18 \cdot 12 = 216$. Add the four side lengths to verify the perimeter: $18 + 12 + 18 + 12 = 60$. ✓

Exercises

Answers and explanations are located at the end of the unit.

1. A technician visits 5 different clients in one day. The technician leaves the office and travels 5 miles to the first client, then twice that distance to the second client, then 3 miles to the third client's office, which is 11 miles from the technician's office. The technician then travels 7 miles to the fourth client, 2 miles to the fifth, and 12 miles back to the office. How far did the technician travel altogether?

2. A rental company charges $39.99 to rent a portable generator for 1 day, $49.99 to rent it for 2 days, and $59.99 to rent it for 3 days, and so on. What does the company charge for a 5-day rental?

3. A patient's bill is reduced by an insurance payment of $126. The patient pays her portion at the time of the appointment and receives a $20 discount. The original bill also included a $7 parking fee. If the amount the patient pays is $56, what was the original total medical bill, not including parking?

4. A medication label states that the medication should be stored at a temperature between 2°C and 8°C. Use the formula $F = \frac{9}{5}C + 32$ to find these temperatures in degrees Fahrenheit.

5. A computer network specialist has 6 computers in a network. How many different connections between the computers are there?

6. An electrical technician makes $22 per hour on a project. He pays $41 plus $4 per hour to rent some special equipment for the job. How many hours must the technician work in order to break even?

Summary

To solve problems, you may choose to use one or more of these strategies. Deciding on which strategy to use depends on what the problem gives and what it is asking for as a solution.

- Find a pattern: The problem describes a relationship between pairs of numbers.
- Make a picture or diagram: The problem involves distances, objects, geometric figures or other items that can be better understood with a visual.
- Work backward: The problem gives the end result and you are asked to find the starting value.
- Use a formula or rule: The problem asks for a quantity that can be found by using an existing formula or rule.
- Make a list or a table: The problem gives a large amount of information that would make more sense if it were organized.
- Solve a simpler problem: The problem is complex, has many conditions, or has numbers that are very large and difficult to compute.
- Guess and check: The problem doesn't show a pattern, and there is no straightforward way to find the solution.

To solve word problems, you can follow a five-step problem solving process.

- State what the problem is asking for as a solution.
- Identify the information that is given.
- Make a plan.
- Carry out the plan.
- Answer the question and look back.

Solving Problems Involving Decimals, Ratios, and Proportions

Decimals

Any time you have worked with money, you have used decimals. In a money amount such as $19.76, the whole number (19) represents the dollar amount, and the decimal part (.76) represents the cents. Decimals are needed to express numbers that are between whole numbers.

Decimals have the same purpose as fractions; for example, 25 cents is $\frac{1}{4}$ of dollar and can be written as 0.25. Many people prefer to work with decimals. You might not know that $\frac{494}{25}$ is a little less than 20, but if you write $\frac{494}{25}$ in its decimal form, 19.76, it is easy to see that it is.

As you saw in Unit 9, operations with decimals are very similar to operations with whole numbers. Operations with decimals are often easier to complete than operations with fractions, because decimal operations do not need the extra step of conversion that is required by fraction operations. For example, to add $\frac{3}{8}$ and $2\frac{1}{4}$, you must find the lowest common denominator for both fractions. However, if you write the numbers as 0.375 and 2.25, all you have to do is line up the decimal points and add the numbers as if they were whole numbers.

> **Points to Remember**
>
> A decimal number has two parts, separated by a decimal point. The digits to the left of the decimal point are ones, tens, hundreds, thousands, and so on infinitely. The digits to the right of the deci-mal point are tenths, hundredths, thousandths, and so on infinitely.

Fractions

$$\frac{3}{8} + 2\frac{1}{4} = \frac{3}{8} + 2\frac{1 \times 2}{4 \times 2} = \frac{3}{8} + 2\frac{2}{8} = 2 + \frac{3 + 2}{8} = 2\frac{5}{8}$$

Decimals

$$
\begin{array}{r}
{}^{1} \\
0.375 \\
+\ 2.250 \\
\hline
2.625
\end{array}
$$

Building **Background**

To add or subtract decimal numbers:

- Line up the decimal points.

- Insert trailing zeros, if necessary, so that all numbers have the same number of decimal places.

- Add or subtract as for whole numbers. Regroup, if necessary.

- Place the decimal point in the answer directly below the decimal point in the numbers.

To multiply decimal numbers:

- Multiply the numbers as if they were whole numbers.

- Count the total number of digits that are to the right of the decimal point in *both* factors.

- Place the decimal point in the whole number product so that it has the same number of digits to the right of the decimal point as counted above. Add leading zeros, if necessary.

To divide decimal numbers:

- Set up the long division problem.

- Count the number of digits to the right of the decimal point in the divisor.

- Move the decimal point in the dividend the number of places found in the divisor.

- Place the decimal point in the quotient directly above the new decimal point in the dividend.

- Divide as if there were no decimal points.

- Add trailing zeros in the dividend, if necessary, to find the answer.

When you solve problems involving decimals, you may use the strategies already described. However, sometimes the problems involve only one or two mathematical operations. So, instead of a strategy, you need to choose which operation to perform to find the answer. This process is sometimes called *Choose the Correct Operation.*

> **A patient sees three specialists in a clinic and asks to have just one bill sent. The specialists' bills are $256.50, $353, and $119.65. What is the total bill?**

State what the problem is asking for as a solution. **The total amount of the bill.**

Identify what is given. **The costs of three bills.**

Make a plan. **Choose the correct operation.** *Add* **the three amounts together.**

Carry out the plan.

Line up the numbers on the decimal points. Insert two 0's after 353.

Add each column. Regroup as needed.

$$
\begin{array}{r}
256.50 \\
353.00 \\
+\ 119.65 \\
\end{array}
$$

$$
\begin{array}{r}
{\scriptstyle 1\ 1\ 1} \\
256.50 \\
353.00 \\
+\ 119.65 \\
\hline
729.15 \\
\end{array}
$$

(continued on next page)

Answer the problem and look back. The patient's total bill is $729.15.

Check by working backward, and subtracting: 729.15 − 119.65 = 609.5; 609.5 − 353 = 256.5; 256.5 − 256.50 = 0. ✓

> The contractor's cost for an outlet box is $34.76. A contractor buys 5 outlet boxes for a project, and marks up the price by 10%, or 1.1 of the cost. What is the customer's cost for the outlet boxes?

State what the problem is asking for as a solution. How much the customer pays.

Identify what is given. The contractor's cost; the number of boxes bought; the markup price.

Make a plan. Choose the correct operation. *Multiply* to find the total cost of the 5 boxes. Then *multiply* that cost by the markup amount.

Carry out the plan.

Multiply the cost of one box by 5.

$$
\begin{array}{r}
\overset{2\ 3\ 3}{34.76} \leftarrow \text{2 decimal places} \\
\times \quad 5 \leftarrow \text{0 decimal places} \\
\hline
173.80 \leftarrow \text{2 decimal places}
\end{array}
$$

To mark up the price by 10%, multiply 173.80 by 1.1.

$$
\begin{array}{r}
173.80 \leftarrow \text{2 decimal places} \\
\times \quad 1.1 \leftarrow \text{1 decimal places} \\
\hline
17380 \\
17380 \\
\hline
191.180 \leftarrow \text{3 decimal places}
\end{array}
$$

Answer the problem and look back. The cost to the customer is $191.18.

Check by solving with another method. Find the total cost of 1 box, including markup: 34.76 × 1.1 = 38.236. Then multiply that cost by 5 boxes: 38.236 × 5 = 191.18. ✓

> The bill for a patient's dental procedure is $425.94. The patient's insurance company will pay $319. How much does the patient pay?

State what the problem is asking for as a solution. The amount the patient pays.

Identify what is given. The cost of the procedure; the amount the insurance company pays.

Make a plan. Choose the correct operation. *Subtract* the insurance payment from the cost of the procedure.

Carry out the plan. Find the *difference* between the amounts.

Line up the numbers on the decimal points. Insert two 0's after 319.

$$
\begin{array}{r}
425.94 \\
- \ 319.00 \\
\hline
\end{array}
$$

Subtract each column. Regroup as needed.

$$
\begin{array}{r}
\overset{1\ 15}{42\cancel{5}.94} \\
- \ 319.00 \\
\hline
106.94
\end{array}
$$

Answer the problem and look back. The patient pays $106.94.

Check whether the answer is reasonable by estimating: 425.94 rounds to 430, and 319 rounds to 320. Subtract 430 − 320 = 110, which is close to 106.94. So, the answer is reasonable. ✓

> An HVAC technician has 26.25 ft of flexible ducting. If equal lengths of ducting are used for three projects, how much can be used for each project?

State what the problem is asking for as a solution. The ducting needed for each project.

Identify what is given. The total amount of ducting; the number of projects; the same amount of ducting at each project.

Make a plan. Choose the correct operation. *Divide* to separate the ducting into 3 equal pieces.

Carry out the plan. Divide the number of feet of ducting by 3.

$$
\begin{array}{r}
8.75 \\
3\overline{)26.25} \\
\underline{24} \\
22 \\
\underline{21} \\
15 \\
\underline{15} \\
0
\end{array}
$$

← Place the decimal point in the answer above the point in the dividend.

Multiply 3 × 8 = 24. Write 8 in the answer. →

Multiply 3 × 7 = 21. Write 7 in the answer. →

Multiply 3 × 5 = 15. Write 5 in the answer. →

Answer the problem and look back. Each project uses 8.75 ft of ducting.

Check by working backward. Multiply the quotient by the number of projects: 3 × 8.75 = 26.25. ✓

Ratios

A dentist's office assistant records that 45 of the 80 children seen in the practice have cavities. Comparing two quantities such as the number of children with cavities to the total number of children in the practice is an example of a ratio. A **ratio** is a comparison of two numbers. Ratios are written three different ways. The ratio that compares *a* and *b* can be written as:

$$\frac{a}{b} \qquad\qquad a : b \qquad\qquad a \text{ to } b$$

> Write the ratio 45 to 80 in two different ways.

$$45 : 80 \qquad\qquad \frac{45}{80}$$

A ratio is in *simplest form* when the numbers in the ratio are both integers and they have no common factors. Because a ratio can be written as a fraction, use the same process for simplifying a ratio as you did for simplifying a fraction. For example, both numbers in the ratio 45 to 80 have a factor of 5. Dividing both numbers by 5 gives the ratio in simplest form, 9 to 16. This can also be written as $9 : 16$ or $\frac{9}{16}$.

List the factors of 24:   1, 2, 3, 4, 6, 8, 12, and 24.

List the factors of 36:   1, 2, 3, 4, 6, 9, 12, 18, and 36.

The common factors of 24 and 36 are 1, 2, 3, 4, 6, and 12.

The greatest common factor (GCF) is 12.

Divide both numbers by 12.   24 ÷ 12 = 2 and 36 ÷ 12 = 3

The simplest form of 24 to 36 is 2 to 3.

Points to Remember

To *simplify* a ratio, find the greatest common factor (GCF) of the two numbers in the ratio.

1. List all the factors of each number.
2. List the factors that the numbers have in common.
3. The GCF is the greatest of the factors listed in step 2.

Two ratios are equal if they have the same simplest form. They may also be called **equivalent ratios.** In order to write a ratio that is equal to a given ratio, you can multiply or divide both numbers in the ratio by the same factor.

Write each ratio in simplest form.

To write 35 : 80 in simplest form, divide each number by their GCF, 5.

35 : 80 = 7 : 16

To write 14 : 32 in simplest form, divide each number by their GCF, 2.

14 : 32 = 7 : 16

The ratios are equal.

Be careful when working with ratios. Although they can be written as fractions, there are some important differences. A fraction always represents a comparison between a part and a whole, and uses the words *out of.* A ratio may also compare two parts of the same whole, and uses the word *to.* For example, using simpler numbers, suppose there are 10 clinic patients, consisting of 3 males and 7 females.

Fraction is always: $\dfrac{\text{part}}{\text{whole}}$ → $\dfrac{3}{10}$ → 3 males out of 10 patients

Ratio can be: $\dfrac{\text{part}}{\text{whole}}$ → $\dfrac{3}{10}$ → 3 males to 10 patients

    $\dfrac{\text{part}}{\text{part}}$ → $\dfrac{3}{7}$ → 3 males to 7 females

    $\dfrac{\text{whole}}{\text{part}}$ → $\dfrac{10}{3}$ → 10 patients to 3 males

Also, you can compare ratios only if they represent similar quantities. It makes sense to compare the ratios of male to female patients at two different clinics, but not to compare the ratio of male to female patients at one clinic to the ratio of insured to uninsured patients at another. For example, using simpler numbers, suppose Clinic A has 5 males and 8 females. Clinic B has 6 males and 8 females. Of the 14 people at Clinic B, there are 2 uninsured patients and 12 insured patients.

Clinic A	Clinic B		Clinic A	Clinic B
$\dfrac{\text{males}}{\text{females}} \rightarrow \dfrac{5}{8}$	$\dfrac{\text{males}}{\text{females}} \rightarrow \dfrac{6}{8}$		$\dfrac{\text{males}}{\text{females}} \rightarrow \dfrac{5}{8}$	$\dfrac{\text{uninsured}}{\text{insured}} \rightarrow \dfrac{2}{12}$

Because these ratios have the same units and because $\frac{6}{8} > \frac{5}{8}$, you can say that Clinic B has a greater ratio of males to females than Clinic A.

You cannot compare these two ratios because they don't have the same units. Knowing the number of insured does not tell you how many of those insured are male or female.

If it makes sense to compare two ratios, write each one in fraction form. If they have the same denominator, you can compare their numerators. If not, then write the ratios with a common denominator.

Points to Remember

To find a *common denominator* of two fractions, list multiples of the denominators of the fractions. Then look for a number that appears on both lists.

A computer installer spent 4 hours out of 15 work hours on repair calls one week. The next week the technician spent 3 hours out of 10 work hours on repair calls. Which ratio is greater?

State what the problem is asking for as a solution. The greater ratio of time spent on repair calls.

Identify what is given. Two ratios indicating hours spent on repair calls.

Make a plan. Write each ratio as a fraction. Then compare the fractions by writing them with a common denominator.

Carry out the plan.

Write each ratio as a fraction: $\frac{4}{15}$ and $\frac{3}{10}$.

Find a common denominator. Use 30, because 30 is a multiple of both 15 and 10.

Write each ratio with the common denominator.

$$\frac{4}{15} = \frac{4 \times 2}{15 \times 2} = \frac{8}{30} \text{ and } \frac{3}{10} = \frac{3 \times 3}{10 \times 3} = \frac{9}{30}$$

Because 9 is greater than 8, then $\frac{9}{30} > \frac{8}{30}$.

Answer the problem and look back. The ratio $\frac{3}{10}$ is greater than $\frac{4}{15}$.

Check by writing the fractions as decimals and comparing: $\frac{3}{10} = 3 \div 10 = 0.333...$ and $\frac{4}{15} = 4 \div 15 = 0.2666...$. Because 0.333 is greater than 0.2666, then it's reasonable to say that $\frac{3}{10}$ is greater than $\frac{4}{15}$. ✓

Unit Rates. A **rate** is a special type of ratio in which the two quantities have different units. In earlier examples, you have seen the cost per outlet box and the amount of ducting per project. Both of those are rates, because they consist of two different units. Rates are used very often in everyday life. You have probably heard of the annual percentage rate charged by a credit card or loan company, for example.

A **unit rate** is a rate whose denominator is 1. Some unit rates that you have probably used are miles per hour and heartbeats per minute. To write any rate as a unit rate, write the rate as an equivalent rate with a denominator of 1.

> **An IV order is for 1,000 cc of solution every 8 hours. Write this as a unit rate.**

State what the problem is asking for as a solution. A unit rate.

Identify what is given. The rate: 1,000 cc for 8 hours.

Make a plan. Write the rate as a fraction and simplify.

Carry out the plan. Write the amount of solution over the number of hours. Divide the numerator and denominator by the GCF, 8.

$$\frac{1000 \text{ cc}}{8 \text{ hours}} = \frac{1000 \text{ cc} \div 8}{8 \text{ hours} \div 8} = \frac{125 \text{ cc}}{1 \text{ hour}} = 125 \text{ cc per hour}$$

Answer the problem and look back. 125 cc per hour

Check by working backward. Multiply the rate by the number of hours:
125 cc per hour × 8 hours = 1000 cc. ✓

Notice that to write a unit rate, you divide the numerator and the denominator by the same number. Because you want the denominator to be 1, this is the same as dividing the numerator by the denominator.

When you want to compare two rates, write each rate as a unit rate. If the rates do not use the same unit, first rewrite them so they do.

> **A corrections officer walks 6 miles in 2 hours one morning, then walks 2 miles in 30 minutes after lunch. Which rate is faster?**

State what the problem is asking for as a solution. The faster rate of walking.

Identify what is given. The walking rate for the morning; the walking rate for the afternoon.

Make a plan. Write each rate as a unit rate. Then compare.

Carry out the plan.

Write each rate as a unit rate, using hours as the denominator unit.

Morning: $\quad \dfrac{6 \text{ miles}}{2 \text{ hours}} = \dfrac{6 \text{ miles} \div 2}{2 \text{ hours} \div 2} = \dfrac{3 \text{ miles}}{1 \text{ hour}} = 3 \text{ miles per hour}$

Afternoon: $\quad \dfrac{2 \text{ miles}}{30 \text{ minutes}} = \dfrac{2 \text{ miles} \times 2}{30 \text{ minutes} \times 2} = \dfrac{4 \text{ miles}}{1 \text{ hour}} = 4 \text{ miles per hour}$

Answer the problem and look back. The afternoon rate is faster.

Check by solving with another method. Write the morning rate in the units (30 minutes) of the second rate, and then compare number of miles. First, write 2 hours as 2 × 60 minutes = 120 minutes. Then simplify the morning rate to have 30 min as the denominator: $\dfrac{6 \text{ miles}}{120 \text{ minutes}} = \dfrac{6 \text{ miles} \div 4}{120 \text{ minutes} \div 4} = \dfrac{1.5 \text{ miles}}{30 \text{ minutes}} =$
1.5 mi per 30 min. The afternoon rate is 2 mi per 30 min, which is faster. ✓

Putting It **Together**

Unit Pricing

A very common use of unit rates is comparing unit prices. Is the price per item really lower if you buy a "Giant Economy Size" than if you buy a smaller size? You can decide by finding the unit price for each size.

- **A paralegal assistant can buy 30 file folders for $13.11 or 25 file folders for $10.09. Which is a better price?**

  State what the problem is asking for as a solution. The better price for folders.

  Identify what is given. Two rates indicating price and number of folders.

  Make a plan. Find the price per folder for each size package. Then compare.

  Carry out the plan. Notice that "per folder" means that the number of folders is in the *denominator* of the rate, even though it is given first in the problem.

  $$\frac{\$13.11}{30 \text{ folders}} = \$0.437 \text{ per folder} \qquad \frac{\$10.09}{25 \text{ folders}} = \$0.4036 \text{ per folder}$$

  0.4036 is less than 0.437.

  Answer the problem and look back. The smaller size (25 folders) has a slightly lower price per folder.

  Check by solving with another method. Use another common denominator ($30 \times 25 = 750$), and then compare the numerators: $\frac{\$13.11 \times 25}{30 \text{ folders} \times 25} = \frac{\$327.75}{750 \text{ folders}}$ and $\frac{\$10.09 \times 30}{25 \text{ folders} \times 30} = \frac{\$302.70}{750 \text{ folders}}$. The rate for 25 folders is less expensive. ✓

Proportions

If you are paid by the hour, your pay is *proportional* to the number of hours that you work. A **proportion** is an equation showing that two ratios or two rates are equal. The ratios in a proportion are usually written in fraction form: $\frac{a}{b} = \frac{c}{d}$.

> Can the ratios $\frac{105}{3}$ and $\frac{350}{10}$ be used to write a proportion?

Write each ratio in simplest form.

$$\frac{105}{3} = \frac{105 \div 3}{3 \div 3} = \frac{35}{1} \qquad\qquad \frac{350}{10} = \frac{350 \div 10}{10 \div 10} = \frac{35}{1}$$

The ratios are equal, so they can be used to write a proportion: $\frac{105}{3} = \frac{350}{10}$.

The numbers in a proportion are called the *terms* of the proportion. When one term of a proportion is not given, you can solve the proportion to find the missing value. One way to do this is to use equal ratios.

> Solve the proportion $\frac{15}{3} = \frac{c}{9}$ using equal ratios.

Rewrite the ratios using 9 for the common denominator.

$$\frac{15 \times 3}{3 \times 3} = \frac{c}{9}$$

Simplify.

$$\frac{45}{9} = \frac{c}{9}$$

Since the ratios are equal and the denominators are equal, the numerators are equal.

$$45 = c$$

Another strategy for solving proportions is to use **cross products.** You find the cross products of a proportion by multiplying the numerator of one side of the proportion by the denominator of the other. To understand this method, look at a proportion that you know is true, such as $\frac{5}{10} = \frac{2}{4}$. The cross products are 5×4 and 10×2, which you know equal each other. In general, if $\frac{a}{b} = \frac{c}{d}$, then $a \cdot d = b \cdot c$. This process is called cross-multiplying or finding the cross products.

$$\frac{5}{10} \diagdown \frac{2}{4} \qquad 5 \times 4 = 10 \times 2 \qquad 20 = 20 \qquad \frac{a}{b} \diagdown \frac{c}{d} \qquad a \cdot d = b \cdot c$$

As you learned in Unit 9, there are several different symbols for multiplication. When working with variables, avoid using the symbol $\times$, as it can be mistaken for the letter x. Other ways to write $5 \times z$, for example, are $5(z)$, $5 \cdot z$, and just $5z$.

Solve the same proportion $\frac{15}{3} = \frac{c}{9}$ that was in the last example, but this time use cross products.

$$\frac{15}{3} = \frac{c}{9}$$

Cross-multiply. $\quad \rightarrow \quad 15 \cdot 9 = 3c$

Divide both sides by 3. $\quad \rightarrow \quad \dfrac{135}{3} = \dfrac{3c}{3}$

Simplify. $\quad \rightarrow \quad 45 = c$

Solve $\frac{12}{25} = \frac{15}{x}$.

$$\frac{12}{25} = \frac{15}{x}$$

Cross-multiply. $\quad \rightarrow \quad 12x = 25 \cdot 15$

Divide both sides by 12. $\quad \rightarrow \quad \dfrac{12x}{12} = \dfrac{375}{12}$

S implify. $\quad \rightarrow \quad x = 31.25$

Building **Background**

Solving equations with division

To solve proportions using cross products, you will have to solve simple linear equations of the form $ax = b$ for x. The properties of equality allow you to multiply or divide both sides of an equation by the same number without changing the solution.

	General Case	Example
■ Solve the equation for x.	$ax = b$	$3x = 21$
■ Divide both sides of the equation by a, or 3.	$\dfrac{ax}{a} = \dfrac{b}{a}$	$\dfrac{3x}{3} = \dfrac{21}{3}$
■ Simplify each side.	$x = \dfrac{b}{a}$	$x = 7$

■ Depending on the context of the problem, you might want to write $\frac{b}{a}$ as a mixed number, a decimal, or an improper fraction.

Solving Problems

Ratios, rates, and proportions have many practical applications on the job. When you read a problem involving ratios or rates, remember that the word "per" tells you what the denominator of the ratio or rate is.

> A medical assistant takes a patient's pulse. The assistant counts 17 heartbeats in 15 seconds. How many beats per minute is this?

State what the problem is asking for as a solution. The number of beats in a minute.

Identify what is given. The number of beats in 15 seconds.

Make a plan. Write the rate and convert the time to 1 minute.

Carry out the plan. Because the problem specifies "per minute," you know that the units of time are in the denominator of the rate.

Write the rate.	To convert 15 seconds to 60 seconds, multiply by $\frac{4}{4}$.	Simplify.

$$\frac{17 \text{ beats}}{15 \text{ seconds}} = \frac{17 \text{ beats} \times 4}{15 \text{ seconds} \times 4} = \frac{68 \text{ beats}}{60 \text{ seconds}} = 68 \text{ beats per minute}$$

Answer the problem and look back. The rate is 68 beats per minute.

Check by solving with another method. First, find the beats per second.

$\frac{17 \text{ beats} \div 15}{15 \text{ seconds} \div 15} = \frac{1.1333... \text{ beats}}{1 \text{ second}}$. Then, multiply by 60 to find beats per minute:

$\frac{1.333... \text{ beats} \times 60}{1 \text{ second} \times 60} = \frac{68 \text{ beats}}{60 \text{ seconds}} = 68 \text{ beats per minute.}$ ✓

> A medical coding specialist is paid $417.96 for 27 hours of work. A medical office assistant is paid $495.36 for 32 hours of work. Which employee has a greater hourly rate?

State what the problem is asking for as a solution. The employee with the greater hourly rate.

Identify what is given. Two employees and their earnings for certain hours of work.

Make a plan. Change each rate to a unit rate by dividing. Compare the unit rates.

Carry out the plan. Write each rate as a fraction and divide.

$$\frac{\$417.96}{27 \text{ hours}} = \$15.48 \text{ per hour} \qquad \frac{\$495.36}{32 \text{ hours}} = \$15.48 \text{ per hour}$$

$$\$15.48 = \$15.48$$

Answer the problem and look back. The two employees have the same hourly rate.

Check by setting up a proportion and cross-multiplying: $\frac{\$417.96}{27 \text{ hours}} = \frac{\$495.36}{32 \text{ hours}}$. Does $(417.96)(32) = (27)(495.36)$? Yes, because $13{,}374.72 = 13{,}374.72$. ✓

When solving word problems involving proportions, you can usually set up the proportion in more than one way. Be sure that corresponding units are either above one another or directly across from one another. For example, if each ratio in a proportion represents a speed, make sure that the units of time are in corresponding positions.

> A dental assistant can prepare 5 supply trays in 30 minutes. At this rate, how many supply trays can the assistant prepare in 45 minutes?

State what the problem is asking for as a solution. **The number of trays prepared in 45 minutes.**

Identify what is given. **The number of trays (5) prepared in 30 minutes.**

Make a plan. **Set up a proportion and solve for the missing value.**

Carry out the plan.

Write the proportion.

$$\frac{5 \text{ trays}}{30 \text{ minutes}} = \frac{t \text{ trays}}{45 \text{ minutes}}$$

Cross-multiply. $\longrightarrow$ $5 \cdot 45 = 30t$

Divide both sides by 30. $\longrightarrow$ $\dfrac{225}{30} = \dfrac{30t}{30}$

Simplify. $\longrightarrow$ $7.5 = t$

Answer the problem and look back. **The assistant can prepare 7 supply trays in 45 minutes.**

Look back at the result. You need to find the number of trays, but the value of *t* is 7.5. Because a half of a supply tray is not very useful, round the answer down.

Points to Remember

Some problems ask you to find the number of objects, but the object can't be divided into parts. For example, the number of people, cars, light bulbs, dogs, etc., cannot be a fraction or decimal number.

You need to evaluate the mathematical answer to see whether it makes sense in the problem. If it does not, you may have to round either up or down to answer the question.

> A parking lot has 3 security lights on every 45 ft of its perimeter. If the total perimeter of the lot is 500 ft, how many lights are there?

State what the problem is asking for as a solution. **The number of lights in the parking lot.**

Identify what is given. **The perimeter of the lot; the number of lights (3) for every 45 feet.**

Make a plan. **Set up a proportion and solve for the missing value.**

Carry out the plan.

Set up the proportion.

$$\frac{3 \text{ lights}}{45 \text{ feet}} = \frac{x \text{ lights}}{500 \text{ feet}}$$

Cross-multiply. $\longrightarrow$ $3 \cdot 500 = 45x$

Divide both sides by 45. $\longrightarrow$ $\dfrac{1500}{45} = \dfrac{45x}{45}$

Simplify. $\longrightarrow$ $33\dfrac{1}{3} = x$

Answer the problem and look back. **There are 33 lights in the parking lot.**

Look back at the result. You cannot have a third of a light. Without seeing a sketch of the parking lot, you can't know exactly how many lights are on the perimeter. So round down to 33.

Scale Drawings. Have you ever looked at a map with a "You Are Here" label at a superstore or a shopping mall? These floor plans are called **scale drawings.** The **scale** is the ratio of the size of the drawing to the actual size of the object. A scale such as 1 in. : 50 ft may be written on the scale drawing. The first number represents a distance on the scale drawing or map, and the second represents the actual distance.

Proportions are used when working with scale drawings. Just as you work with other proportion problems, make sure that corresponding units are in corresponding positions.

TrueStory

"I'm an electrical contractor, and I do both new construction and small remodels. No matter what size the project, I use math each and every day on the job. It is a vital tool that I use constantly. For big projects, I start by reading blueprints that show where to put wires, electrical equipment, and outlets for plugs. Since the blueprints are drawn to scale, if any part needs to be changed, I can scale the drawing to find the right measurements and make the adjustments. It's an important skill to have at any level of electrical work."

> The scale on a map of a store is 1 in. : 10 ft. If the actual distance from the cashier stand to the exit is 36 ft, what is the distance on the map?

State what the problem is asking for as a solution. The map distance from the cashier stand to the exit.

Identify what is given. The scale of the map; the actual distance.

Make a plan. Set up a proportion and solve for the missing value.

Carry out the plan.

Set up the proportion.

$$\frac{1 \text{ in.}}{10 \text{ ft}} = \frac{x \text{ in.}}{36 \text{ ft}}$$

Cross-multiply. $\rightarrow \quad 1 \cdot 36 = 10x$

Divide both sides by 10. $\rightarrow \quad \dfrac{36}{10} = \dfrac{10x}{10}$

Simplify. $\rightarrow \quad 3.6 = x$

Answer the problem and look back. On the map, the distance is 3.6 in.

Check by substituting the value of x into the right ratio, and simplify:

$$\frac{3.6 \text{ in.}}{36 \text{ ft}} = \frac{3.6 \text{ in.} \div 3.6}{36 \text{ ft} \div 3.6} = \frac{1 \text{ in.}}{10 \text{ ft}}.$$

You get the scale of the map. ✓

An HVAC technician is planning to install a room air conditioner that is recommended for areas that are 180 to 270 sq ft. The technician is using blueprints of the room. On the blueprints, the dimensions of the room are $2\frac{3}{4}$ in. by $4\frac{1}{2}$ in. Is this air conditioner the right size for the room?

State what the problem is asking for as a solution. Whether the air conditioner can cool the amount of space.

Identify what is given. The dimensions of the room; the scale on the blueprint; the dimensions of the room on the blueprint.

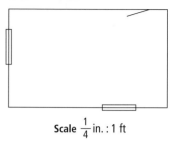

Scale $\frac{1}{4}$ in. : 1 ft

Make a plan. Find the actual dimensions of the room by using proportions. Then find the area of the room. Compare the area to the air conditioner's range.

Carry out the plan.

You may find it easier to work with decimals than fractions. Write $\frac{1}{4}$ as 0.5, $2\frac{3}{4}$ as 2.75, and $4\frac{1}{2}$ as 4.5.

Set up a proportion for the width.
$$\frac{0.25 \text{ in.}}{1 \text{ ft}} = \frac{2.75 \text{ in.}}{x \text{ ft}}$$

Cross-multiply. $\longrightarrow$ $0.25x = 2.75$

Divide both sides by 0.25. $\longrightarrow$ $\frac{0.25x}{0.25} = \frac{2.75}{0.25}$

Simplify. $\longrightarrow$ $x = 11$

The actual width of the room is 11 ft.

Set up a proportion for the length.
$$\frac{0.25 \text{ ft}}{1 \text{ ft}} = \frac{4.5 \text{ in.}}{x \text{ ft}}$$

Cross-multiply. $\longrightarrow$ $0.25x = 4.5$

Divide both sides by 0.25. $\longrightarrow$ $\frac{0.25x}{0.25} = \frac{4.5}{0.25}$

Simplify. $\longrightarrow$ $x = 18$

The actual length of the room is 18 ft.

Find the area of the room. $\qquad$ 11 ft $\times$ 18 ft = 198 ft²

Answer the problem and look back. Since 198 ft² is between 180 ft² and 270 ft², the air conditioner is the right size for the room.

Check by working backward to verify the width of the room. Divide each room area (180 ft²; 270 ft²) that the air conditioner can cool by the length (18 ft) of the room. Determine whether the actual width (11 ft) of the room is within the range of the air conditioner. Smallest room to cool: 180 ft² ÷ 18 ft = 10 ft. Largest room to cool: 270 ft² ÷ 18 ft = 15 ft. The width of the room must be between 10 ft and 15 ft in order for the air conditioner to work. The actual width is 11 ft, so it will work. ✓

Exercises

Answers and explanations are given at the end of the unit.

7. One brand of a heart medication costs $36.35 to fill, and another brand costs $28.68. What is the difference between the prices?

8. The cost of renting a truck for 4 days is $165.91. What is the cost of renting the truck for one day?

9. A medical assistant is planning an exercise program for a patient. The patient uses 7.9 calories per minute on an exercise bicycle and 11.3 calories per minute on a stair machine. If the patient exercises for 15 minutes on each machine, how many calories does the patient use in total?

10. Write the ratio 4 to 19 in three different ways.

Write each ratio in simplest form.

11. $\dfrac{9}{114}$

12. $\dfrac{16}{100}$

13. 3.8 to 0.75

14. 244 adult patients to 56 pediatric patients

15. The price of 25 ft of flat speaker wire is $79.99. What is the unit price?

16. A truck travels 200 miles in 3 hours. What is the speed in miles per hour?

Solve each proportion.

17. $\dfrac{40}{18} = \dfrac{15}{c}$

18. $\dfrac{a}{21} = \dfrac{2}{3}$

19. $\dfrac{x}{1.10} = \dfrac{4}{0.8}$

20. $\dfrac{1}{500} = \dfrac{2\frac{1}{4}}{d}$

21. A medical assistant draws 18 vials of blood in 2 hours. At this rate, how many vials of blood can the assistant draw in 5 hours?

22. A doctor orders 200 mg of a medication every 8 hours for an infant who weighs 15.4 lb. What amount would the doctor order for a child who weighs 20 lb?

23. An electrical blueprint calls for a wire to go around the perimeter of a room. On the blueprint, the room is a rectangle that is $3\frac{1}{2}$ in. by 4 in. The scale of the blueprint is $\frac{1}{4}$ in. : 1 ft. How much wire is needed for the perimeter?

Unit Summary

- To solve word problems, you can follow a five-step problem solving process.
  1. State what the problem is asking for as a solution.
  2. Identify the information that is given.
  3. Make a plan.
  4. Carry out the plan.
  5. Answer the question and look back.

- Because ratios involve the same unit but rates have quantities with different units, pay close attention to the units used and what each term represents.

- Some problem-solving strategies include:
  - Find a pattern
  - Make a picture or diagram
  - Work backward
  - Use a formula or rule
  - Make a list or a table
  - Solve a simpler problem
  - Guess and check

- To solve a proportion, you can use cross-multiplication or equivalent ratios. When solving problems with proportions, be sure that the corresponding units are either above one another or directly across from one another.

Important Terms

How well do you know these terms? Look them up in the glossary if you need help remembering them.

five-step problem solving process

ratio

equivalent ratios

rate

unit rate

proportion

cross products

scale drawing

scale

Answer Solutions to Exercises

1. *State what the problem is asking for as a solution.* The number of miles the technician traveled.

Identify what is given. The distances from the office to clients and between clients.

Make a plan. Use the strategy *Make a Diagram*. Then add the distances.

Carry out the plan. The diagram does not have to be to scale, or show any details other than the distances. Each point represents a client and each line represents a distance.

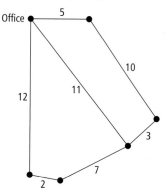

Add the lengths of the sides: $5 + 10 + 3 + 7 + 2 + 12 = 39$.

Answer the problem and look back. The total distance traveled is 39 miles.

In looking back, notice that the distance from the third client's office to the technician's office was extraneous information. Check by working backward: $39 - 12 = 27$; $27 - 2 = 25$; $25 - 7 = 18$; $18 - 3 = 15$; $15 - 10 = 5$; $5 - 5 = 0$.

2. *State what the problem is asking for as a solution.* The cost of renting a portable generator for 5 days.

Identify what is given. The cost for renting for 1, 2, and 3 days.

Make a plan. Use the strategy *Find a Pattern*. Look at the costs and find a pattern for the prices of the first three days. Then continue the pattern to 5 days.

Carry out the plan. Use a table to organize the information.

Day	1	2	3	4	5
Rental Cost	39.99	49.99	59.99	?	?

For each day, another $10 is added to the cost. Continue the pattern for Day 4 and Day 5 by adding $10 to the previous day's cost. The rental cost for 5 days is $59.99 + 10 + 10 = 79.99$.

Answer the problem and look back. A 5-day rental costs $79.99.

Check by estimating. Round the first day cost of $39.99 to $40. Each additional day costs $10. Since there are 4 more days on the rental to get to 5 days, add $4 \cdot 10$ to the first day cost: $40 + (4 \cdot 10) = 80$. The estimate 80 is close to $79.99, so the answer is reasonable.

3. *State what the problem is asking for as a solution.* The amount of the original medical bill, which does not include the parking fee.

Identify what is given. The final amount of the bill; three adjustments to the bill: the insurance payment, the discount, and the parking fee.

Make a plan. Use the strategy *Work Backward.* Start with the amount the patient paid, and subtract the parking payment, add the discount, and add the insurance payment.

Carry out the plan. Start with the patient's payment.

Payment by patient	$56
Subtract the parking fee. It's not a medical cost.	$-\ \ 7$
	$49
Add the discount. It's part of the original bill.	$+\ \ 20$
	$69
Add the insurance payment. It's part of the original bill.	$+\ 126$
	$195

Answer the problem and look back. The original medical bill was $195.

Check by starting with $195 and work to get the patient's payment. The insurance paid $126, so $195 - 126 = 69$. The patient received a $20 discount, so $69 - 20 = 49$. The patient paid a $7 parking fee, so $49 + 7 = 56$.

4. *State what the problem is asking for as a solution.* Two temperatures in degrees Fahrenheit.

Identify what is given. The two temperatures in degrees Celsius; the conversion formula.

Make a plan. Use the strategy *Use a Formula.* Substitute the known values into the formula and solve.

Carry out the plan. Use the formula $F = \frac{9}{5}C + 32$. To use a calculator, write $\frac{9}{5}$ as 1.8. The formula is $F = (1.8)C + 32$. Substitute 2 for C: $F = (1.8)(2) + 32 = 35.6$. Substitute 8 for C: $F = (1.8)(8) + 32 = 46.4$.

Answer the problem and look back. The medication should be stored between 35.6°F and 46.4°F.

Check by working backward. Substitute the values for F into the formula and solve for C.

$$35.6 = (1.8)C + 32 \qquad 46.4 = (1.8)C + 32$$
$$3.2 = (1.8)C \qquad\qquad 14.4 = (1.8)C$$
$$2 = C \qquad\qquad\qquad 8 = C$$

5. *State what the problem is asking for as a solution.* The number of connections between computers.

Identify what is given. 6 computers in the network.

Make a plan. Use the strategies *Solve a Simpler Problem* and *Find a Pattern.* Make a table with the number of connections for 2, 3, 4, and find a pattern. Then extend the pattern to 6 computers.

Carry out the plan. Each point represents a computer and each line represents a connection between computers.

Number of Computers	Diagram	Number of Connections
2		1
3		3 = 1 + 2
4		6 = 1 + 2 + 3
5		10 = 1 + 2 + 3 + 4

Notice that the number of connections for 4 computers is the sum of the whole numbers less than 4, or 1 + 2 + 3. The pattern is the number of connections for n computers is the sum of the whole numbers that are less than n.

So, the number of connections for 6 computers is 1 + 2 + 3 + 4 + 5 = 15.

Answer the problem and look back. There are 15 different ways to connect 6 computers.

Check your answer by drawing a diagram to verify the number of connections.

6. *State what the problem is asking for as a solution.* The number of hours a technician must work in order to pay for equipment rental.

Identify what is given. Earnings per hour; initial rental payment; rental cost per hour.

Make a plan. Use the strategy *Make a List or Table.* In a table, write the amount the technician makes and how much he pays. Then find out how many hours pass before the income is greater than the expenses.

Carry out the plan. List the technician's income and expenses for each number of hours.

Hours Worked	Income	Rental Cost
0	0	4 × 0 + 41 = 41
1	22 × 1 = 22	4 × 1 + 41 = 45
2	22 × 2 = 44	4 × 2 + 41 = 49
3	22 × 3 = 66	4 × 3 + 41 = 53

(continued on next page)

After 3 hours, the amount the technician earns exceeds the amount he pays.

Answer the problem and look back. The technician needs to work 3 hours to pay for the equipment rental.

Look back at the problem. Another way to solve is with the *Guess and Check* strategy, by guessing a number of hours, then finding the corresponding income and expenses.

7. *State what the problem is asking for as a solution.* The difference between two prices.

Identify what is given. The two prices.

Make a plan. Choose the correct operation. *Subtract* the lower price from the higher price.

Carry out the plan.

$$
\begin{array}{r}
36.35 \\
-\,28.68 \\
\hline
7.67
\end{array}
\qquad
\begin{array}{r}
{\scriptstyle 2\ \ 15\ \ 12\ \ 15} \\
\cancel{3}\,\cancel{6}\,.\,\cancel{3}\,\cancel{5} \\
-\,2\ 8\,.\,6\ 8 \\
\hline
7\,.\,6\ 7
\end{array}
$$

Answer the problem and look back. The difference in prices is $7.67.

Check by adding the difference to the lower price: $7.67 + 28.68 = 36.35$.

8. *State what the problem is asking for as a solution.* The cost of renting a truck for one day.

Identify what is given. The cost of renting a truck for four days.

Make a plan. Choose the correct operation. *Divide* the cost for four days by 4.

Carry out the plan. Divide.

$$
\begin{array}{r}
41.477 \\
4\overline{)165.910} \\
\underline{16} \\
05 \\
\underline{4} \\
19 \\
\underline{16} \\
31 \\
\underline{28} \\
30 \\
\underline{28} \\
2
\end{array}
$$

Although the division problem continues, you can stop because you will round to the nearest cent.

Answer the problem and look back. The cost of renting a truck for one day is $41.48.

Check by estimating. Write 165.91 as 160, which is compatible with 4. Divide: $160 \div 4 = 40$, which is close to the answer.

9. *State what the problem is asking for as a solution.* The total number of calories used in 15 minutes when exercising on two machines.

Identify what is given. The number of calories used for one minute on each machine.

Make a plan. Choose the correct operation. *Multiply* the number of calories used for one minute on each machine by 15. *Add* the products.

Carry out the plan. Calories used on the exercise bike: 15 minutes × 7.9 calories per minute = 118.5 calories

Calories used on the stair machine: 15 minutes × 11.3 calories per minute = 169.5 calories

Total: 118.5 + 169.5 = 288

Answer the problem and look back. The patient uses 288 total calories.

Check by solving with another method. Add the number of calories for one minute on each machine, then multiply the sum by 15 min: (7.9 + 11.3) × 15 = 19.2 × 15 = 288.

10. The ratio 4 to 19 can be written as 4 : 19, 4 to 19, and $\frac{4}{19}$.

11. $\dfrac{9}{114} = \dfrac{9 \div 3}{114 \div 3} = \dfrac{3}{38}$

12. $\dfrac{16}{100} = \dfrac{16 \div 4}{100 \div 4} = \dfrac{4}{25}$

13. In simplest form, both terms in a ratio should be whole numbers. Multiply both terms in the ratio 3.8 to 0.75 by 100 to clear the decimal places. The result is 380 to 75. The GCF of 380 and 75 is 5, so divide both terms by 5. The result is 76 to 15.

14. Find the GCF of 244 and 56. The factors of 244 are 1, 2, 4, 61, 122, and 244. The factors of 56 are 1, 2, 4, 7, 8, 14, 28, and 56. The common factors are 1, 2, and 4. The GCF is 4. Divide both terms by 4: 244 ÷ 4 = 61 and 56 ÷ 4 = 14. In simplest form, the ratio is *61 adult patients to 14 pediatric patients.*

15. *State what the problem is asking for as a solution.* The unit price of wire.

    Identify what is given. The price for 25 feet of wire.

    Make a plan. Write the given information as a rate and simplify.

    Carry out the plan. Divide both terms by 25. $\dfrac{\$79.99}{25 \text{ ft}} = \dfrac{\$79.99 \div 25}{25 \text{ ft} \div 25} = \dfrac{\$3.1996}{1 \text{ ft}}$

    Answer the problem and look back. The unit price is about $3.20 per foot.

    Check by multiplying: $3.20 × 25 ft = $80, which is close to $79.99.

16. *State what the problem is asking for as a solution.* The speed in miles per hour.

    Identify what is given. The speed for 3 hours.

    Make a plan. Write the given information as a rate and simplify.

    Carry out the plan. Divide both terms by 3. $\dfrac{200 \text{ miles}}{3 \text{ hours}} = \dfrac{200 \text{ miles} \div 3}{3 \text{ hours} \div 3} = \dfrac{66.666... \text{ miles}}{1 \text{ hour}}$

    Answer the problem and look back. The speed is about 67 miles per hour.

    Check by multiplying: 67 miles per hour × 3 hours = 201 miles, which is close to 200 miles.

17. Write the proportion. $\dfrac{40}{18} = \dfrac{15}{x}$

    Cross-multiply. $40x = 18 \cdot 15$

    Divide both sides by 40. $\dfrac{40x}{40} = \dfrac{270}{40}$

    Simplify. $x = 6.75$

18. Write the proportion.

$$\frac{a}{21} = \frac{2}{3}$$

Cross-multiply.

$$3a = 21 \cdot 2$$

Divide both sides by 3.

$$\frac{3a}{3} = \frac{42}{3}$$

Simplify.

$$a = 14$$

19. Write the proportion.

$$\frac{x}{1.10} = \frac{4}{0.8}$$

Cross-multiply.

$$0.8x = (1.10)(4)$$

Divide both sides by 0.8.

$$\frac{0.8x}{0.8} = \frac{4.4}{0.8}$$

Simplify.

$$x = 5.5$$

20. Write the proportion.

$$\frac{1}{500} = \frac{2\frac{1}{4}}{d}$$

Cross-multiply.

$$1 \cdot d = (500)\left(2\frac{1}{4}\right)$$

Simplify.

$$d = 1{,}125$$

21. *State what the problem is asking for as a solution.* The number of vials drawn in 5 hours.

Identify what is given. The number of vials (18) drawn in 2 hours.

Make a plan. Set up a proportion and solve for the missing value.

Carry out the plan.

Write the proportion.

$$\frac{18 \text{ vials}}{2 \text{ hours}} = \frac{x \text{ vials}}{5 \text{ hours}}$$

Cross-multiply.

$$2x = 18 \cdot 5$$

Divide both sides by 2.

$$\frac{2x}{2} = \frac{90}{2}$$

Simplify.

$$x = 45$$

Answer the problem and look back. Write the answer with units. The assistant can draw 45 blood vials in 5 hours.

Look back at the problem. Another way to solve is to set up the proportion as $\frac{18 \text{ vials}}{x \text{ vials}} = \frac{2 \text{ hours}}{5 \text{ hours}}$. Cross-multiplying this proportion gives the same equation, $18 \cdot 5 = 2x$, as the one above.

22. *State what the problem is asking for as a solution.* The amount of medication needed for a child who weighs 20 lb.

Identify what is given. The medication (200 mg) for a 15.4 lb child.

Make a plan. Set up a proportion and solve for the missing value.

Carry out the plan.

Write the proportion.

$$\frac{200 \text{ mg}}{15.4 \text{ lb}} = \frac{x \text{ mg}}{20 \text{ lb}}$$

Cross-multiply.

$$200 \cdot 20 = 15.4x$$

Divide both sides by 15.4.

$$\frac{4{,}000}{15.4} = \frac{15.4x}{15.4}$$

Simplify.

$$259.74 = x$$

Answer the problem and look back. A child who weighs 20 lb needs about 260 mg of the medication.

Look back at the problem. Another way to solve is to set up the proportion as $\dfrac{200 \text{ mg}}{x \text{ mg}} = \dfrac{15.4 \text{ lb}}{20 \text{ lb}}$.
Cross-multiplying this proportion gives the same equation, $200 \cdot 20 = 15.4x$, as the one above.

23. *State what the problem is asking for as a solution.* The length of wire needed for a room.

Identify what is given. The dimensions of the room on a blueprint; the scale of the blueprint.

Make a plan. Use proportions to find the actual dimensions of the room. Then find the perimeter of the room.

Carry out the plan. Find the dimensions of the room. You might find decimals easier to work with than fractions.

Width:
$$\frac{0.25 \text{ in.}}{1 \text{ ft}} = \frac{3.5 \text{ in.}}{x \text{ ft}}$$
$$0.25x = 3.5$$
$$\frac{0.25x}{0.25} = \frac{3.5}{0.25}$$
$$x = 14$$

Length:
$$\frac{0.25 \text{ in.}}{1 \text{ ft}} = \frac{4 \text{ in.}}{x \text{ ft}}$$
$$0.25x = 4$$
$$\frac{0.25x}{0.25} = \frac{4}{0.25}$$
$$x = 16$$

The room is 14 ft × 16 ft.

The perimeter is $14 + 16 + 14 + 16 = 60$ ft.

Answer the problem and look back. 60 feet of wire are needed.

Check by using another method. First find the perimeter of the room on the blueprint: $3.5 + 3.5 + 4 + 4 = 15$ in. Then use the scale of the blueprint to find the actual perimeter: $\frac{0.25 \text{ in.}}{1 \text{ ft}} = \frac{15 \text{ in.}}{x \text{ ft}}$; $0.25x = 15$; $x = 60$.

Credits

Glossary

academic skill   a learned ability that helps people succeed in school

active listening   the act of making a conscious effort to hear and comprehend others in conversation

addend   one of the numbers you are adding

adjective   a word that describes a noun

adverb   a word that modifies a verb, an adjective, or another adverb

affix   an attachment added to the beginning or end of a word

age diversity   a range of different generations

application   a computer program

article   an adjective that indicates whether a noun being referenced is general or specific

behavior   the way a person acts and reacts in response to his or her environment

bias   a preference or inclination that prevents impartial judgment

blog   short for *weblog;* a personal website that combines the functionality of a daily diary with the ability to post photos and videos online; usually offered in a fixed template

body   the part of a piece of writing that includes the main ideas and supporting details

bookmark   a favorite website that you save so that you can return to it quickly later on

brainstorming   an active, energetic method of generating ideas

cite   to give credit to the original source of a quotation or idea

classify   to divide objects or information into groups

complex fraction   a fraction that has a fraction in its numerator, its denominator, or both

conclusion   the part of a piece of writing that leaves the final impact of your message

conjunction   a word that joins two or more parts of sentences, such as words or phrases, and expresses the relationship between those parts; for example, *and, but, either, or, than, wherever*

coping strategy   a behavior pattern that arises in response to anxiety

copyright   a body of law that gives authors control over their work and guarantees their right to be paid for its use

cross products   the products obtained by multiplying the numerator of one side of the proportion by the denominator of the other

cultural diversity   a range of cultures

culture   the customs, values, and beliefs that are shared among a group

denominator   the number below the fraction bar in a fraction

difference   the result when you subtract two numbers

diversity   a range of differences

dividend   the number you are dividing

divisor   the number you are dividing by

domain extension   the letters at the end of a URL; for example, *.edu* or *.com*

drafting   the second stage of the writing process, in which you implement your plan and do the bulk of your writing

editing   a writing phase in which you address sentence clarity, word choice, repetition, and rules of grammar

ego   according to Freudian psychology, the part of the human personality that consists of reasoning and caution

email etiquette   a set of guidelines for using email professionally and courteously

equivalent ratios   two ratios that have the same simplest form

evaluation   a judgment process that determines the quality or reliability of a source

external customer   an outside party doing business with your company

factor   one of the numbers you are multiplying

feedback   a verbal or nonverbal response to an action or a communication

field   a rectangular window in which you type text on a computer screen

file   a set of data that is stored on a computer

five-step problem solving process   a process for solving word problems that consists of these steps: state what the problem is asking for, identify what information is given, make a plan, carry out the plan, and answer the question

folder   a named location where computer files are stored

font   a style of type, such as Times New Roman or Arial

formatting   the aspects of the way text is arranged on a page, such as margins, title placement, type size, and line spacing

fraction   a rational number in the form $\frac{a}{b}$

gram   the base unit for mass in the metric system

grammar   the study of words and how they function

graphic organizer   a visual tool, such as a chart, that helps you organize your thoughts and notes when reading or learning new information

hard drive   a device that stores data in a computer

hardware   the physical parts of a computer

homophones   words that sound the same but have different meanings

icon   a small picture or symbol that represents an object, such as an application or a file, on a computer screen

id   according to Freudian psychology, the part of the human personality that consists of instinctual urges and drives

improper fraction   a fraction in which the numerator is greater than the denominator

input port   a type of outlet in a computer, used to attach peripherals

instant messaging (IM)   an electronic method of communication in which people type, send, and receive messages in real time

interjection   a sudden word or phrase that expresses surprise or emotion

internal customer   a person or department within your organization that receives support from something that you do

Internet a worldwide network composed of smaller, connected computer networks and other computer organizations

introduction the part of a piece of writing that announces the subject and grabs, or hooks, the reader

keyboard a panel, usually flat, used for typing letters, numbers, and commands on a computer

keyword qualifiers words or characters (such as *and* or quotation marks) that help refine or limit a keyword search

keyword a word or phrase entered into a library catalog or online search engine to find sources on a certain subject

least common denominator (LCD) the least common multiple of the denominators of two or more fractions

link a block of text or an image that leads to another location on the World Wide Web

liter the base unit for capacity in the metric system

mechanics the conventions of writing, such as spelling, punctuation, and capitalization

meter the base unit for length in the metric system

metric system the system of measurement used worldwide, based on the decimal system; also known as the International System of Units (SI)

mixed number a number consisting of a whole number and a fraction

monitor a device that receives information from a computer and displays it on a screen

mouse a handheld device used to move a pointer or a cursor on a computer screen and to send commands to the computer

negotiation a process of discussion and compromise

nonverbal communication the signals a person gives, such as body language, facial expressions, eye contact, and so on, that send a message without using words

noun a word that names a person, place, or thing

numerator the number above the fraction bar in a fraction

optical drive a device in a computer that reads DVDs and CDs

organizational behavior the way individuals and groups act in organizations, such as businesses and schools

partial product the result when you multiply one digit of one number by the other number

part of speech a category of words, based on their functions

peripheral an external device that cooperates with a computer

personality the set of behaviors, values, and attitudes that distinguish an individual or a group

personality test a survey or questionnaire used to determine an individual's dominant traits and behavior patterns

personality type one of several predetermined categories used to group people who have common traits

phrasal verb   a group of words that expresses a single action, such as *turn off* or *settle up*

place value   a system that shows the value of each digit in a number

plagiarism   the act of using someone else's information, ideas, or words without crediting him or her

planning   the first stage of the writing process, in which you gather and organize ideas and information

portable drive   an external device that stores and transfers digital data

prefix   a word part attached to the beginning of a word

preposition   a word that expresses the relationship between two words in a sentence

processor   a device that receives, calculates, manipulates, and resolves most of a computer's data; also called a central processing unit (CPU)

product   the result when you multiply two or more numbers

pronoun   a word that takes the place of one or more nouns

proofreading   the process of reviewing a piece of writing for grammatical and mechanical errors

proper fraction   a fraction in which the numerator is less than the denominator

proportion   an equation showing that two ratios are equal

psychologist   a scientist who studies the human mind and behavior

quotient   the result when you divide two numbers

RAM (random access memory)   memory that programs use while running on a computer

rate   a special type of ratio in which the two quantities have different units

ratio   a comparison of two numbers

reciprocal   the multiplicative inverse of a number; $\frac{a}{b}$ is the reciprocal of $\frac{b}{a}$

remainder   the number left over after a division problem is completed and the quotient is not a whole number

research   a focused collection of facts; an investigation into a specific topic

revising   the third and final stage of the writing process, in which you revamp and fine-tune your work

root   the main part of a word; a word with no affixes

scale   the ratio of the size of an object in a drawing to the size of the actual object

scale drawing   an enlarged or reduced drawing of an object in the same proportions as the object; for example, blueprints, maps, and floor plans

simplest form   the form of a fraction in which the only common factor of the numerator and denominator is 1

skill   an ability or aptitude that you learn, develop, and master through practice and effort

software   the programs and operating systems that are used on a computer; also called applications

stereotype   a generalized assumption that is made about members of a particular group

suffix   a word part attached to the end of a word

sum the result when you add two or more numbers

superego according to Freudian psychology, the part of the human personality that consists of moral and ethical awareness; the conscience

talent a natural, inborn ability

temperament an overall attitude or mood; one's inborn personality

tone a writer's overall attitude toward his or her audience and subject matter

total the value when you combine two or more numbers

trackpad a rectangular, touch-sensitive keyboard panel used to move a pointer or cursor on a computer screen and to send commands to the computer

traits personal characteristics or qualities, such as honesty or maturity

transition a word or phrase that connects ideas or indicates a change in topic

U.S. customary system the system of measurement used in the United States; includes measures such as feet and inches for length, fluid ounces and cups for liquid capacity, and pounds and ounces for weight

unit rate a rate whose denominator is 1

URL (uniform resource locator) the address of a website

verb a word that expresses an action or a state of being

verb tense an indication of the timing (past, present, or future) of a particular action

verbal communication the use of words to speak or write in order to exchange information exchanged between two or more people

websites specific online locations hosted by individuals or organizations

World Wide Web the collection of websites accessible via the Internet

Index

A

Abbreviations, 101
Academic Search Premier link, 112
Academic skills, 3–12
  application of, 7–8
  communication skills, 5, 29–39, 121–135
  computer skills, 9–10, 43–60
  definition of, 4
  importance of, 4–5
  language arts skills, 7, 65–83
  listening skills, 5, 36–37, 39, 124–125, 128, 136
  math skills, 10–12, 139–167, 173–196
  presentation skills, 5, 32, 125–126
  research skills, 7, 91, 94–95, 106, 111–118
  types of, 5–7
  writing skills, 11, 12, 79–80, 87–102, 126
Academic subjects, 78
Accessories, as nonverbal communication, 34–35
Accessory programs, 48
Acronyms in email, 101
Actions, as nonverbal communication, 33
Active listening, 5, 36–37, 39, 124–125, 133, 136
Addends, 140
Addiction, 24
Addition, 140
  of decimals, 141–142, 185
  of fractions, 151–152
  of mixed numbers, 152–153
  of whole numbers, 140–141
Adjectives, 68, 72
Adobe Acrobat Pro, 48
Adobe Reader, 48
Adverbs, 69, 72
Affixes, 81–83, 84
Age, influence on personality, 20–21
Age diversity, 134–135

Agreeableness, 19
American Psychological Association citation format (APA), 95, 117
And (keyword qualifier), 110
And not (keyword qualifier), 110
Animations tab, 58
APA citations format, 95, 117
Apostrophe, 75, 76
Appearance
  influence on personality, 19
  as nonverbal communication, 33, 34–35
Apple Mail, 48
Applications, computer programs, 48, 53–60
Archives, 113
Area, metric units of measure, 158, 161
Articles (part of speech), 67
Ask.com, 108
Associative Property, 140, 145
Attachments to email, 100
Audience
  communicating with, 38, 39
  of email, 97, 102
  understanding internal/external customers, 126–127
  of written work, 89, 102

B

Baby Boom, 135
Back button, 107, 108
Bcc field in email, 98–99
Behavior
  career and, 26
  definition of, 23
  patterns on the job, 25
  personality and, 23–25
  positive/negative patterns of, 25
Bias, 114
Big Five, 19
Bing, 108

Biological influences on personality, 18–21
Birth order, influence on personality, 20
Blogs, 115
Body
    of email, 100
    of writing project, 92, 93
Body language, 34, 133
Body type, influence on personality, 20
Boldface type, 54, 55, 101
Bookmarks, computer, 49
Booting computers, 45
Boss, conflict with, 129–130
Brainstorming, 90
Browsers, 10, 48–49, 106–107, 118
Building Background
    adjectives in pronoun clothing, 68
    avoiding plagiarism, 7
    clarity of speech, 32
    computers, 44
    coping strategies, 24
    Internet, 106
    operations with decimals, 185
    properties of numbers, 140, 145, 147
    purposes/types of writing, 89
    solving equations with division, 192
    websites/Internet access, 106

C

Calculator, 48
Call to action, 94
Cameras, 47
Cancelling in proportions, 155
Capacity, 158, 159
Capitalization, 7
    to be fancy/emphasize words, 78
    in email, 78, 101
    proofreading for, 97
    rules for, 77–78
Career, personality and, 17–18, 26
Carrying, 140, 145
CC field in email, 98

Centimeters, 158, 159
Choosing the correct operation, 185
Citing sources, 7, 94–95, 115, 116–117
Clarity, of speech, 32
Classifying, 5
Climate, influence on personality, 21
Closing
    files, 55
    windows, 48, 55
Closing of email, 100
Clothing, as nonverbal communication, 34–35
Colon, 75
Comma, 75, 76–77
Commercial sites, 109
Common denominator, 151, 189
Common nouns, 66–67, 78
Communication skills, 5, 29–39, 121–135.
    See also Speech; Writing process
    active listening, 36–37, 39, 124–125, 136
    basics of, for work, 124–126
    expression vs. communication, 30
    getting through rough patches, 128–129
    making a good first impression daily,
        122–124
    nonverbal communication, 33–35, 39,
        123–124
    recognizing nonverbal cues, 35, 124
    understanding diversity, 131–135
    understanding internal/external customers,
        126–127
    verbal communication, 31–33, 37–38, 39,
        123
    when negotiation/compromise fails, 129–131
    in workplace, 37–39, 121–135
    writing process, 79–80, 88–97, 126
Commutative Property, 140, 145
Company names, capitalization of, 77
Complex fractions, 157
Compound words, 75, 77
Compromise, 128
Computer programs, 10, 48, 53–60

Computer skills, 9–10, 43–60. *See also*
  Personal computer
  basic personal computer tasks, 44
  basic user skills, 9
  email, 97–102
  finding information on Internet, 111–116
  identifying computer components, 9, 45–48
  Instant messaging, 101–102
  Internet basics, 48–49, 106–110, 118
  software programs, 48
  using Microsoft Office, 53–60
  using programs, 10
  using spell/grammar checkers, 80
  writing papers on, 95
Conclusion of writing project, 92, 93–94
Conflict-resolution skills, 6, 128–131, 136
Conjunctions, 71
Conscientiousness, 19
Contact information, 114
Contractions, 75, 76
Converting measurements
  within metric system, 162–164
  between systems, 165–167
Coping strategies, 24
Copying text/images, 54, 55
Copyright, 117
Co-workers
  communication with, 122–129
  conflicts among, 129–131
Creating
  bookmarks, 49
  Excel workbook, 59–60
  files, 51, 53, 55
  folders, 52
  lists/charts/groups of data, 59
  PowerPoint presentation, 57–59
  Word documents, 55–56
Critical thinking, 5
Cross products, 192
Cultural diversity, 131–133
Cultural influences on personality, 20–21

Culture, 131–132
Customers, 126
Cutting text/images, 54, 55

D

Dash, 75, 77
Database programs, 48
Data tab, 60
Days of the week, capitalization of, 77
Decimals
  addition of, 141–142, 185
  division with, 148–149, 185
  multiplication of, 146–147, 185
  solving problems involving, 184–187
  subtraction of, 144, 185
Decision making, 5
Deleting folders, 52
Denial, 24
Denominator, 151
Dependable students, 127, 144
Design tab, 58
Desktop, 47–48, 61
Determining reasonableness of measurements, 161
Diagrams, 177–178
Difference, 142, 174
Direction arrows, 60
Direct quotation, 75, 77
Diversity
  age diversity, 134–135
  communicating with others, 6
  cultural diversity, 131–133
  definition of, 131
  language diversity, 133
  stereotyping, 131, 135
  in workplace, 136
Dividend, 147
Division, 147–150
  of decimals, 148–149, 185
  of fractions, 156–157
  by powers of ten, 150

solving equations with, 192
of whole numbers, 147–148
Divisor, 147
Documents, 50, 52, 55–56
Domain extension, 114
Drafting
  avoiding plagiarism, 95
  citing sources, 94
  email, 98–100
  using transitions, 94
  writing projects, 88, 92–94, 102
Duplicate Selected Slides, 57

E

Ebscohost, 112
Editing, 88, 95, 96–97, 101
Ego, 24
Ellipsis, 75, 77
Email, 97–102
  attachments to, 100
  drafting, 98–100
  forwarding, 98
  planning, 97–98
  revising, 101
  timely answering, 98
  using all capital letters in, 78
Email address, 98
Email etiquette, 97, 98, 101, 102
Emoticons, 101
Emotional stability, 19
Emotions, controlling, 128
Empowered students, 20, 34, 35, 175
Engaged students, 80, 111
Entertaining writing, 89
Environmental influences on personality, 21–22
Equations, 192
Equivalent ratios, 188
Equivalent units of measure, 166
Estimating, 142
Evaluating sources, 7, 113–116
Excel. *See* Microsoft Office: Excel

Exclamation point, 75, 76, 101
Expanding a window, 48
Experiences, influence on personality, 21–22
Expression, 30, 39, 123–124, 133
External customers, 127
Extraversion, 19
Eye contact
  when listening, 5, 36
  when speaking, 34, 123, 133

F

Facial expressions, 34
Factors, 144
Family, influence on personality, 22–23
Favorites, computer, 49
Feedback, 33
Field, in browser, 49
Files, computer, 50–51, 53, 61
Find Articles and E-Books link, 112
Five-step problem-solving process, 174–175
Five Ws, 91
Folders, computer, 51–53, 61
Fonts, 54, 56, 57–58, 59
Format, checking, 97, 101
Format Painter button, 54
Formatting text, 54
Formulas, 179
Formulas tab, 60
Forward button, 107
Fractions
  addition of, 151–153
  complex fractions, 157
  converting to decimals, 184
  division of, 156–157
  multiplication of, 155–156
  ordering, 154
  parts/types of, 151
  proportions as, 191–196
  ratios as, 187–191
  simplifying, 155
  subtraction of, 153–154

Freewriting, 95
From field in email, 98

G

Gathering ideas, 90
Gathering information, 91
Gender, influence on personality, 19
Generations X, Y, and Z, 135
Genetics, influence on personality, 19
Geography, influence on personality, 21
Gestures, 34
Goal-oriented students, 10, 47, 98
Google, 108
Google Chat, 48
Government, influence on personality, 21
Grammar, 7, 38
    confusing adverbs/adjectives, 72
    confusing past tenses of verbs, 72
    confusion with helping verbs, 73
    in email, 101
    misusing pronouns, 72
    noun/verb agreement, 73
    parts of speech, 66–71
    proofreading for, 97, 126
    sentence fragments, 72
    themselves/theirselves, 73
Grammar checkers, 80, 97, 101
Grams, 158, 160, 165, 166
Graphic organizers, 91–92
Greatest common factor (GCF), 188
Grievance policy, 131

H

Hard drive, 45
Hardware, 45, 61
Health, influence on personality, 19–20
Help button, 53
Helping verbs, 69, 73
History command, 107
Holidays, capitalization of, 78
Home page, 107

Home tab
    in Excel, 60
    feature common to Microsoft Office
        components, 53–54
    in PowerPoint, 57, 58
    in Word, 56
Homophones, 73
Hook, 92–93, 94
Human behavior, 15–25
Hyphen, 75, 77

I

I, 77
Icons, 47, 61
Id, 24
Identity Property, 140, 145, 147
Images, 56, 59, 109, 110
IM etiquette, 101
Improper fractions, 151
Inches, 165, 166
Inflection, 32, 123
Information superhighway. *See* Internet
Informative writing, 89
Input ports, 47
Insert tab
    in Excel, 60
    in PowerPoint, 58
    in Word, 56
Instant messaging (IM), 101
Instant messaging programs, 48
Intended message, matching nonverbal
    cues to, 35
Interjections, 71
Internal customers, 126–127
Internet, 48–49, 105–117
    citing sources from, 116–117
    email, 97–101
    evaluating sources on, 113–116
    instant messaging, 101–102
    reliable sources, 116
    researching a topic, 111–116

search engine savvy, 108–111

using online sources, 111–116

using your browser, 106–107

Internet Explorer, 10, 48–49, 106

Internet Generation, 135

Introduction of writing project, 92–93

Italic type, 54, 55, 101

J

Job Search Tip, 60

K

Kaplan Quad, 112, 115

Keyboard, 45, 46, 61

Keyboard shortcuts, 55, 56

Keys to Success

academic skills, 3

communication in the workplace, 121

communication skills, 29

computer skills, 43

human behavior/personality, 15

Internet applications, 105

language arts, 65

math skills, 139, 173

writing skills, 87

Keyword qualifiers, 110, 118

Keyword searches, 108, 110, 118

Kilograms, 158, 160

Kilometers, 158, 159

L

Language arts skills, 7, 65–83

grammar roadblocks, 72–73

parts of speech, 66–71

proofreading process, 79–80

punctuation roadblocks, 75–76

spelling roadblocks, 73–74

word parts, 81–83

Language diversity, 133

Languages, capitalization of, 78

Laws, influence on personality, 21

Leadership skills, 6, 15

Least common denominator, 151

Length, metric units of measure, 158, 159

Letters, capitalization in, 78

Links, 106, 108, 114

Listening skills

active listening, 5, 36–37, 39, 124–125, 133, 136

effect on speaker, 37

keys to, 36–37, 124–125

showing respect, 36

using to smooth rough patches, 128

Lists, solving math problems with, 179–180

Liters, 158, 159, 165, 166

M

Mailings tab, 56

Manners, 38

Maps, on the Internet, 109

Mass, metric units of measure, 158, 160

Math skills, 10–11, 139–167, 173–196

addition, 140–142, 151–153, 185

decimals, 141–142, 144, 146–147, 148–149, 185–187

division, 147–150, 156–157, 185, 192

fractions, 152–157

identifying/applying problem-solving strategies, 174–182

multiplication, 144–147, 150, 155–156, 185

operations, 11

solving mathematical problems, 11, 162–167, 184–196

subtraction, 143–144, 153–154, 185

systems of measure, 11, 157–161

Measurement problems, 164–167

Mechanics, 84

capitalization roadblocks, 77–78

definition of, 72

proofreading for, 97

punctuation roadblocks, 75–77

spelling roadblocks, 73–74

Media programs, 48
Menus, computer, 47–48
Meters, 158, 159, 165, 166
Metric system, 157–158
    adjusting measurements, 164–165
    converting measurements within, 162–164
    converting to/from U.S. customary system,
        165–167
    equivalent U.S. customary measures, 166
    prefixes for units of measure, 158
    units of area, 161
    units of capacity, 158, 159
    units of length, 158, 159
    units of mass, 158, 160
Microsoft Office, 53–60
    common features, 53–55
    common keyboard shortcuts, 55
    Excel, 50, 59–60, 61
    Outlook, 48
    PowerPoint, 10, 50, 51, 57–59, 61
    Word, 10, 50, 51, 55–56, 61
Miles, 166
Millennials, 135
Milligrams, 158, 160
Milliliters, 158, 159
Millimeters, 158, 159
Mind mapping, 90, 91
Minimizing a window, 48
Minus sign (keyword qualifier), 110
Mixed numbers
    addition of, 152–153
    definition of, 151
    division of, 156–157
    multiplication of, 155–156
    subtraction of, 153–154
MLA citation format, 95, 117
Modem, 45
Modern Language Association citation format
    (MLA), 95, 117
Monitor, 45
Months, capitalization of, 77

Morals, influence on personality, 21
Mouse, 46, 61
Mozilla Firefox, 10, 48–49, 106
MP3 players, 47
Multiples, 151
Multiplication, 144–147
    of decimals, 146–147, 185
    of fractions, 155–156
    of mixed numbers, 155–156
    by powers of ten, 150
    of whole numbers, 144–145
Myers-Briggs Type Indicator (MBTI), 20

N
Naming files, 51
Navigating between websites, 106
Near-homophones, 73
Negotiations, 128
News, on the Internet, 109
New Slide, 57
Nonverbal communication, 39, 123–124
    recognizing cues, 35
    types of cues, 33–35
Notepad, 48
Note taking, 7
Nouns
    common, 66, 78
    forming plurals, 76
    forming possessives, 76
    function of, 66–67
    proper, 66, 77
    verb agreement with, 73
Noun/verb agreement, 73
Numerator, 151

O
Office button, 53
Online library, 112–113
Online Resources
    academic skills, 13
    behavior/personality, 27

computer skills, 62
 Internet applications, 119
Online sources
 citing, 116–117, 118
 evaluating, 113–116, 118
 for research, 111–116
 types of, 112–113
Online stores, 109
On the Job
 communication, 39
 cultural differences, 134
 email, 101
 Internet searches, 113
 Myers-Briggs type indicator, 20
 proofreading, 79
Opening
 computer programs, 48
 files, 53
Openness, 19
Operations. *See* Addition; Division;
 Multiplication; Subtraction
Optical drive, 47
Or (keyword qualifier), 110
Organizational behavior, 17
Organization of ideas/information, 91
Organizations, capitalization of, 77
Original sources, 113
Ounces, 166
Outline, 91–92, 95

P

Page Layout tab
 in Excel, 60
 in Word, 56
Parentheses, 75
Partial product, 145
Parts of speech, 66–71, 84
 adjectives, 68, 72
 adverbs, 69, 72
 articles, 67
 conjunctions, 71

interjections, 71
 nouns, 66–67, 73
 prepositions, 70
 pronouns, 67, 72, 73
 verbs, 68–69, 72, 73, 74
Pasting text/images, 54, 55
Patterns, in math, 175–177
PC. *See* Personal computer
PDF-viewing programs, 48
Period, 75, 77
Peripherals, 47
Person, verbs and, 68
Personal computer, 60, 61. *See also* Computer
 skills
 booting (loading/starting), 45
 desktop, 47–48
 files and folders, 50–53
 functions of, 44
 hardware, 45–47, 61
 Internet basics, 48–49
 Microsoft Office, 53–60
 mouse/trackpad commands, 46
 software, 48, 53–60, 61. *See also* Microsoft
  Office
 spelling/grammar checkers, 80
 writing projects on, 95, 97
Personality, 26
 behavior and, 23–25
 career and, 17–18, 26
 definition of, 16–17
 influences on, 18–23, 26
 traits of, 16
 types of, 17
Personality tests, 17–18, 20, 26
Personality type, 17
Personal names, 77
Personal space, 35, 133
Personal websites, 115
Persuasive writing, 89
Phrasal verbs, 69
Physical appearance, influence on personality, 19

Pictures of math problems, 177–178
Pitch, 32, 37
Place value, 140, 184
Plagiarism, avoiding, 7, 95, 116–117
Planning writing projects, 88–92, 97, 102
Plural nouns, 66, 76
Plural pronouns, 67
Plural verbs, 74
Plus sign (keyword qualifier), 110
Portable drives, 47
Possessive nouns, 75, 76
Posture, 123
Pounds, 160, 165, 166
PowerPoint. *See* Microsoft Office: PowerPoint
Powers of ten, 150
Practice Now
    dependable, 127, 144
    empowered, 20, 34, 35, 175
    engaged, 80, 111
    goal-oriented, 10, 47, 98
Predictions, in conclusion of writing project, 93
Prefixes
    for metric units of measure, 158
    word analysis, 81–82
Prepositions, 70
Presentation programs, 10, 48, 57–59
Presentation skills, 5. *See also* Presentation
    programs; Speech
Preview, 48
Printers, 45, 47
Printing a file, 53
Problem solving, 5
Problem-solving strategies for math
    find a pattern, 175–177, 183
    five-step problem-solving process, 174–175
    guess and check, 181–182, 183
    make a list/table, 179–180, 183
    make a picture/diagram, 177–178, 183
    solve a simpler problem, 181, 183
    use a formula/rule, 179, 183
    work backward, 178, 183

Processor, 45
Product, 144, 151, 174
Programs, 10, 48, 53–60
Pronouns, 67, 72, 73
Proofreading process, 79–80, 84, 95, 97, 101
Proper fractions, 151
Proper nouns, 66, 77–78
Properties of numbers, 140, 145, 147
Property of One, 147
Property of Zero, 145, 147
Proportions, 191–192, 194–196
    cross products, 192
    solving problems with, 194–196
Psychologists, 16
Punctuation, 7, 75–77, 97
Purpose for writing, 89, 97, 102

Q
Quarts, 159
Question mark, 75
Questions
    asking in conclusion of writing, 93
    asking speakers to clarify, 37, 124–125
    evaluating Internet sources, 114
    punctuation of, 75
    starting research with, 111
Quick Access Toolbar, 53
Quotation marks
    as keyword qualifier, 110
    use in direct address, 75
Quotient, 147, 174

R
Race, influence on personality, 20
RAM (random access memory), 45
Rates, 189–191, 192–194
Ratios, 187–191
    equivalent ratios, 188
    simplifying, 188
    solving problems with, 192–194
    unit pricing, 191

unit rates, 189–191
Reading Internet materials, 113–116
Reciprocal, 156
Redoing actions, 53, 55
Reference tab, 56
Reference tools, 80
Refreshing the screen, 107
Regression, 24
Regrouping, 140, 143, 144, 145
Reliability, of Internet material, 111, 113–116
Religion, influence on personality, 21
Remainder, 147
Research skills, 7
    avoiding plagiarism, 7, 116–117
    citing sources, 7, 94–95, 115, 117, 118
    evaluating sources, 7, 113–116
    gathering information, 91, 106
    general tips for, 111–112
    Internet searches, 106–111, 118
    using online sources, 111–118
    for writing, 91
Respect
    communication and, 38
    listening and, 36
Resumes, 66, 69
Review tab
    in Excel, 60
    in PowerPoint, 58
    in Word, 56
Revising, 88, 95–97, 101, 102
Ribbon, 53
Root words, 81, 84
Rounding numbers, 142
Rules for math, 179
Run-on sentences, 76

S
Safari, 48–49, 106
Salutation of email, 100
Save As, 51
Saving files/images, 51, 53, 55, 56

Scale, 195
Scale drawings, 195
Scanners, 47
Scholarly (Peer Review) Journals link, 112–113
Schooling, influence on personality, 21
Screen name, 101
Search engines, 107, 108–111, 118
Search field, 107, 108
Selecting text/images, 55
Semicolon, 75, 77
Sending a file, 53
Sentence fragments, 72
Sentences
    capitalization of first word, 77
    fragments, 72
    punctuation of, 75, 76–77
    run-on, 76
Setting Home page, 107
Signature on email, 100
Silent Generation, 134, 135
Simplest form of fractions, 152
Simplifying
    complex fractions, 157
    fractions, 155
    ratios, 188
Singular nouns, 66
Singular pronouns, 67
Skill, 4, 12
Skin color, influence on personality, 20
Skype, 48
Slang, 38
Slide show, 50, 57–59
Slide Show tab, 58
Slides tab, 57
Small caps, 54
Social influences on personality, 22–23
Software, 48, 53–60, 61
Sources
    citing, 7, 94–95, 115, 116–117
    evaluating, 7, 91, 113–116
    finding, 7, 91, 106, 111–113

list of reliable sources, 116

taking notes from, 7

types of online, 112–113

Spacing button, 56

Speakers, computer, 45

Specialized information, 113

Speech, 31–33, 37–38, 39, 123, 125–126. *See also* Communication skills

Speed of speech, 32, 37, 123

Spell checkers, 80, 97, 101

Spelling, 7

commonly misspelled words, 74

in email, 101

forming verb tenses/plurals, 74

homophones/near-homophones, 73

proofreading for, 126

Spreadsheet, 48, 50, 59–60

Square meters, 158, 161

Square yards, 161

Stage in life, influence on personality, 20–21

Standard English, 38, 97, 101

Start button, 45, 47–48

Start menu, 47–48

Stereotyping, 131, 135

Stop button, 107

Stress in speech, 32

Strikethrough text, 54

Subject line of email, 99–100

Subtraction

of decimals, 144, 185

of fractions, 153–154

of whole numbers, 143–144

Suffixes, 81, 83

Sum, 140, 174

Superego, 24–25

Surfing the Web, 106

Systems of measurement, 11

converting measurements between systems, 165–167

converting measurements within metric system, 162–164

determining reasonableness of measurements, 158, 159, 160

metric system, 157–161

U.S. customary system, 157, 165–167

System unit, 45

T

Tables, solving math problems with, 179–180

Tabs, 53

Talent, 4

Temperament, 19

Tense of verbs, 68–69, 72

Text alignment, 54

Themselves/theirselves, 73

Thinking skills, 5

Titles, capitalization of, 78

To-Do List

academic skills, 12

communication skills, 40, 136

computer skills, 61

Internet applications, 118

personality/behavior, 26

To field in email, 98

Tone

of email, 97–98

of voice, 32, 123, 126

of written work, 89

Topic selection, 89–90

Total, 140, 174

Trackpad, 46, 61

Trademarks, capitalization of, 78

Traits, 16, 26

Transitions, 94

True Story

communication on the job, 125

computer skills, 47

email, 99

evaluating Internet sources, 115

instant messaging, 102

listening, 37

math skills, 146, 195

metric measure, 160
nonverbal communication, 35
power of research skills, 8
resumes, 66, 80
social influences on personality, 22
Type size, 54, 58

U

Underlining text, 54
Undoing actions, 53, 54–55
Unit pricing, 191
Unit rates, 189
URL (uniform resource locator), 49, 106, 115
U.S. customary system, 157
converting to/from metric system, 165–167
equivalent metric measures, 166
units of area, 161
units of capacity, 159
units of length, 159
units of weight, 160

V

Verbal communication, 31–33, 39, 123,
125–126
Verbs
agreement with nouns, 73
forming plurals, 74
function of, 68
helping verbs, 69, 73
person and, 68
phrasal verbs, 69
tenses, 68–69, 72, 73, 74
Videos, on the Internet, 109
Video viewing programs, 10, 48
View tab
in Excel, 60
in PowerPoint, 58
in Word, 56
Voice, qualities of, 123, 32–33, 37
Volume, of voice, 33, 37, 123

W

Weather, influence on personality, 21
Web browsers, 10, 48–49, 106–107, 118
Websites, 106, 111, 113–114. *See also* Internet
Whole numbers
addition of, 140
division of, 147–148
multiplication of, 145–146
subtraction of, 143
Wikis, 115
Windows Live Messenger, 48
Windows Media Player, 10, 48
Windows Picture and Fax Viewer, 48
Withdrawal, 24
Word. *See* Microsoft Office: Word
Word analysis, 7, 81–84
Word choice, 31, 123
Word problems
with decimals, 184–186
five-step problem-solving process, 174–175
with ratios/proportions, 192–196
strategies for solving, 174–183
Word processors, 10, 48, 55–56
Workbook, digital, 50, 59–60
Workplace communication. *See* Communication
skills
World Wide Web, 106. *See also* Internet;
Websites
Writing, using when language barriers exist, 133
Writing process, 11, 87–102. *See also* Grammar
drafting, 88, 92–95, 98–100, 102
email, 97–101
planning, 88–92, 97–98, 102
proofreading process, 79–80
purposes/types of writing, 89
revising, 88, 95–97, 101
in workplace, 126

Y

Yahoo! 108
Yards, 159, 165, 166